THE ART & SCIENCE

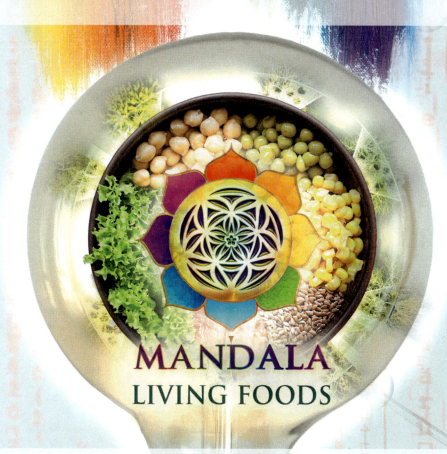

OF LIVING FOODS

Micah Skye

The Art & Science of Living Foods

by
Micah Skye
of
Mandala Living Foods

Publisher's Note

This book details the author's personal experiences and opinions about general health, prevention of disease, nutritional supplements, and/or exercise. The author is not your healthcare provider. Mandala Living Foods including Micah Skye is providing this book and its contents as a story on an "as is" basis with no representations or warranties of any kind with respect to this book or its contents. The authors and publisher disclaim all such representations and warranties including, for example, warranties of merchantability and healthcare for a particular purpose. In addition, the author and the publisher do not represent or warrant that the information accessible via this book is accurate, complete or current.

The statements made about products and services have not been evaluated by the U.S. Food and Drug Administration. They are not intended to diagnose, treat, cure, or prevent any condition or disease. Please consult with your own physician or healthcare specialist regarding the suggestions and recommendations made in this book. Except as specifically stated in this book, neither the authors, nor Mandala Living Foods, nor any contributors or other representatives will be liable for damages arising out of or in connection with the use of this book. This is a comprehensive limitation of liability that applies to all damages of any kind, including (without limitation) compensatory; direct, indirect or consequential damages; loss of data, income or profit; loss of or damage to property and claims of third parties.

Understand that this book is not intended as a substitute for consultation with a licensed healthcare practitioner, such as your physician. Before you begin any healthcare program, or change your lifestyle in any way, you should consult your physician or another licensed healthcare practitioner to ensure that you are in good health and that the examples contained in this book will not harm you. This book provides content related to physical and/or health issues. As such, use of this book implies your acceptance of this disclaimer.

Copyright © 2023 by Micah Skye

All Rights Reserved. No part of this book may be reproduced in any manner without the express written consent of the publisher, except in the case of brief excerpts in critical reviews or articles. All inquiries should be addressed to Pierucci Publishing, PO Box 2074, Carbondale, Colorado, 81623.

Pierucci Publishing books may be purchased in bulk at special discounts for sales promotion, corporate gifts, fund-raising, or educational purposes. Special editions can also be created to specifications. For details, contact the Special Sales Department, PO Box 2074, Carbondale, CO 81623, via email at publishing@pieruccipublishing.com or by phone at 1-855-720-1111.

Visit our website at www.PierucciPublishing.com
Library of Congress Cataloging-in-Publication Data is available on file.
Paperback ISBN: 978-1-962578-01-1
Ebook ISBN: 978-1-962578-10-3

Cover Design by Micah Skye
Edited by Russell Womack
Printed in the United States of America

CONTENTS

Forward by Ronnie Landis. 5

Introduction 7

Chapter 1
The Geometry of Protein 11

Chapter 2
The Tools of the Technology. 21

Chapter 3
The Meditation of Preparation 25

Chapter 4
The Science of Herbometry & Spiceology. . . .41

Chapter 5
Dictionary 98

Chapter 6
Book of Tonic Alchemy 154

Chapter 7
Rawvelations of Dairy 175

Chapter 8
Dressings, Sauces, & Sides 217

Chapter 9
Bread & Snacks 257

Chapter 10
Bulk Proteins 275

Chapter 11
Healfast 297

Chapter 12
Pupus 305

Chapter 13
Entrees 313

Chapter 14
Desserts. 323

Reflections of a Living Foods Chef... 347

FORWARD

BY RONNIE LANDIS

It's an honor and privilege that I have the opportunity to introduce this revolutionary, paradigm shifting body of work, from my dear brother Micah Skye. When Micah asked me to review the book and write the foreword, my gut response was an automatic yes simply because of the immense respect and admiration I had for his work in almost ten years of knowing him. I met Micah in 2015 in Los Angeles through a close mutual friend of ours that insisted that we needed to meet, and within 5 minutes of us meeting, it was clear that we were kindred brothers with a shared passion for the full spectrum of holistic health, ancient & modern healing arts, & spiritual development. I was introduced to his healing modality called NMRT, which is still to this day the most advanced and powerfully effective touch based therapeutic approach to whole systems healing of the physical body I have ever experienced.

In the summer of 2015 I left LA to move to the Garden Island of Kauai, HI to move in with Micah to do further therapeutic work and collaborate on various projects together. I have a very unique insight into the rarified genius that is Micah Skye, because I have spent extended containers of time with him in various capacities, such as receiving advanced treatments in his healing modalities, living with him on multiple occasions, speaking on conference stages with him, watching him raise his now 4 children, & witnessing the undeniably magnetic field that emanates from him, that people are energetically drawn into, as a direct effect of his unwavering passion, wisdom, & expertise for holistic healing & human potential. Micah would be described as a 'polymath', which is a unique individual that has not only developed mastery in multiple disciplines of study but has found a way to weave these areas of focus together and create something brand new that had not existed before it.

I think it's useful to mention a bit about myself & my background to further emphasize the importance of Micah's work and this book in particular. I have been a professional nutritionist, holistic health practitioner, author, & speaker for almost 15 years. I have written multiple books centered around the raw living foods lifestyle, given hundreds of lectures on health, worked with countless clients & students in my online programs, & have interviewed almost 250 of the world's leading experts in all areas of holistic health & personal development. I have either met, spoken alongside on stages or workshops, been personally mentored by, interviewed on my podcast, and/or developed close friendships with virtually every single major proponent & leader of the raw food lifestyle & super food revolution in the world today. I have read most of what are considered the bibles of this movement from every prominent leader over the last 20 years and many of them have written endorsements for my own books on the subject as well. I say all of this not to impress you but to impress upon you, that when I say Micah's book, The Art & Science of Living Foods, is a revolutionary work in this field, you can rest assured it's not just words, but a matter of undeniable fact.

This book is the culmination of Micah's knowledge & direct experience in the fields of living foods nutrition, super foods & herbalism, & combined with a foundational understanding in the gourmet culinary arts. This is not just another book on raw food recipes or repetitive information on another dietary approach that everyone has heard a hundred times over. This is the most complete, comprehensive, & easily accessible book to ever put together the full scope of this incredible lifestyle that combines the most up to date scientific research, practical wisdom for easily upgrading your health routines, a full scale super food & herbal dictionary, the most unique & delicious gourmet recipes anyone can master in your own kitchen, and inspired writing that will motivate you to pursue a life of opulent health, unlimited vitality, & more creative enjoyment in the kitchen.

This is not just a book to teach you how to make delicious food recipes but how to use the power of living foods to take back your own power to choose how you want to feel in your body and how much energy you wish to have for the totality of your life. This is a priceless resource book that contains a treasure vault of timeless wisdom & easy to access recipes that can change the trajectory of your entire family's health for generations to come. You can finally put down all of the other books on theoretical health philosophies & complicated recipes, because you now have the absolute best of both worlds combined in one, yet the difference is that this book removes all the fluff and impractical filler information and guides you directly into what is immediately accessible, what is easy to understand and take action on, and most importantly, what actually works!

INTRODUCTION

My love for the art of food began as a dishwasher in my home state of Michigan for the five-star Gandydancer restaurant kitchen. As fate would have it, I was given a chance to cook at the gourmet omelet station for the five-star brunch on Sunday mornings. I loved making omelets for people to order, watching peoples' faces light up as they saw their omelet made to order creation. It was through this I made an impression on a chef at another five-star restaurant in the area. I was then offered an apprenticeship in a full service gourmet restaurant called the Common Grill.

I was sixteen years old, and had found one of my passions in life, the *art of gourmet*. A month into my apprenticeship, I was transferred onto the line and with an ambitious vigor a year flew by in the world of American Bistro / Pacific Northwest Gourmet Cuisine. It was one crazy Saturday night service where I was literally 'burnt out' of the kitchen. I severely burned myself from hot oil and was instantly pulled out of the wonder and awe of culinary artistry and faced with the new reality of healing and high school graduation. My fire for the art of culinary expression was far from extinguished.

I moved to Los Angeles at eighteen to pursue a career in the film industry as a writer and actor, all the while continuing my independent studies of the cultural cuisines of the world. Along with a multitude of other jobs, I would work as a private chef always polishing my ever developing skills as a young chef in training. Simultaneously, my path of the healing and yogic sciences had begun with the enrollment to become certified in a spectrum of healing modalities and practices at the Touch Therapy Institute. It wasn't until I met one of my teachers, a yogic practitioner who trained me in the biochemistry of plant based nutrition, that I began my journey into the world of the vegan diet and plant based nutrition. I began to adapt my traditional culinary techniques to this new diet and its ingredients. It was a challenge at first, but because it was my diet, I had no choice but to evolve. Over half a decade into the lifestyle of being vegan, my teacher introduced the next step in the evolution of nutrition... Raw or Living Foods.

Food that was alive and enriched with its own enzymes. It was then that I embarked upon the next chapter in my attempt to fuse the concept of traditional gourmet cuisine with raw living plant based nutrition. I was blessed to cross the path of many Raw chefs on my journey, studying and learning what they had figured out so far and how to keep the movement of raw food in constant evolution and ultimately soaring to new heights. From here, I began developing my recipe archives of gourmet raw food.

WHAT'S THE PURPOSE OF THIS BOOK?

The Art & Science of Living Foods is the most extensive guide of raw plant-based nutrition to date. It contains a superfood dictionary, spice & herb dictionary, and a full raw cook book inundated with the science & methodologies of raw food technology. It takes you through a journey of defining what raw means, what you will need to create raw food, and how to create a schedule to incorporate it functionally into your lifestyle.

The science of sacred geometry is that geometry and mathematical ratios, harmonics, and proportion are also found in music, light, cosmology...and you guessed it...food! This book is more of a metaphorical expression of sacred geometry but is also full of sacred geometry through beautiful photographs, elaborate designs, and in the food itself.

INTRODUCTION

Provided with easy to follow detailed recipes that inspire and excite the taste buds, this is a divine guide into the world of the medicinal, artistic, and scientific revolution of raw plant-based nutrition. *The Art & Science of Living Foods* is everything that every other raw or living foods book hasn't been for me as a raw food explorer on the path to learning and integrating raw food in my life and into my community.

What truly sets this book apart from all others is that it has a superfood dictionary, Herb & Spice guide, and an extensive gourmet cook book.

So many living food books are full of elaborate beautiful pictures and artistic layouts but are lacking in the fundamental, practical, and applicable information on procedure, technique, and methodology of its ingredients.

The first of its kind, this raw centered text breaks down the methodologies and technologies in the processing of making raw food recipes as well as providing a structured system / schedule to integrate the production of raw foods into your personal lifestyle. Another interesting characteristic to this book is a kind of spiritual essence that embodies the book itself. It's subtle, but also present and in alignment with the natural evolution of consciousness that develops from eating higher conscious food. When you combine this spirit with the user friendly structure, it makes for easy reading, yet an intensely informative guide to understanding and integrating raw food in everyone's lifestyle.

CHAPTER 1
THE GEOMETRY OF PROTEIN

With all the controversy around protein these days, I was tempted to label this chapter, 'THE CONTROVERSY OF PROTEIN'. Upon reflection I realized that addressing the mythology of the manufactured concept "that to be nutritionally balanced and healthy, you must ingest a specific requirement of meat protein", and the exploration of the truth about proteins and their role in the human body was what really needed to be innerstood (my evolution of 'understood'). Unfortunately, because the innerstanding just really hasn't happened yet, I am constantly contacted by health conscious nutritional pioneers that are feeling lost in a sea of protein based controversy. My intention in this chapter is to reflect the basic facts, as well as some information you may not know, or have been desensitized to by your environment. Either way, with all the misinformation out there, we deserve a scientific foundation of truth to ground our nutritional understanding and overstanding of what our body needs biochemically to function at the highest vibration achievable.

So let us get into it...there are a few aspects to the reality of subjective perspective i.e. ego, and the foundational structure of nutrition. First, be present and sit with the awareness that any diet can be looked at negatively, especially a raw food or vegan diet, if it is not structured and applied correctly. Plenty of raw food practitioners do not get sufficient amounts of protein on a daily basis. This is usually for two different reasons: (1) they do not consume a large enough amount of calories/proteins, *or* (2) they consume too much raw food without protein substance and higher sugar (like excess amounts of fruit and not enough protein and fiber rich vegetables). In order to live healthy on a raw food diet, you have to almost double your caloric intake...In short, you have to eat lots of food. I always tell people I work with that it is the food lover's diet because you have to eat a lot. Because this food is enzyme enriched, it digests itself a.k.a, it is processed quickly. This gives you energy instantly and takes you back to the roots of humanity's diet schedule...which is snacking throughout the day. This greatly conflicts with the current American programming of a daily three meal routine. Alternatively, many of these trendy diets are based around an organic 'traditional' meal schedule of small consistent meals or snacks throughout the day. In the case of raw food, because as mentioned before, the food itself is digested so quickly that each snack leads to the next. Unfortunately, most raw foodists' have either not been taught or do not follow a harmoniously healthy raw diet based on this structure of ancestral consumption, and ultimately reflects in their appearance being super thin, emaciated, and weak. It is they who create a negative image for those curious and exploring this divine path of nutrition.

It takes a lot of work to make up for not having all those amino acids and proteins from muscle tissue. In any truly healthy diet the odds of you accumulating any substantial amount of muscle mass have very specific limitations due to simply your own genetic makeup...unless you incorporate some destructively unhealthy and potentially dangerous practices. In all truth, if you don't have your cup in the gene pool for that type of build you desire, all the exercise and working out in the world will not build your muscle mass and sculpt you to what 'your mind' envisions. Speaking of working out, most of the 'muscle men' you see in the gyms who have these super hero builds are in no way genetically 'blessed'. They are using drugs and growth stimulants in one form or another. Everything from forcing anabolic growth hormone stimulation to full on steroids shots or some other synthetic supplemental measures. These toxifying superficial devices of illusion may create rapid muscle growth and an increase in the overall size but are highly destructive to a multitude of systems in the body.

Where so many will righteously proclaim that they do NOT take steroids or growth hormones, 99% of them are using and for the most part don't have a clue of the mutation and modification going on within their bodies. How you may be wondering? Simply put *the meat* and *the dairy*. Generally, animal products when consumed in large quantities are full of antibiotics, growth stimulants, and hormones leading to your own bodies tissue, like a sponge, absorbing these chemicals and hormones. The disturbing fact that Europe now refuses import of American beef after learning of the high levels of hormones in it should tell you enough.

CHAPTER 1 THE GEOMETRY OF PROTEIN

Reality check...The actual accumulation of real muscle that a human being can build naturally, is about 1% of muscle a month, and that is with consistent and diligent effort (nutritionally and physically). A lot of the increase in muscle size that people see is due to fluid accumulation rather than muscle growth. One of the main reasons that the human body requires more protein, specifically athletes and bodybuilders, is really very elementary. Their caloric intake is too low, and they are not eating enough carbohydrates. During physical training, carbs (the body's primary energy source) burn up or begin to run low. In order to sustain a base supply of carbs, the body will initiate the consumption of its protein supply for energy. Multitudes of studies reveal an increase of protein in the diet ends up primarily being utilized for energy as opposed to muscle growth and regeneration. In fact, if there is any effect on the muscles at all it is most likely from the hormones and steroids in the animal's muscle tissue. What's interesting though is that if the same person were to simply increase their consumption of healthy carbohydrates, they would expand their supply of glycogen (reserve carbs) and would find themselves more adaptable to the conservation and reduction of the false protein requirements of their confused body. Since most all carbohydrates are made up of some protein, they would still be getting more than enough protein resulting in a better prepared body for athletics.

When we break down the statistics and run the numbers, it becomes apparent how *sold* we've become on an overabundance of protein, ($product$), in our diet. The complication being that the primitive tradition/practice/ritual of the hunt toward survival was then industrialized along with the rest of the world's food completely eradicating the spirit within the substance. It became a product to be sold, it became a numbers game of profits and margins. That's why when the nutritional studies were done and it was discovered that the body does not require high levels of animal proteins to be healthy or that is does not necessarily get any calcium from milk at all, it was swept under the rug and the dawn of industrialization of nutrition began. It began with a false foundational chart of what your body NEEDS to be healthy. The birth of media, through radio, television, to quick news at the touch of your fingertips, turned our nutritional programming into the constant barrage of false information given to the masses that trust in their government. With ad slogans like, "Drink milk for healthy teeth and strong bones'—for which it does quite the opposite, with some third world countries leading our rank it is no wonder we are ranked 35th in the world for health. Now we could get lost in a multitude of reasons to why that is, but in staying focused on the mythology told to us of protein... Let's run some numbers.

THE ART & SCIENCE OF LIVING FOODS

CHAPTER 1 THE GEOMETRY OF PROTEIN

The amount of protein a human being supposedly requires based on U.S. RDA's chart is 0.8 grams per kilogram (2.2 pounds) of body weight. Now, this doesn't apply to someone who is overweight, this is factored off of a classic model body weight. Someone with excess body fat doesn't need to feed that excess protein. Please also take into account that the .8 grams/kg is an overestimation that has a safety factor calculated in. The actual amount needed to sustain a nitrogenous balance is roughly .3 grams—.4 grams per 2.2 pounds of body weight. When you look at the studies and reports done in regard to how much protein an athlete or bodybuilder requires, the calculations range from .8 grams per kg (2.2 pounds), showing that they don't require anymore protein than your average folk.

So, lets crunch some of these guesstimates on yours truly; I am 5'11" and my weight is a super healthy 187. My BMI is 26, which is by the machine's standards technically overweight. Since it's .8 gram per 2.2 pounds, we need to split my weight in half to 85 pounds and multiply it by .8 (the low estimate) which equals 68 grams. Now, when we do the numbers for the high estimate: 85 x 1.5 (high estimate), it equals 127.5; this is the amount of protein I require by their calculations to be healthy. Take note that by me eating fruits, vegetables, nuts, and some raw hummus, I was well over the low estimate of protein required for daily consumption. In choosing to increase my quantities of nuts and add a raw dessert, I ran the figures again and was comfortably soaring above the bodybuilders' requirement of protein intake with a whopping 2,800 calories, and 129 grams of protein.

The truth of the matter is that even if these numbers were exact, acquiring enough protein on a raw food diet is *easily* achievable. When you factor in that these calculations are excessive and that we don't even really need this much protein in the first place, it starts to become clear that something is not right in the world of food information. It has been provided that there is more death and disease in the world from an overabundance of protein then there is from a depletion of protein. In fact, a variety and number of health conditions can be attributed to this, including osteoporosis, gout, hypertension, strokes, heart disease, kidney stones, and a surge in the death toll of many types of cancers. It is clear something isn't working here, and it's time to explore our options. I believe that's what you're doing even reading a book like this.

Congratulations for breaking the generational / traditional / cultural programming and tuning into the disharmony between your living human body and the dead matter you've been told your whole life was food. In that respect, let's explore a few examples that I implore you to expand upon that are alternative, viable sources of protein to muscle tissue.

It must be addressed that most vegetables are exceptional sources of protein, specifically any of the green leafy specimens such as kale, collard greens, Swiss chard, etc. Why is it we deter from eating enough of these green protein gold mines? Not the easiest to get down? As a true ADULT, it is your responsibility to put substance over taste on the same note we can have our green cake and eat it too. There are several methodologies to ingesting strong greens from juicing them to sneaking them in a smoothie. There are a multitude of recipes from pizza to hummus wraps that incorporate these powerful greens in without you really even noticing. Kale has the highest protein content of any of the green vegetables, making it irresistible going down the hatch. Broccoli is right behind as 1,200 calories of raw broccoli provide an astounding 131 grams of protein. Now I know that's a lot of protein, but the point is to reflect upon the fact that RAW veggies have a lot of protein. Why don't most people know this about veggies? Simple... because they cook them, and by doing so, they cook most of the proteins right out of them. In conclusion, if you want more protein in your diet, eat more RAW greens.

Make no mistake, I'm not saying that the raw vegan diet is the RIGHT diet and everything other diet is wrong. If I did, I would be just like every other intellectually righteous person in the diet psychosis of the modern day listening to their mind when they eat instead of their bodies. Rather, I state for the record that you should always listen to your body and eat what it expresses its needs intuitively, and if that means some meat one week, then who is your brain (ego) to stand in the way of that? I would recommend that you eat all food as full of life force as possible; remember as you cook anything over 117 degrees, you literally cook the life out of it. It's not black and white though, some vegetables, legumes, and leafy greens have bio-chemical elements—even neuro toxins—that require some breakdown with heat to be able to digest. This information can be overwhelming in revealing that animal proteins are truly *unnecessary* in our modern day and in this age of food technology, science, and consciousness. It is quite literally a dying practice. On the following page, I have listed a finite list of key protein statistics based off of the most recent, more accurate system called the Protein Digestibility Corrected Amino Acid Score (PDCAAS). While not 100% accurate, it is a great improvement and more precise in relation to the true requirements of humans and the statistical scoring of food.

CHAPTER 1 THE GEOMETRY OF PROTEIN

Utilizing the PDCAAS method, the protein quality rankings are calculated by comparing the amino acid profile of the specific food protein against a basic amino acid profile. The highest possible score is a 1.0, means that after digestion of the protein, it provides per unit of protein, 100% or more of the indispensable amino acids required.

whey (1.0)
egg white (1.0)
casein (1.0)
milk (1.0)
soy protein isolate (1.0)
beef (0.92)
soybean (0.91)
tubercules (0.74)
vegetables (0.74)
legumes in general (0.69)
kidney beans (0.68)
rye (0.68)
cereals (0.58)
whole wheat (0.54)
lentils (0.52)
peanuts (0.52)
seitan (0.25)

THE ART & SCIENCE OF LIVING FOODS

MICAH SKYE

CHAPTER 1 THE GEOMETRY OF PROTEIN

NOTES

CHAPTER 2
THE TOOLS OF THE TECHNOLOGY

As with all technologies, Raw food requires a certain assortment of tools. These tools will become your assistants—your companions—along the journey of raw culinary exploration, and are worth investing in. Don't skimp or cut corners with quality because it will cost you more in the long run. Since there is no cooking involved in the process of raw food, all of our 'companions' are for prep work, excluding the dehydrator which is a major pillar in a raw foodists diet as it allows for the preparation and preservation of larger quantities of raw food to be made for future consumption. Throughout this chapter, we will define, understand, and integrate the various tools used in the art of incorporating raw food cuisine into our journey. I have created icons for the various categories of tools. These icons you will see throughout the recipe section when they are required. I have found this to be easier, especially when starting out, to approach and successfully complete some of the more process-oriented raw recipes—especially when it requires more than one preparation tool or device. Eventually, it will become second nature to you, for instance, to know that when making bread, you will need to use a food processor and a dehydrator, but when just beginning or when approaching a recipe for the first time...it helps.

The following page lists the icons next to which are the categories that they represent and a brief description of their role in the raw food process and how to use them. Some icons/categories represent several tools, for instance, cutlery doesn't just represent knives but also cutting devices such as a mandolin which is used to cut raw pasta. It is clarified in the recipe and will again become second nature, but in the beginning be very conscious of what each recipe requires in regard to your tools. Today's technology has taken the possibilities with raw food to another level of manifestation. Many of these 'modern' devices are evolutions to age old methodologies of preserving food from the harvest for the winter. I am currently working on one such device to create a solar based dehydration system. I want to reiterate the FACT that you should choose your tools and equipment very consciously as they are a vital part of the process, and it is worth getting the premium quality. For example, I burned through 3 food processors until I finally got one with the wattage and motor capacity to handle the caliber of processing I was doing. Keep in mind, you are going to be grinding up nuts, dates, avocados; heavy duty and dense foods that will put your motors to the test, both blenders and food processors. I do recommend getting both. Though they may seem similar in functionality, they actually serve very different purposes in the kitchen. For this reason they are separate icons on our list.

FOOD PROCESSOR – An appliance consisting of a container housing interchangeable rotating blades and used for preparing foods by shredding, slicing, chopping, or blending. This device is much more effective for grinding up dense materials such as nuts, grains, etc. than a blender. It's much more effective for breads, pie crusts, and so on.

CUTLERY – A wide variety of edged cutting tools for cutting food ranging from a chef knife to a mandolin (stationary cutting device).

COFFEE GRINDER – A device traditionally used for pulverizing or powdering coffee beans. In a raw foodist's hands it becomes a lucrative tool for powdering anything from spices and herbs to flaxseeds.

SPROUTING DEVICE – A tool or device that enables the growth or gestation of seeds, legumes, grains, and so on. These devices range from sprouting jars, trays, and even actual mechanical devices for higher volume. They are cheap, simple, and easy to use.

BLENDER – An electrical appliance with rotating blades for chopping, mixing, or liquefying foods. Blenders are much more effective in liquefying substances such as smoothies, dressings, and puddings.

DEHYDRATOR – An appliance or a designed system engineered to remove H20 from substances such as absorbents or food. This device will 'uncook' everything from cookies to bread while leaving all the enzymes and nutrients. Cooking removes by heating over 115 degrees.

CHAPTER 2 THE TOOLS OF THE TECHNOLOGY

MANDALA LIVING FOODS

THE ART & SCIENCE OF LIVING FOODS

I want to again remind you of the importance of the quality when acquiring your various tools of technology. These are your ovens and stoves, and for this reason you will be using them to fullest capacity (daily), and at times pushing them to the limit of their capability. They are going to be your most significant investment in your future outside of your time and effort in the raw food transformation.

Herre are a few recommendations in regard to specifications for purchasing equipment. With food processors, make sure the wattage of your motor is at least 700 watts. I only use a 1,000 watt industrial food processor, but like I said... it's about quality. In regard to a blender, I would go with nothing but a Vitamix. It has the equivalent of a race car motor in it and creates the most effective consistency needed for creams, puddings, and other puree based components of various raw dishes. Knives are a very personal decision to a chef as they are an extension of yourself, but if I could make one recommendation it would be to make sure they have a full tang through the handle and have rivets. With dehydrators, I would recommend the Excaliber as it is the most functional in its design. Coffee grinders are pretty standard, but I would recommend checking the wattage on the motor. Well, now it's official, you have more guidance than I did trying to figure this brave new world out for myself. I hope it helps you on your road to evolution!

It is an interesting journey of transformation evolving your lifestyle into the raw food diet. Letting go of a lot of the destructive crutches we feel such a dependency on like our ovens, microwaves, and stoves. I remember it was strange for me to think, "Wow, I really don't need these tools of the past to provide food for myself and others." It was almost more unsettling how programmed to use them I was as I reflected on the fact that we are the only species on the planet that cooks its food. We are also the unhealthiest species on the planet, and what's worse is our diet is affecting other species as well... our pets! All of the food we raise our pets on and feed them is also cooked. These tools, although based in technology, are our way of getting back to our roots. So learn them, know them, and apply them to your process. Evolution is a choice for humanity, just as the word 'human being' is actually two words. 'Human' and 'being', and you have a choice...To live toward the 'human' (lower vibrational animalistic side of our consciousness), or the 'being' (the evolving higher vibrational spiritualistic side of our consciousness). One of the key factors that resonates with me is that a diet that is in alignment with the ascending vibratory levels of the planet is going to allow for our simultaneous ascension much more easily than a diet that is based in the lower vibrational resonance. That is why there has been this explosion of raw food technology into the mainstream. That's why you purchased this book, and probably several others. It is time to go higher as a species. Who would of thought it should start with the food? Well as the famous saying goes, "You are what you eat."

CHAPTER 3
THE MEDITATION OF PREPARATION

There are many definitions for the concept of meditation, and in many contexts, it can be applied. The definition I resonate with is a mental discipline by which one attempts to get beyond the conditioned 'thinking' mind into a deeper state of relaxation or awareness. Meditation often involves turning attention to a single point of reference. In that sentence lies the true essence of one of the greatest secrets to connecting with the divinity of each moment. If meditation is based around turning one's attention to a single point of reference, then that point of reference can be anything and everything! Everything can be a meditation: doing your laundry, painting your fence, and preparing your food. Hey, even drinking a glass of H20 can be a meditation... or it could just be drinking a glass of H20. This is the free will dimension, so you do have a choice. I'll elaborate on the simple task I've already introduced, drinking a glass of H20. So I could just gulp it down quenching my thirst...Or I could tune into the sensation of the H20 and its vibration as it passes over my tongue, feel the vibration of its molecules as it passes my throat and enters my H20 vessel only to return to itself, and explore the effects of it being absorbed into my being. Wow, that sounds like a complicated drink of H2o, but you know what? It's so simple. It just takes slowing down into the 'present'. That word, 'present', also means gift, and that's exactly what each and every one of them is manifested. Unfortunately we are raised in a world of fast paced, moment to moment stimulation and restlessness. We have no idea how to slow down -to receive this gift-but it's easier than we think. In fact some of us already do this and don't even know it. In the context of our journey in this book, we are going to tune in with cooking-or uncooking in our case. Either way cooking or not the process and ritual of making food is also an amazing meditation that can calm and center the mind, body, and soul...Or you can just make yourself some food. Again, the choice is yours.

THE ART & SCIENCE OF LIVING FOODS

CHAPTER 3 THE MEDITATION OF PREPARATION

There are many definitions for the concept of meditation, and with many contexts it can be applied. The definition I resonate with is a mental discipline by which one attempts to get beyond the conditioned, 'thinking' mind into a deeper state of relaxation or awareness. Meditation often involves turning attention to a single point of reference. In that sentence lies the true essence of one of the greatest secrets to connecting with the divinity of each moment. If meditation is based around turning one's attention to a single point of reference, then that point of reference can be anything and everything! Everything can be a meditation: doing your laundry, painting your fence, and preparing your food. Hey, even drinking a glass of H20 can be a meditation... Or it could just be drinking a glass of H20. This is the free will dimension, so you do have a choice. I'll elaborate on the simple task I've already introduced, drinking a glass of H20. So I could just gulp it down quenching my thirst...Or I could tune into the sensation of the H20 and its vibration as it passes over my tongue, feeling the vibration of its molecules as it passes my throat and enters my H20 vessel only to return to itself, and explore the effects of it being absorbed into my being. Wow, that sounds like a complicated drink of H2o, but you know what? It's so simple. It just takes slowing down into the 'present'. That word, 'present', also means gift, and that's exactly each and every one of them is manifested. Unfortunately we are raised in a world of fast paced, moment to moment stimulation and restlessness. We have no idea how to slow down to receive this gift, but it's easier than we think. In fact some of us already do this and don't even know it. When you read a book, create (painting, drawing, etc.), and the list goes on. In the context of our journey in this book, we are going to tune in with cooking-or uncooking in out cases. Either way cooking or not the process and ritual of making food is also an amazing meditation that can calm and center the mind, body and soul...Or you can just make yourself some food. Again, the choice is yours.

Now all types of food have preparation that takes place along the journey to the plate, but with raw food our preparation also a lot of the times is our "uncooking" so to speak. Now you are going to learn the plethora of items you can make that are in some sense of the word, "cooked", or "baked". Just not over 115 degrees, so that all the enzymes and nutrients remain in the food. After all, that is why you're eating food right? For nutrition that is. Too often we eat for sensory gratification and not for substance. The goal of this book is to show you functional foods that satisfy both taste and substance that are fairly easy to prepare. The focus in evolving your eating habits has to be both anticipation and preparation. Meaning, if I am on my last couple pieces of raw bread, I should already have another batch of grains sprouting and ready to make more bread. If I'm on my last few pieces of cheese or at the end of my raw almond, I should have the ingredients already prepared to make sure my nutritional momentum is not halted by a lack of preparation and anticipation. Those who choose the path of living food have much "meditation" that lies ahead. Outside of the prepared raw food you can buy in a store (which is rapidly expanding), if you want raw almond milk or cheese...You're going to have to make it yourself. It's as simple as that. It definitely takes more time and energy to create food that gives you more time and energy on this planet. The goal of this chapter, and for you as a self-practitioner is to get into a tempo of preparation that flows with your evolving schedule and lifestyle.

Before we can go into setting up a customized raw schedule for you. We need to go through a sprouting chart of the units of life that needed to be awakened. Our nuts, seeds, grains, and legumes. They each have their own activation (soak) time in which the life awakens from the slumber. This is the principle of nut and seed hydration (soaking). All raw seeds, grains and nuts should be soaked before using. Raw nuts and seeds have enzyme inhibitors on their surface that protect them while they grow. Soaking releases the inhibitors and significantly boosts the nutrition and digestibility of nuts and seeds. Your digestive system will feel better after eating them soaked than after eating them unsoaked. Some of you might like to add a little salt to the H20 before soaking to help speed up the process. After soaking, be sure to rinse seeds and nuts thoroughly with fresh pure H20 until it runs clear to remove the enzyme inhibitors that have been released into the H20. It is also recommended to rinse soaking seeds and nuts 2-3 times during the soak. After soaking, you can dehydrate at 105 degrees until the nuts/seeds are completely dry. Store in the refrigerator or freezer to keep them fresh. Use within 3-5 days.

The following chart gives a good guideline for soaking and sprouting times of the most common seeds, nuts and grains. You'll notice that some nuts are not soaked or sprouted. I have experienced otherwise, but I have labeled them as such because they are.

Learn this chart on the following page and absorb these hydration cycles so that there is no need to reference this chart eventually when contemplating what you'd like to soak for the week. On the following pages we're going to go through everything from the basics of sprouting to the various methodologies of sprouting techniques. I recommend experimenting with what resonates with you the best, and then build form there.

Put on your lab coats, because the raw experiment has begun!

CHAPTER 3 THE MEDITATION OF PREPARATION

BASICS OF SPROUTING:

1. Obtain seed for sprouting. Store in bug-proof containers, away from extreme heat/cold. Seed should be viable, and, to extent possible, free of chemicals.

2. Basic steps in sprouting are:

   - Measure out appropriate amount of seed, visually inspect and remove stones, sticks, weed seed, broken seeds, etc.
   - Rinse seed (if seed is small and clean, can usually skip this rinse)
   - Soak seed in H20 for appropriate time
   - Rinse soaked seed, put in sprouting environment for appropriate time
   - Service seeds (rinse) in sprouting environment as needed
   - When ready, rinse seeds. Store in refrigerator, in sprouting environment or in other suitable container until ready to use. If not used within 12 hours, seeds should be serviced (rinsed) every 24 hours in refrigerator. Best to eat as soon as possible, as freshness is what makes sprouts so unique!

HYDRATION CHART

Seed, Nut, or Grain	Soak Time	Sprout Time
Adzuki	12 hours	3-5 days
Alfalfa	8 hours	2-5 days
Almonds	8-12 hours	12 hours
Barley	6-8 hours	2 days
Brazil Nuts	Do not soak	N/A
Buckwheat	6 hours	2 days
Cashews	2-2 ½ hours	N/A
Chickpeas	12 hours	12 hours
Clover	4-6 hours	4-5 days
Corn	12 hours	2-3 days
Fenugreek	8 hours	3-5 days
Flax	8 hours	N/A
Green Peas	12 hours	2-3 days
Hemp Seeds	Do not soak	N/A
Kamut	7 hours	2-3 days
Lentils	8 hours	12 hours
Macadamia Nuts	Do not soak	N/A
Millet	8 hours	2-3 days
Mung Beans	1 day	2-5 days
Mustard	8 hours	2-7 days
Nuts (all others)	6 hours	N/A
Pecans	4-6 hours	N/A
Pine Nuts	Do not soak	N/A
Pistachio Nuts	Do not soak	N/A
Pumpkin Seeds (hulled)	8 hours	1 day
Rye	8 hours	3-5 days
Quinoa	2 hours	1 day
Sesame Seeds	8 hours	1-2 days
Spelt	7 hours	2 days
Sunflower Seeds (hulled)	2 hours	2-3 days
Walnuts	4 hours	n/a
Wheat Berries	7 hours	2-2 ½ days
Wild Rice	9 hours	3-5 days

CHAPTER 3 THE MEDITATION OF PREPARATION

TWO RECOMMENDED SPROUTING METHODS: JARS AND CLOTH

Jars: I use a wide-mouth, glass canning jars. These are available at many hardware stores anywhere in the country. Now I have found both plastic screen lids made for sprouting in these canning jars, and sprouting jars that come ready to sprout. Otherwise, you will need to create a screen lids—cut pieces of different (plastic) mesh screens and place them on the top of the jar underneath the metal ring. Sprouting in jars is very easy when you get the process down. It's really all about being attentive to the sprouts: simply put your nuts, grains, etc. in the jar, add H20, and twist the lid on. I recommend filling your jar half way with your desired sprout because if you fill it too much then it cramps the sprouts from growing in the bottom of the jar and they can get funky or moldy. It's illusive, because you'll think that you haven't put enough in, but after the soak it'll be almost double in size. Then as the days go on the jar will be full to the top. When soak is over, invert jar, drain the H20, and then rinse again. Then prop the jar up at 45 degree angle for H20 to drain. Keep out of direct sunlight. Rinse seed in jar 2–3 times per day until ready, always keeping this angle when draining. The more you rinse the healthier the sprouts will be. The next method is in my opinion less efficient and leaves room for more bacterial development but is the old school method of sprouting.

Cloth: soak sprouts to be in a flat-bottom container, containing a shallow volume of H20. When their soak time is finished, empty the sprouts into strainer and rinse. Then take a flat-bottom bowl or dish, line the bottom with wet 100% cotton washcloth, and spread the sprouts on the wet cloth. Now take a second wet cloth and put it on top of sprouts, or, if your bottom cloth is large enough you can fold it over the sprouts. Now comes the attentiveness to add additional H20 to washcloths every 12 hours by either: (a) sprinkling it over top, or (b) if they have gotten very dehydrated, then remove the sprouts from the cloth, wash them off, re-wet cloth, and put the sprouts back in between the wet cloths. Cloths used should be 100% cotton (terry cloth) or linen, used only for your sprouting process, and of lighter colors. Cheap cotton washcloths (and cheap plastic bowls) work well and will last a long time.

MANDALA LIVING FOODS

THE ART & SCIENCE OF LIVING FOODS

IN COMPARISON: JARS VS. CLOTH METHODS

In my experience, the jar method has more versatility. For instance, you can grow greens in the jar (i.e., 6–8 day old clover greens), and the jar is less likely to mold than the cloth method for sprouts that require more than a couple days of soaking. Nonetheless, the jar method needs a consistent drain system (otherwise, mold can develop). The cloth method can withstand some direct sunlight, whereas direct sunlight in early stages of sprouting can cook the seed in jars, and on top of that, cloth needs no drainage system. The methods require roughly the same time, although the second service of cloth is very fast. Some nuts and grains fare better in cloth to the jar method, such as almonds, buckwheat, and walnuts. They all do better in cloth. In fact, for your almonds and walnuts, I suggest soaking them in a big glass bowl with a plate flush over the top. Simple is better sometimes. Especially with almonds, as they're one of the only nuts that can easily sprout and are in their most nutritious state when they sprout.

OTHER METHODS OF SPROUTING:

1. **Sprouting bags** - usually made of cotton or linen; I've also seen plastic mesh. You soak sprouts in the bag in a bucket of H20, and then hang the bag inside of a plastic bag. It's basically your own little greenhouse.
2. **Trays** - great for growing greens. You need a system to drain though.
3. **Clay saucer** - mostly used for mucilaginous seeds such as flax, psyllium, etc.
4. **Commercial sprouters** - wide variety available. Often fairly expensive; most don't work as well as cloth/jar methods.
5. **Plastic tube** - variation on jar method; opens at both ends ~ easier to remove long sprouts like greens from a tube than from a jar.

CHAPTER 3 THE MEDITATION OF PREPARATION

WHAT IS THE LIFESPAN OF MY SPROUTS?

Well, the ultimate answer is...YOU will only know by experimenting, growing sprouts, and eating them at a variety of ages/lengths. My personal preference is different with each sprout. With a few exceptions, like almonds, I prefer when the tail or root is, on average, a little under the length of the seed. You may like them better when the sprout is just popping out. I will say that the more life that grows and strengthens in the sprout the more nutritious it gets. Remember, if you planted this life capsule in the ground, it would grow into a plant or a tree. Instead, you plant it in you... in your soil to grow and bring life to your world...

There are many organizational systems that can aid the raw food practitioner, from a weekly/monthly calendar or schedule to a note pad on the fridge that says, "weekly prep". This is one of the key foundations of integrating a well-rounded cycle of food mindfulness for your week. Eventually, you will customize your own system that will work best for you, but I've found that it's always nice to a have a functional structure as a beginning foundation. So I've enclosed my weekly and monthly raw calendar/schedule for you. This is something that all other Raw books have lacked. The main focus of this book is to integrate the lifestyle of living nutrition which requires a schedule. There are some basic guidelines that I recommend with which you build your raw schedule:

Designate at least two prep days a week for soaking nuts and grains at least three days apart. For example, let's say you assign Monday as a soak day. Then, you should soak enough nuts to last you until at least Friday and should be soaking your next batch by Saturday. Now every nut, grain, seed, legume, etc. has a different soak/sprout time which can be referenced in the chart on the previous page.

MANDALA LIVING FOODS

Calculate when you want your processed raw food in your week so that you can know when to start your prep for it. For instance, if you want your bread for the start of the week (Monday), then you need to start soaking the grains for the bread on Tuesday of the previous week so they will be sprouted by Saturday and ready to be prepped and unbaked (dehydrated). As you'll learn in the recipe sections of the book, dehydrating some raw food products can range anywhere from 6–17 hours and need to be factored in to your calculation. In the current example of our bread, it takes 8–12 hours to dehydrate the raw bread. Therefore, if you started your bread on Saturday at 8 a.m., it would be done around 6 p.m.–8 p.m. and ready for your week. Something to take note of is that as you start your week stocked with bread, come Tuesday, you should be soaking your grains for the next week if you want to have bread for the following week. The same goes for all the other foods on your list. The highlighted categories that are labeled 'on the spot' are labeled that way because they need little to no prep ahead of time and can be made... on the spot.

Inventory your food to know when your finished raw food is good until expiration so that you know how much to make and when to eat it by. Each recipe has a life span marked at the bottom of the recipe that reflects how long it will last. Some things have a shorter shelf life than others, such as almond milk which is at its best within the first four days of making it. With dehydrated food such as cheese, bread, and burgers, the shelf life is longer as they have been preserved to a certain extent.

The below Raw Schedule will allow you to factor in a schedule to stock your refrigerator and cupboards with all the live food you need throughout the week. Feel free to substitute or add any elements that needs to be prepped to the schedule (e.g., tostadas, tacos, etc.)

Raw Schedule

Food to-do list	Monday	Tuesday	Wednesday	Thursday	Friday	Saturday	Sunday
Breads / Pastries		Soak grains				Make dough & dehydrate	Package
Cheeses	Prepare & dehydrate			Prepare non-dry cheese			
Milk			Soak nuts	Process			Soak nuts & process
Cookies		Soak nuts/ legumes	Process & store				
Spreads							
Marinades	Soak (mushrooms)	Store	On the spot	On the spot	On the spot	On the spot	On the spot
Sauces	On the Spot	On the spot	On the spot	On the spot	On the spot	On the spot	On the spot
Desserts	Prepare & serve / store						
Crackers / Shells					Soak seeds	Prepare & dehydrate	Pack & store
Protein	Serve & store for the week					Soak nuts	Prepare / dehydrate

CHAPTER 3 THE MEDITATION OF PREPARATION

Here's your clean slate so to speak. You can model it after mine or modify it to your individuality/preference. I left you a blank row at the bottom for anything else your heart desires. My suggestion? Kombucha tea...But that's just me! Please enjoy this lifestyle tool of transformation. This is my gift to you...Sat Nam!

Food to-do list	Monday	Tuesday	Wednesday	Thursday	Friday	Saturday	Sunday
Breads / Pastries							
Cheeses							
Milk							
Cookies							
Spreads							
Marinades							
Sauces							
Desserts							
Crackers / Shells							
Protein							

MANDALA LIVING FOODS

HERBOMETRY & SPICEOLOGY

OF LIVING FOODS

CHAPTER 4
THE SCIENCE OF HERBOMETRY & SPICEOLOGY

The science of spices and herbs is an ancient practice that spans throughout the world's cultures and civilizations. Folk practitioners, herbalists, and the people of these various cultures alike have used plant-based remedies for centuries in everything from tonics and compresses to the consumption of their daily food, In fact, many common ingredients found in your kitchen have the powerful medicinal properties to heal your body, mind, and soul with great effectiveness. It is for this reason that researchers have recently begun to study the powers of these herbs and spices. Well, the reports are in, and they are all confirming what our ancestors have known for ages... the earth's herbs and spices possess truly powerful preventive and healing properties.

With their origins a mystery, lost in trade from culture to culture, these magical medicines were a symbol, a token, and even a gift of power, of knowledge... of a connection of union with nature to heal, to harness strength, but most of all to activate a union with mind, body, and soul. This was the ancestors' acknowledgement of the herb and the spice. Many of the beliefs of ancient cultures in regard to herbs and spices were based in the more esoteric realms. For example, the Mayans used allspice in their embalming rituals because they believed it would bring wealth and good fortune, and the ancient Chinese believed coriander to be connected with immortality. Now there were also a multitude of more "practical" or 'medicinal' practices and beliefs that these cultures followed such as the Romans who discovered a natural appetite suppressant in chewing fennel seeds. Another example is cumin which was used as a natural cold remedy.

In this chapter, we will explore the history, chemistry, and the functionality of herbs and spices, both on a medicinal and culinary level. The ancient rituals and practices of spices and herbs have been lost in many of the more contemporary societies. Many cultures have maintained their traditions of Herbometry and Spiceology. In fact, it is mainly the Western world that lost their way with the use of spices. More recently, though, with the trend of culinary practices, especially though the media, Americans are becoming more aware of the significance of the age old tools, thus why I felt it was important to create a dictionary of all the herbs and spices that I was raised on, or have been led to, on my journey so far on this earth. So again, I want to state that this collection is not finite. There are no boundaries to this dictionary, and I implore you to keep searching and keep expanding your knowledge of the science of herb and spice!

CHAPTER 4: THE SCIENCE OF HERBOMETRY & SPICEOLOGY

MANDALA LIVING FOODS

ALLSPICE

Allspice is a single berry from the Jamaican Pimenta Dioica tree. With hints of cinnamon, cloves, and nutmeg, allspice can be used as a whole berry or can be ground as needed. When used as a whole berry, one can create seafood stocks, mulled wine, and pickling blends. When ground, allspice adds a warming flavor to fruit dishes, baked desserts, sauces, and marinades. Medicinally, it was used in the Caribbean to remedy colds and cramps. For the Mayans, it was utilized in their embalming rituals and was believed to bring good luck and wealth. Below are some basic statistics of its compatibility and uses, both culinarily and medicinally

Flavor characteristics of allspice:
- Possesses an aromatic warmth with a peppery hint of cinnamon, cloves, and nutmeg.

Culinary applications:
- Jerk seasoning, pickling spices, curries, spiced unbaked goods, and sauces.

Allspice complements:
- Raw walnut meat for jerk recipes, apples, chocolate/cacao recipes, peaches, pears, plums, pumpkins, tomatoes.

Allspice blends well with:
- Garlic, ginger, mustard, cloves, coriander, pepper, rosemary, as well as thyme.

Medicinal benefits:
- anti-inflammatory
- carminative
- anti-flatulent properties
- digestion
- antioxidant
- anti-bacterial
- anti-fungal
- coughs
- bronchitis
- migraines

ANISE

Anise seeds, also known as Star of Anise from the shape of its seed pod, originate out of the Mediterranean and Middle East. They hold a unique licorice taste and can specifically be used to season raw breads and soups. Anise is also used to bake into cookies, crackers, and even our raw cake recipe. Its medicinal qualities range from aiding in digestion and freshening the breath to relieving chronic pain and severe coughing. The whole seeds can also be mixed with coriander, cumin, cinnamon, or ginger to create a pickling spice blend. The seeds can be dehydrated to increase the aroma and flavor for raw curries and stews.

Flavor characteristics of anise:
- Sweet, warm, and fruity with hints of licorice.

Culinary applications:
- Raw sausage & other raw nut meat seasonings, unbaked goods, and sauces.

Anise complements:
- Almond, apricot, black pepper, cocoa butter, fig, honey, lemon, orange, peach, agave, nut meat, and vanilla.

Anise blends well with:
- Allspice, cardamom, cinnamon, cloves, cumin, dill, fennel, ginger, nutmeg, and pepper.

Medicinal benefits:
- Intestinal spasms
- Lactation disorders
- Flatulence
- Muscle cramps
- Asthma
- Nausea
- Cancer
- Coughs
- Bronchitis
- Migraines
- Colic
- Hiccups
- Irregular menstrual cycle
- Menstruation
- Dyspepsia
- Distention

BASIL

This herb is thought to have originated out of Africa and India. On an esoteric level, it was revered with ties to the Hindu goddess Tulsi which, in connection to her, Basil was honored as a symbol of love, faithfulness, and eternal spirit or life. The name Basil originates from the Greek *basileus* which means "king". Basil is a relative of the mint family, and like many mints, is primarily utilized medicinally for its digestive and anti-gas properties, but has other benefits listed below. On a culinary level, its harmonious relationship to other herbs makes it one of the most versatile and widely used herbs in our spice rack. There are a variety of types of basil with slight variations in essence and flavor. Here are a few I have explored: African Blue basil, Bush basil, Cinnamon basil, Opal basil, Purple Ruffles. And then there are an array of Asian basils including Thai, Licorice, Lemon, Lime, Holy, and Thai Lemon.

Flavor characteristics of Basil:
- Sweet with the essence of anise and clove. The flavor of basil is warm and contains underlying mint tones.

Culinary applications:
- An essential element to pesto, blends well with tomatoes, raw cheeses, breads, dehydrated nuts, and nut meats.

Basil complements:
- Tomatoes, raw cheeses, olives, olive oil, raw pastas, pasta sauces, raw pizza, salads, and tomatoes.

Basil Blends Well With:
- Chives, cilantro, garlic, marjoram, oregano, mint, parsley, rosemary, and thyme.

Medicinal benefits:
- Stomach cramps
- Vomiting
- Flatulence
- Constipation
- Headaches
- Anxiety
- Distention

CHAPTER 4 THE SCIENCE OF HERBOMETRY & SPICEOLOGY

BAY LEAF

In the Roman and Greek empires, the Bay leaf was a symbol of wisdom and glory. Generally, bay leaves are infused to flavor soups and stews. They are also used for pickling and work well with tomatoes, often utilized to flavor tomato sauces. Bay leaves can be used in any nut loaf creation, including the nut meatloaf in this book. One recommendation is to be conscious of how much you use as they provide an intense flavor and need to be removed before serving any dish.

Flavor characteristics of bay leaves:
- Bay leaves have a sweet and slightly balsamic smell. The leaves are slightly bitter and have a high potent flavor with hints of camphor; so use sparingly.

Culinary applications:
- Flavorful accent to sauces, soups, and marinades.

Basil complements:
- Tomatoes, raw cheeses, lentils, white beans, raw pastas, sauces, soups, and dressings.

Bay leaves blend well with:
- Allspice, garlic, juniper, marjoram, oregano, parsley, sage, savory, and thyme.

Medicinal benefits:
- Relaxation
- Sleep disorders
- Appetite stimulant
- Antifungal
- Diuretic
- Aids in digestion
- Anti-bacterial
- Antioxidant
- Lowers blood sugar

MANDALA LIVING FOODS

CARAWAY

Caraway qualities were realized by the ancient Egyptians, Greeks, and Romans. The herb was greatly integrated in the Middle Ages. It has been used for centuries in breads and cakes, and with baked fruit, especially roasted apples, as caraway was believed to keep lovers from straying. For this reason, it was once a fundamental ingredient in love potions and tonics. In our raw evolution, we'll use it to flavor our raw rye breads, raw sauerkraut, and even raw fruit dishes. In the nutritional deconstruction of caraway seeds, these ancient seeds reveal that they contain protein, fat, a sufficient amount of carbohydrates, besides ash, calcium, phosphorus, sodium, potassium, iron, thiamine, riboflavin, and niacin. It also contains vitamins C and A.

Flavor characteristics of caraway:
- Sweet with the essence of anise and clove. The flavor of basil is warm and contains underlying mint tones.

Culinary applications:
- An essential element to pesto, it blends well with tomatoes, raw cheeses, breads, dehydrated nuts, and nut meats.

Caraway complements:
- Tomatoes, raw cheeses, olives, olive oil, raw pastas, pasta sauces, raw pizza, salads, and tomatoes.

Caraway blends well with:
- Chives, cilantro, garlic, marjoram, oregano, mint, parsley, rosemary, and thyme.

Medicinal benefits:
- Eases dyspepsia
- Eases hysteria
- Flatulence
- Constipation
- Relieves earaches
- Aids with colic in babies

CHAPTER 4 THE SCIENCE OF HERBOMETRY & SPICEOLOGY

CARDAMOM

Also known as elaichi, cardamom is a tropical fruit from the ginger family called Elettaria Cardamomum. It was given the notorious title "The grains of paradise" throughout India were it is found in the fruit of a large perennial bush. It is a powerful and aromatic herb which has a great versatility to it as it holds several medicinal and therapeutic powers. Its value as a food source alone is excellent as it is low in fat and high in proteins and vitamins A, B, and C. Cardamom seeds are made up of 10% volatile oil. The Ancient Egyptians chewed cardamom seeds to freshen their breath and whiten their teeth. At the bottom of the page is a list of its uses dating back as early as 4th century B.C.

Flavor characteristics of cardamom:
- A fresh fruity aroma with a hint of citrus, followed by a flowery taste with a hint of camphor.

Culinary applications:
- Unbaked goods, curries, garam masala, chai tea, raw ice cream flavor.

Cardamom complements:
- Apples, banana, citrus fruits, curry, raw milks, oranges, pears, peppers, tea, vanilla, raw yogurt.

Cardamom Blends Well With:
- Caraway, cinnamon, cloves, coriander, cumin, ginger, paprika, pepper, saffron.

Medicinal benefits:
- Eases nausea
- Improves appetite
- Flatulence
- Aids with digestion
- Aids with heartburn
- Urinary disorders

MANDALA LIVING FOODS

CELERY SEED

Celery has been in use for over 2,000 years. It was grown by a multitude of cultures from the Chinese to the English. In the 16th and 17th centuries, it was brought into gardens and cultivated first as a medicinal plant, and later it became a flavoring for soups and stews. Celery seeds have a sort of warm yet blunt flavor, almost astringent. It can be used as whole seeds to flavor cabbage, coleslaw, or nut meats. Celery seeds can be ground to flavor soups, curries, and salads. It can also add a nice accent in pickling spices, celery salt, and a variety of dressings.

Flavor characteristics of celery seed:
- Celery seeds possess a warm, slightly bitter essence with accents of mint, nutmeg, and parsley.

Culinary applications:
- Cabbage, coleslaw, cucumbers, raw cheeses, unbaked potatoes, curries, and soups.

Celery seed compliments:
- Raw breads, cabbage, nut sausage, tomatoes, raw egg salad, raw mayonnaise, and dressings.

Celery seed blends well with:
- Cilantro, cloves, cumin, ginger, turmeric, mustard, parsley, and pepper.

Medicinal benefits:
- Cures gout
- Promotes sleep
- Flatulence
- Diuretic
- Liver/bladder
- Eases nausea
- Aphrodisiac
- Relieves arthritis
- Nerve regulator
- Rheumatism

CHERVIL

Chervil frequently symbolizes new life, and in that respect brings new vibrance to everything from raw egg salad to the raw cheeses. It also is a wonderful addition to the raw vegetable soup, any dressings, and salads. Combined with chives, parsley & tarragon, it makes the classic French formula known as Fines Herbes. It should always be integrated at the end of the prep process. As we explore the medicinal world of chervil, we see that it has been used throughout the ages as a diuretic, expectorant, digestive aid, and skin rejuvenator. When making a tea, keep a sealed cover on the cup or pot to contain the volatile oils. This tea may also be applied as an eye wash by immersing in a cotton swab in it and laying it on closed eyes for 10 minutes. You can also dry and pulverize the leaves into a powder to be consumed in capsule form.

Flavor characteristics of chervil:
- Chervil holds a subtle, delicate flavor that adds to salads, soups, raw butter, and cream sauces.

Culinary applications:
- Raw butters (see butter recipes), cream sauces, Fines Herbes, salads, soups, and any vegetables.

Chervil compliments:
- Raw breads, asparagus, raw cheeses, fennel, beans, beets, carrots, and all types of mushrooms.

Chervil blends well with:
- Basil, chives, dill, mint, mustard, parsley, and tarragon.

Medicinal benefits:
- Cures gout
- Heals eczema
- Lowers blood pressure
- Eases kidney stones
- Diuretic
- Relieves pleurisy
- Rejuvenates the skin
- Digestive aid
- Nerve regulator

CHILE PEPPER

Chile pepper is actually the fruit of a plant out of the genus Capsicum family, (the nightshade family). Technically, it's the fruit of capsicum family that are berries. It really is according to the intensity, flavor, and meat in which they are used. Chili peppers origins go back to the Americas, but because of their versatile use as a food and medicine, they are cultivated around the world. Chilies can have a variety of fruity, floral, nutty, and smoky flavors with a heat index ranging from mild to tingling to explosively hot. The unit of measure of a chili's heat is in SHUs (Scoville Heat Units) which are based on the amount of capsaicin in the pepper. We are going to organize them into four categories:

- **Annuum** - A milder pepper - used in paprika, chili powder, and mole.
- **Frutescens** - Small in size, but much hotter - used in tabasco and aji.
- **Baccatum** - Full of flavor, mild in heat, and colorful (long yellows).
- **Chineuse** - The 'fire' chilies - Scotch Bonnet and habaneros.

Culinary applications:
- Jerk seasoning, harissa, romesco sauce, kimchi, sambal

Chile pepper complements:
- Beans, nut meat, raw nacho cheese, coconut, curry, onion, sauces, pastas, and salsa.

Chile pepper blends well with:
- Bay, coriander, cumin, garlic, ginger, rosemary, and sesame.

Medicinal benefits:
- Prostate cancer
- Painful joints
- Toothaches
- Bronchitis
- Stomach ulcers
- Arthritis
- Cluster headaches
- Peptic ulcers
- Frostbite
- Treats pain
- Psoriasis
- Neuropathies
- Endorphin high
- Cholesterol
- Stops bleeding
- Weight loss
- Stimulates circulation

CILANTRO

Cilantro is an herbal plant, also sometimes referred to as Chinese parsley. The seeds of the cilantro plant are called coriander. They both hold the same medicinal basic qualities: they ease indigestion and stop wound infection. Cilantro is a foundational ingredient in Latin American, Portuguese, and Asian cooking, and also in several Thai curries and noodle dishes. The cilantro leaves are integral in sauces, dressings, and as a garnish for many savory dishes like tostadas, tacos, etc. Cilantro can be combined with other herbs and spices to form marinades as well as sweet or spicy chutneys.

Flavor characteristics of cilantro:
- Cilantro gives a spicy flavor with a slight hint of citrus, mint, as well as ginger.

Culinary applications:
- Salsa, garam masala, chutney, lentils, onions, beans, curry powders, chili powders, and raw chili.

Cilantro complements:
- Coconut milk, fennel, garlic, apples, avocados, citrus fruits, ginger, lemon grass, mint, mushrooms, and onions.

Cilantro blends well with:
- Allspice, basil, chives, cinnamon, cloves, cumin, dill, garlic, ginger, mint, and parsley.

Medicinal benefits:
- Lowers Low Density Lipoproteins (LDL). LDL particles contain a large amount of cholesterol and a smaller amount of proteins.
- Heals wounds
- Chelates metals
- Antifungal
- Antioxidant
- Antibacterial
- Relieves colic
- Digestive aid
- Anti-inflammatory

CINNAMON

The name cinnamon originates from the Greek word meaning sweet wood. In its purest state, it is the aromatic sweet inner bark of the cinnamon evergreen tree of the Laurel family. The rolled bark is allowed to dry, forming a scroll shape. There are two basic types of Cinnamon (Cinnamomum Zeylanicum), which is native to Sri Lanka which has a fragrant aroma and a sweet, spicy bite, and Cassia Cinnamon (Cinnamon Cassia/ Verum) which is native to Vietnam and Burma which has a higher oil content, a more reddish brown color, and has a more pronounced aroma and taste. In raw cuisine cinnamon can be integrated to many different cultural dishes. Cinnamon has been utilized both as a culinary spice and for medicinal and other purposes since ancient times, from the Egyptian to the Roman Empire.

Flavor characteristics of Cinnamon:
- Sweet, rustic, and warm, with spicy hints of cloves... and a citrusy zest.

Culinary applications:
- Unbaked goods, desserts, raw hummus, superfood balls, curries, barbecue sauce, and so on.

Cinnamon complements:
- Raw sweet bread, raw yogurt, raw almond milk, apples, apricots, and bananas.

Cinnamon blends well with:
- Anise, cardamom, cloves, coriander, cumin, ginger, nutmeg, and turmeric.

Note: only use H20 soluble cinnamon for medicinal uses.

Medicinal benefits:
- Lowers blood sugar
- Inhibits tumor cells
- Anti-inflammatory
- Eases stomach cramps
- Fights candida
- Anti-fungal
- Rejuvenates the skin
- Digestive aid
- Lowers cholesterol

CLOVES

Cloves are the dehydrated flower buds of the clove tree, a tropical evergreen native to Indonesia. As a result of their strong flavor and aromatic intensity, it is recommended that it be used sparingly mainly as to not to drown out the other flavors in your recipe. Cloves also have many medicinal qualities. To start, they are known to be a stimulant, they are useful in relieving spasmodic disorders, and also alleviating flatulence. In the Ayurvedic system of medicine, cloves are used to treat a variety of ailments either in powder form or an extract made from the essence of clove. Clove oil contains components that help balance blood circulation and body temperature.

Flavor characteristics of cloves:
- Cloves have a powerfully warming, yet spicy taste with accents of camphor.

Culinary applications:
- Raw apple pie, five spice powder, unbaked goods, fudge, garam masala, biryanis, pickles, salad dressings, desserts, ketchup, and, of course, yogi chai.

Cloves complement:
- Apples, beets, red cabbage, carrots, chocolate, chili, fennel, onion, pumpkin, and sweet potatoes.

Cloves blend well with:
- Allspice, bay, cardamom, cinnamon, coriander, fennel, ginger, mace, and nutmeg.

Medicinal benefits:
- Cholera
- Relieves coughs
- Burns / boils
- Eases toothaches
- Asthma
- Relieves earaches
- Headaches
- Digestive aid
- Muscle cramps

CORIANDER

Coriander is a small, erect, sweet smelling annual and perennial herb that grows up to 20 centimeters (close to 8 inches) in length with many branches which are also referred to as cilantro. The stem is thin, smooth, and light green with leaves to match that are also thin. The fruit are spherical – about one centimeter in diameter with some vertical ridges. They are green when tender and brownish yellow when ripe. Coriander seeds are dehydrated when they are ripe. They have a fragrant scent and a nice, zesty taste. Their mineral and vitamin contents consist of calcium, iron, phosphorus, carotene, thiamine, riboflavin, niacin. Coriander juice is highly beneficial in deficiencies of vitamins A, B1, B2, C, and iron.

Flavor characteristics of coriander:
- Cloves have a powerfully warming, yet spicy taste with accents of camphor.

Culinary applications:
- Raw apple pie, five spice powder, unbaked goods, fudge, garam masala, biryanis, pickles, salad dressings, desserts, ketchup, and of course yogi chai.

Coriander compliments:
- Apples, beets, red cabbage, carrots, chocolate, chili, fennel, onion, pumpkin, and sweet potatoes.

Coriander Blends Well With:
- Allspice, bay, cardamom, cinnamon, coriander, fennel, ginger, mace, nutmeg.

Medicinal benefits:
- Hepatitis
- Ulcerative colitis
- Nausea
- Typhoid fever
- Asthma
- Skin disorders
- Dysentery
- Digestive aid
- Lowers blood cholesterol

CUMIN

Cumin seeds are originally from Egypt but are now cultivated in a variety of areas. These seeds are usually brownish-yellow in color and slightly curved. They are utilized either whole, dehydrated, or ground. Cumin is a fundamental element in a multitude of culture dishes from Spanish and Mexican to Indian tandoori dishes. There are also black cumin seeds from Kashmir and Iran which are smaller, have a sweeter smell, and has a softer flavor closer to that of caraway. Their mineral and vitamin contents are calcium, iron, phosphorous, potassium, thiamine, sodium, riboflavin, niacin, and vitamins C and A.

Flavor characteristics of cumin:
- Cloves have a powerfully warming, yet spicy taste with accents of camphor.

Culinary applications:
- Raw apple pie, five spice powder, unbaked goods, fudge, garam masala, biryanis, pickles, salad dressings, desserts, ketchup, and, of course, yogi chai.

Cumin compliments:
- Apples, beets, red cabbage, carrots, chocolate, chili, fennel, onion, pumpkin, and sweet potatoes.

Cumin Blends Well With:
- Allspice, bay, cardamom, cinnamon, coriander, fennel, ginger, mace, nutmeg.

Medicinal benefits:
- Aphrodisiac
- Insomnia
- Morning sickness
- Detoxes the blood
- Diarrhea
- Cold / fevers
- Diabetes
- Digestive aid
- Fatigue

DILL SEED / WEED

Dill seeds are small, flat, and oval in shape. They are easily removed from their husks by rubbing the dried seed heads. With a sharper taste than the dill weed leaves, they have a sweet and citric type flavor. The seeds are recommended in moderation with recipes and pickling brines, but dill is not just for culinary purposes. One tablespoonful of dill seed contains as much calcium as one-third cup of raw milk. It also has specific medicinal qualities as well. Originating from the Norse word *dill*, meaning to soothe or calm, it is no surprise that this herb is used to induce sleep and is a great insomnia reliever. Dill was also used by Hippocrates to treat burns suffered by soldiers in ancient Rome. Let's explore some of the other aspects of dill.

Medicinal benefits:
- Anti-bacterial
- Insomnia
- Morning sickness
- Anti-inflammatory
- Diarrhea
- Strengthens nails
- Freshens breath
- Digestive aid
- Rheumatoid arthritis
- Cold / flu
- Flatulence
- Menstrual cramps

Flavor characteristics of dill:
- Dill seeds are similar to caraway but have a strong anise taste that lingers.

Culinary applications:
- Raw cheeses, raw egg salad, breads, salad dressings, and curries.

Dill complements:
- Cabbage, chili, onion, potatoes, and squash.

Dill blends well with:
- Coriander, cumin, garlic, ginger, mustard seed, and turmeric.

FENNEL

Fennel seeds are greenish yellow in color and are used in pickling brines, soups, cookies, breads, as well as other dishes. Fennel leaves are digestive, appetizing, and stimulating. Fennel's medicinal qualities were uncovered long before its use as an herb. Pliny, the Roman naturalist, explored its qualities as an eye-strengthener. Fennel can also be added to tea as a remedy for indigestion. One of the most interesting things about this ancient seed is that its 'licorice taste' is from a substance called anethole, which has been proven to fight cancer and inflammation. Fennel's nutritional content is made up of calcium, sodium, phosphorus, iron, thiamine, potassium, riboflavin, niacin, and vitamin C.

Flavor characteristics of fennel:
- Fennel seed has a warming licorice flavor, that is fresh and slightly sweet with a tingling aftertaste of bittersweet camphor.

Culinary applications:
- Raw Italian sausage, curry blends, raw tomato sauce, unbaked bread, and salad dressings.

Fennel complements:
- Lentils, beans, beets, cabbage, and lemon.

Fennel blends well with:
- Chervil, cumin, fenugreek, mint, parsley, and thyme.

Medicinal benefits:
- Freshens breath
- Insomnia
- Menstruation
- Flatulence
- Vomiting
- Conjunctivitis
- Relieves colic
- Digestive aid
- Lung conditions

FENUGREEK

Fenugreek seeds are used extensively in the recipes of countries in the Middle and Far East and in the West but are not as well-known as the other spices. Fenugreek leaves are used in many Indian vegetable dishes. They are also used to flavor sauces, lentil dishes (in Bengali and Iranian cuisines), and to flavor breads in Egypt and Ethiopia. Not only does fenugreek impart a distinct flavor and zing to food but it also holds a variety of very important disease preventing characteristics. As with the majority of spices, fenugreek is made-up of many antioxidant and anti-inflammatory compounds such as apigenin, genistein, kaempferol, quercetin, rutin, selenium, and superoxide-dismutase. It also contains compounds such as trigonelline that has been proven to stop the degeneration of nerve cells in all neuro-degenerative diseases.

Flavor characteristics of Fenugreek:
- Fenugreek is aromatic of hay. Its flavor is close to celery or lovage with a subtle bitter after taste.

Culinary applications:
- Raw cheeses, breads, salad dressings, curries, chutneys, and sauces.

Fenugreek compliments:
- Green vegetables, curries, root vegetables, legumes, lemon, and tomatoes.

Fenugreek blends well with:
- Cardamom, chervil, cinnamon, cloves, coriander, cumin, fennel seed, pepper, and turmeric.

Medicinal benefits:
- Antioxidant
- Insomnia
- Anti-tumourigenic
- Anti-viral
- Diabetes
- Neuro-degenerative diseases
- Replenishes energy
- Digestive aid
- Lowers blood cholesterol
- Cancer fighting
- Fights obesity
- Sores / abscesses (poultice)

GARLIC

Allium sativum, generally known as garlic, is a relative of the lily family Alliaceae. Its cousins include the onion, shallot, leek, and chive. Garlic has been utilized throughout the ages for its culinary and medicinal purposes. The bulb of garlic, the most frequently used component of the plant, is divided into numerous fleshy units referred to as cloves. The cloves are cultivated as seeds, as well as for consumption or for medicinal remedies. The leaves of the plant, stems, and flowers on the head are also edible and are usually eaten while young and still tender. The medicinal resume of garlic reads a little something like this: lowers cholesterol, reduces blood pressure, balances blood sugar, fights cancer, combats fungus, eases bronchitis, cures colds, removes warts, and tones and strengthens the immune system. Its abilities are diverse and reach nearly every tissue and system of the human body.

Flavor characteristics of garlic:
- It has a pungent, spicy zest that mellows and sweetens considerably with uncooking and dehydration.

Culinary applications:
- Breads, cheeses, crackers, dressings, hummus, nut meats, pastas, sauces, and so on.

Garlic compliments:
- Citrus, legumes, lentils, ginger, herbs alike... EVERYTHING!!!

Garlic blends well with:
- All types of herbs, all types of spices, citrus, ginger, and vinegar.

Medicinal benefits:
- Anti-bacterial
- Autoimmune
- Antioxidant
- Anti-inflammatory
- Antiviral
- Blood pressure
- Anti-fungal
- Digestive aid
- Arthritis
- Cold / flu
- Flatulence
- Lowers blood sugar
- Cancer combatant
- Heals lungs
- Lowers cholesterol

GINGER

Ginger is the underground stem, also known as a rhizome, of the perennial plant Zingiberaceae. It was originally cultivated in China and India and used in many savory Asian dishes. Fresh ginger can be used sliced, grated, or chopped for cooking fish, meats and poultry. It neutralizes many of the pungent smells of fish and game meats. Larger unpeeled slices or pieces are used for cooking and then discarded. It is used to flavor soups, sauces, dressings and when sliced or grated thinly, used as a garnish.

Flavor characteristics of ginger:
- Fresh ginger has a vibrant and refreshingly woodsy aroma. The flavor can have a range of flavors from hot and spicy to a citrus zest. When ginger is dried, it is less aromatic, but keeps the peppery taste with a slight lemony tone.

Culinary applications:
- Asian dishes, pickled ginger, ginger kombucha, desserts, curries, marinades, sauces, and salad dressings.

Ginger complements:
- Coconut, garlic, unbaked goods, carrots, raw fruit cobblers, lemon, lime, nuts, onions, pumpkins, and scallions,

Ginger blends well with:
- All types of basil, chili, cilantro, galangal, lemon grass, mint, paprika, pepper, and saffron.

Medicinal benefits:
- Anti-bacterial
- Autoimmune
- Antioxidant
- Anti-inflammatory
- Diarrhea
- Circulatory
- Freshens breath
- Digestive aid
- Arthritis
- Cold / flu
- Flatulence
- Menstrual cramps
- Treats migraines
- Nausea
- Morning sickness

GINKGO

The gingko tree is known to be one of the oldest living species of trees. At one time, it may have covered most of the planet, but it was nearly wiped out after the Ice Age, surviving only in areas of Asia. Ginkgo has always traditionally been the honored plant of Chinese monks, who utilized ginkgo for food and herbal remedies. The ginkgo tree of the present day has become a useful urban landscape plant, decorating streets and parks throughout various cities because of its unique resistance to everything from pollution to drought and even disease. It's also an 'elder' tree living as long as a thousand years. On the medicinal side of the leaf, ginkgo most remarkable effect is its ability to expand blood vessels thus improving circulation and vascular integrity in the brain, heart, and the extremities. When circulation is restricted to the head, it leads to a wide spectrum of the mental and neurological symptoms of aging, including memory loss, depression, and impaired hearing. Ginkgo can help these conditions by improving circulation.

It also has other physiological effects on the brain such as strengthening the vessels and amplifying the action of neurotransmitters which are chemical compounds that are in charge of the transmission of nerve impulses between the brain and other nerve cells. Ginkgo also contains potent antioxidants that hold anti-inflammatory effects. It is believed that an array of the signs of aging and chronic disease come from the oxidation of cell membranes by toxic substances known as free radicals. They come are a by-product of man and are a result of everything from pollution in the atmosphere to the production of metabolic by-products and wastes. Ginkgo, like the other medicinal foods in this book, possess the ability to reverse inflammation and destruction or damage to cells from oxidation. Now the seed or nut of the ginkgo is utilized in Chinese medicine, as well as used in Oriental cooking. Let's look at the medicinal benefits first:

Medicinal benefits:
- Memory loss
- Autoimmune
- Antioxidant
- Hearing
- Circulatory
- Anti-inflammatory
- Anti-aging
- Depression
- Brain function

GINSENG

When working with ginseng, as opposed to treating specific conditions, ginseng is rather given to remedy deeper vulnerabilities that lead to a multitude of conditions. For instance, among its many uses, ginseng is given as an herbal remedy to someone who is regularly exhausted, fragile, or stressed, like someone whose immune system is weak and gets colds and flu repeatedly. Like many of these ancient medicines we've gone through, ginseng is an adaptogen, which means it's able to 'adapt' by protecting the body from physical and mental stress and helping bodily functions return to normal. Ginseng is an herbal remedy for fatigue, stress, and other afflictions, thus aiding the body in reclaiming harmony.

The spirit over ginseng was sparked thousands of years ago in China where the Asian species of ginseng, Panax ginseng, was discovered. The demand became so great for China's native species that the plant was almost completely wiped out from overharvesting due to the increased demand. Now there are two types of ginseng, A mature woods-grown root, and an a mature wild woods-grown root of Panax ginseng. The farmed Panax will sometimes go for $1,000 or more but a mature wild woods-grown root of Panax ginseng will easily go for up to $200,000 or more! Many people believe that cultivated ginseng has distinctly different properties from the natural wild specimens. The Asian species is said to be the true supreme medicine in comparison to the American species, but the two species have individually different applications based on what is referred to as "Yin and Yang". In the age old tradition of Chinese medicine, our vital qi (Chi) is composed of a duality of two opposing life forces—the yin and the yang. These dualistic opposites spin and cycle in not just all life, but all matter. The yang life forces are the blazing, fiery, external, expansive, dynamic pole. The yin aspect is the deep dark, damp, internalized, contracted, mystifying pole. In Chinese medicine, all living things—all matter—even all diseases, possess the yin and yang aspects. Within the dynamic of ginseng, the Asian Panax ginseng is known as a yang tonic which activates the internal fire (warming) where as the American Panax quinquefolius is known to be more a of a yin tonic which is a H20 energy (cooling). They are both honored as qi tonics, qi strengtheners, but it's all about the goal of the individual in finding harmony within their yin and yang duality.

MICAH SKYE

GOLDENSEAL

Goldenseal is the root of this woodland plant that is harvested in the fall as a powerful and versatile antimicrobial agent. As a matter of fact, because of its intense effectiveness, goldenseal was almost completely wiped out. Goldenseal is a strong herbal remedy that improves health in many ways. It is a strong antimicrobial, an anti-inflammatory, and a digestive cleanser! It possesses powerful astringent qualities that make it very effective for healing the throat, stomach, and vagina, when these tissues are inflamed, swollen, or infected. An effective infusion to treat sore throats can be made by mixing goldenseal, echinacea, and myrrh together in a tonic with lemon H2O or even a homemade raw lemonade. If you're ready to get extreme, gargling with goldenseal is the most effective treatment as direct contact with the infected area brings the best results.

If you're looking for a good antiseptic, look no further, as goldenseal is a very effective skin wash for wounds as well as an internal skin surfaces such as in the vagina and ear canal. Goldenseal can also be used as an eye wash for conjunctivitis. Since we've established that goldenseal is an effective astringent and is both anti-inflammatory and antimicrobial, it is especially beneficial to the digestive system. This includes everything from the oral mucosa to the intestinal tract and is also helpful for canker sores in the mouth as well as a mouth wash for irritated / infected gums. Goldenseal also relieves irritable bowel diseases as well as diarrhea. A combination of goldenseal and cayenne pepper in equal amounts either in a tonic or in capsule form are an effective cure for general ailment of digestion such as chronic gas, indigestion, and difficulty with assimilation of nutrients. Goldenseal has shown to be effective in fighting a number of disease-causing organisms which include staphylococcus, streptococcus, chlamydia species, E. coli, salmonella typhi, entamoeba histolytica, and many others.

Goldenseal has also proven effective in the promotion of circulation in liver and spleen which is attributed to an array of alkaloids in goldenseal, but one in particular, Berberine, is thought to be responsible for the increased white blood cell activity attributed to goldenseal use. New studies show that Berberine aids in the treatment of brain tumors and skin cancers, along with improving cardiovascular health, lowering LDL and triglycerides, decreasing blood pressure, and improving the function of the heart muscle.

HORSERADISH

Horseradish (Armoracia rusticana, Cochlearia armoracia) is a perennial plant that belongs to the same family as mustard, wasabi, broccoli, and cabbage which is in the Brassicaceae family. The unprocessed root has barely any smell, but as soon as it's shredded or cut, it must be preserved in vinegar preferably immediately or it loses its potency. Horseradish has been used medicinally for centuries to clear sinuses, increase circulation of the face and head, and activates the release of mucus from upper respiratory pathways. Horseradish also has a moderate antibiotic effect as well as the ability to stimulate urine production. For this obvious reason, it has been given to people to treat urinary infections. One of the benefits is that horseradish is considered safe for long-term usage. Horseradish is also used externally to relieve the pain of arthritis, nerve irritation, and is also made into a poultice to heal infected wounds.

Flavor characteristics of horseradish:
- Horseradish has a very mild aroma until cut, upon which it gives off a pungent vapor of spice and a robustly overwhelming spice flavor with hint of radish or cabbage.

Culinary applications:
- Dressings, pickled in vinegar as a garnish, spicy raw mayonnaise.

Horseradish compliments:
- nut meats, veggies, mushrooms

Horseradish Blends Well With:
- Bay, garlic, marjoram, Thai basil, rosemary, sage, savory, thyme.

Medicinal benefits:
- Circulation
- Insomnia
- Clears sinuses
- Anti-inflammatory
- Influenza
- Urinary infections
- Antibacterial
- Cold / flu
- Lung congestion

JUNIPER BERRY

Juniper berries grow on the evergreen shrub grown throughout the hills of Europe. They traditionally mixed with other seasonings to be rubbed on meats. We will be using them to enhance the flavor of sauces, raw stuffings, and dressings. Whole juniper berries can also be infused in elixirs and tonics. With their warm analeptic, and disinfecting qualities, juniper berries have a variety of medicinal uses. For instance, Juniper berries hold an antiseptic quality and are frequently used to treat chronic and repeated UTI's (urinary tract infections).

Flavor characteristics of the juniper berry:
- Juniper berries have a woodsy scent similar to gin, and their flavor refreshes the palette with a sweetness that is followed by a piney zest.

Culinary applications:
- Dressings, sauces, and soups.

Juniper berry compliments:
- Cabbage, apples, and nut meats.

Juniper berry Blends Well With:
- Bay, caraway, garlic, marjoram, pepper, rosemary, sage, savory, thyme.

Medicinal benefits:
- anti-bacterial
- insomnia
- bladder infections
- anti-inflammatory
- gout
- aids kidneys
- stimulant
- digestive aid
- rheumatoid arthritis
- cold / flu
- flatulence
- tones tissue / organs
- astringent
- relieves UTI
- uterine stimulant

LAVENDER

Lavenders Lavandula is a broad family of 39 species of aromatic flowering plants in the mint family. It has been treasured and utilized for centuries for its sweet, relaxing aroma and essence. Its name originates from the Latin root lavare, meaning "to wash," as lavender was commonly used in soaps and hair rinses. Outside of its significance as an aroma and fragrance, lavender has a multitude of medicinal purposes. Generally, it is considered to relax and calm nervous tension. For instance, lavender oil can be rubbed into the temples for head pain or mixed into bath H20 for a stress relieving bath. Lavender has a moderately sedating effect and can act as a mild antispasmodic to help with muscular tension. Like many herbs high in volatile oils are reported to do, lavender can also alleviate bloating and flatulence in the intestines. One volatile oil specifically, linalool, has shown to relax the bronchial passages which reduces inflammatory and allergic reactions. Linalool is also known as an antiseptic.

Flavor characteristics of lavender:
- Lavender has a warm, floral fragrance that is powerful, so use sparingly. Its flavor is a spicy floral sweetness that is followed by traces of lemon and camphor.

Culinary applications:
- Raw cheeses, unbaked goods, raw milks, ice cream, desserts, raw milks, salad dressings, and teas.

Lavender complements:
- Blueberries, strawberries, cherries, plums, and tea infusions.

Lavender blends well with:
- Basil, marjoram, oregano, parsley, rosemary, savory, thyme, sugar, and vanilla.

Medicinal benefits:
- Antiseptic
- Insomnia
- Antispasmodic
- Bloating
- Calms nerves
- Flatulence
- Asthma
- Allergies
- Cough

MARJORAM

Marjoram comes from mint species just the same as oregano. The difference is it has a significantly milder scent and flavor. I would describe it as spicy, sharp, and a little bittersweet with hints of camphor. It is frequently added to salads and raw vegan egg salad, soups, as well as dressings. Be aware that because of its subtle flavor, it is recommended to integrate it at the end of preparation. Now, on a medicinal level, marjoram has a multitude of functions toward treating health conditions and ailments. From aiding in the release of phlegm from the mucous membranes of both the nasal and bronchial passages to regulating and promoting menstruation, as well as increasing the lactation and secretion of milk in nursing mothers. Now externally, the oil of marjoram can be helpful in array of skin conditions from bruises and sprains to paralytic appendages. It has been known to relieve everything from toothaches to gas and diarrhea.

Flavor characteristics of marjoram:
- Spicy, sharp, and a little bittersweet with hints of camphor.

Culinary applications:
- Raw cheeses, raw egg salad, breads, salad dressings, and sauces.

Marjoram complements:
- Beans, cabbage, carrots, legumes, mushrooms, and onions.

Marjoram blends well with:
- Basil, bay leaf, coriander, cumin, garlic, paprika, parsley, rosemary, sage, and thyme.

Medicinal benefits:
- Menstruation
- Insomnia
- Toothache
- Anti-inflammatory
- Diarrhea
- Skin conditions
- Cold / flu
- Digestive aid
- Respiratory system

MINT

Mint (Lamiaceae or Labiatae) describes a broad spectrum of the plant family which includes Mentha along with many other species. Historically, mint was the name of Hades' lover, who was transformed into an earth-growing herb by his wife Persephone so that she would be tread upon for everlasting life. In the present day, mint is one of the most favored herbs in the world. It can be integrated with a variety of dishes such as salads, tomatoes, fruit desserts, and raw ice cream. It is used in Mediterranean dishes such as salads and tabbouleh. Mint is also used for enhancing lamb dishes, grilled fish, and traditional Asian sauces and marinades. Fresh mint sprigs often accompany summertime cocktails.

Flavor characteristics of mint:
- Mint has an aromatic and refreshing fragrance which releases even more when the leaves are rubbed. The taste of mint is sweet and sharp with hints of lemon for spearmint and a fiery, biting camphor for peppermint.Culinary applications:
- Fresh mint is used in sweet desserts, salads, salsas, and elixirs.

Mint complements:
- Raw chocolate, desserts, elixirs, fruit and syrups, raw dairy, and salsa.

Mint blends well with:
- Basil, cardamom, cumin, dill, fenugreek, ginger, marjoram, oregano, parsley, pepper, and thyme.

Medicinal benefits:
- Burns
- Insect bites
- Appetite stimulant
- Anti-inflammatory
- Fever
- Flatulence
- Freshens breath
- Digestive aid
- Rheumatic aches

MUSTARD SEED

The mustard seed is the seed from the mustard plant. Mustard seeds come in an array of different colors pertaining to their regions of origin. Black mustard and white / yellow mustard seeds are indigenous to Europe and western Asia. Brown mustard seeds are indigenous to India. The potency of a mustard seed is affected by an enzyme called myrosinase. Mustard seeds are soaked in H20 to activate this enzyme and then are smashed and mixed with vinegar or H20 and other ingredients such as lemon and herbs. Mustard was one of the earliest spices to be used in folk medicine. From being used to treat war wounds in the Middle Ages to being used in the Italian renaissance to cure stomach cramps. It is also a key ingredient in our raw food marinades, dressings, etc.

Flavor characteristics of marjoram:
- The whole seed itself has no fragrance, but upon being ground, they become pungent. Black seeds are the most powerful in flavor. The brown seeds are not as intense but are somewhat bitter. The white mustard seeds, upon being ground, have a slightly sweet taste, but have a somewhat hot and spicy finish.

Culinary applications:
- Raw cheeses, raw egg salad, breads, salad dressings, marinades, and sauces.

Mustard seeds complement:
- Raw chili, more aged raw cheeses, and raw nut sausage.

Mustard seeds blend well with:
- Bay, coriander, cumin, dill, fenugreek, garlic, nigella, parsley, pepper, tarragon, and turmeric.

Medicinal benefits:
- Antiseptic
- Disinfectant
- Toothache
- Anti-inflammatory
- Stimulant
- Skin conditions
- Cold / flu
- Digestive aid
- Respiratory system

MYRRH

Myrrh is a fragrant spiny shrub with yellow-red flowers, followed by pointed, ellipsoid fruits. Myrrh is an anti-inflammatory, antioxidant, and an antimicrobial, making it ideal for painful or swollen tissues. It activates circulation to mucosal tissues, specifically in the bronchial tract, throat, tonsils, and gums. Myrrh is also useful for bleeding gums, gingivitis, tonsillitis, sore throat (especially strep throat), as well as bronchitis. The increase in circulation aids in fighting infection and accelerates healing, especially when you have a cold or infection of the throat and mouth. Myrrh is also known to aid in the discharge of excess mucus in cases of bronchitis and lung congestion. Myrrh is optimal for long-term conditions with swollen tissues because it carries tannins and resins, which work as astringents on tissues.

Aromatherapy and essential oil use:
- Myrrh essential oil aids to relieve emotionally or spiritually stagnancy and is beneficial in the detox of especially mucus as well as preventing putrefaction and infection. It also promotes cell and tissue growth.
- It is valuable for the stomach as well as the mouth and gums, while at the same time working as a uterine stimulant. Myrrh also aids in menstrual promotion.
- Topically, it is a great treatment for wounds and sores, especially in healing eczema, skin ulcers, and bed sores, because of its regenerative cell properties.
- Myrrh possesses an anti-catarrhal, astringent, balsamic, carminative, cicatrisant, emmenagogue, expectorant, fungicidal, sedative, digestive, stomachic, tonic, as well as uterine and vulnerary qualities.

Medicinal benefits:
- Antioxidant
- Fungicidal
- Antiseptic
- Anti-inflammatory
- Antimicrobial
- Throat / gums / mouth
- Stomach
- Cold / flu
- Lung conditions

NETTLE

Nettle is an herb from my childhood that I had to include in our herb and spice handbook. It's a plant that leaves a sting that keeps on stinging (it's also known as stinging nettle), but don't let that ruin your impression of this unlikely medicine plant. Its benefits far outweigh its offensiveness. For ages, it has been used by healers as a food and in herbal remedies. First off, all throughout Europe, nettle was known to nurture and stimulate the immune system, but let's explore more specific uses. Making a tea from nettle was used to remedy intestinal weakness, diarrhea, and malnutrition. In addition, nettle works as a diuretic and is helpful in healing kidney weakness as well as bladder infections. Wait, there's more; it also works to aid in ridding the body of excess fluid (e.g., edema), specifically in a patient who has a poor heart condition and deficient circulation.

There are a number of external uses for nettles, including the treatment of eczema, skin rashes, as well as relieving arthritic and rheumatic joints. As a matter a fact, the nettle plant has sparked the most interest in its ability to treat arthritis and gout. Gout is actually when uric acid, which is a product of protein digestion, collects in the joints and tissues which inflames them severely. To aid in elimination of uric acid from the tissues and the body, it takes only one tablespoon of freshly juiced nettle multiple times a day. Now, true to the nature of homeopathy, fresh nettle compounds, ointments, and other medicines have a sting on them, which is what creates the healing effect. In fact, it is the irritating and stinging of the epidermis that relieves the inflammation of a series of skin ailments, from eczema to arthritis. Chemically, this is because nettle is rich in flavonoids which are anti-inflammatory, and they hold trace amounts of plant sterols. They are also very high in an array of essential nutrients, such as vitamin D (not usually found in plants), vitamins C and A, as well as an assortment of minerals, including iron, calcium, phosphorus, and magnesium.

Medicinal benefits:
- Arthritis
- Diuretic
- Appetite stimulant
- Anti-inflammatory
- Circulation
- Malnutrition
- Gout
- Digestive aid
- Rheumatic ache

NUTMEG

Nutmeg, to be more specific, is the seed of the nutmeg tree. In fact, it is the only tropical fruit tree that is also the source of two different spices: nutmeg and mace. Now nutmeg and mace are similar in flavor, but mace is more pungent. The nutmeg seed is surrounded by a spotted yellowish edible fruit that's about the size of a small peach. The fruit separates in half to expose a web-like, vibrant red sheath covering the seed. This is called the aril which is what is gathered, dehydrated, and sold as mace. Underneath the aril lies the dark glossy nut-like pit, and inside this pit is an ovoid seed which is true nutmeg. Even though the origins trace back to the islands of Indonesia, nutmeg has managed to migrate all across the planet and is widely used in Western cuisines. From sweet cakes and fruit desserts to spiced drinks. On a medicinal level, it holds a long list of functionalities: Sedative, stimulant, relaxant, anti-inflammatory, antiseptic, bactericide, etc.

Flavor characteristics of nutmeg:
- Hints of clove and a deep, slightly bittersweet pine flavor.

Culinary applications:
- Unbaked goods, raw eggnog, raw pies, raw breads, raw puddings, nut sausage, and meatballs.

Nutmeg compliments:
- Cabbage, carrots, raw cheese, fruit desserts, onion, potato, pumpkin, and sweet potato.

Nutmeg blends well with:
- Cardamom, cinnamon, cloves, coriander, cumin, ginger, mace, pepper, thyme.

Medicinal benefits:
- Antiseptic
- Insomnia
- Respiratory
- Bactericide
- Sex tonic
- Brain booster
- Relaxant
- Cardiovascular
- Freshens breath

OREGANO

Oregano, or 'mountain joy' in Greek, is a species of Origanum, which originates out of Europe, the Mediterranean region, and southern and central Asia. It has become one of the most diversely utilized herbs found in kitchens around the world. In Greek mythology, oregano was believed to be a particular favorite of the Greek Goddess Aphrodite. Traditionally, people throughout the ages regarded oregano as a magical herb that can create good luck and health. The warming aroma and flavor of oregano establishes it as a necessity in every Mexican, Italian, and Mediterranean kitchen. Greek oregano is a strong, peppery herb from the Mediterranean that is frequently utilized in Italian and Greek cooking. In Italian cuisine, it is prepared in pasta sauces, pizza, nut meatballs, and vegetables. In Spanish and Latin American cuisines, it is used with cumin and chili peppers to flavor nut meat dishes and soups. Oregano is also highly regarded for a variety of medicinal benefits ranging from treating infections to relieving inflammation.

Flavor characteristics of oregano:
- Oregano has a warming and somewhat peppery aroma with an essence of camphor. Its flavor is strong and peppery with a light bitter taste. It has a higher potency than marjoram.

Culinary applications:
- Nut meat and vegetable stews, tacos, raw meat, Greek salad, nut sausage, and meatballs.

Oregano complements:
- Artichokes, beans, cabbage, carrots, mushrooms, onion, and spinach.

Oregano blends well with:
- Basil, chili, cumin, garlic, parsley, pepper, rosemary, and sage.

Medicinal benefits:
- Antiseptic
- Insomnia
- Anti-inflammatory
- Bactericide
- Antioxidant
- Brain booster
- Relaxant
- Colon cancer
- Digestive aid

PAPRIKA

Paprika is from the capsicum annuum family. Paprika is commonly stored in the form of a fiery red powder that is made from the ground dry fruits of the pepper plant. The flavors of paprika vary according to the types of pepper, the temperature / climate, and the region of their origin. Hungarian paprika is typically considered the highest in quality. Hungarian paprika comes out of two regions: Szeged and Kalosca. There are more than just the red and yellow colors at the market. Check the labels carefully to ensure that you are purchasing the flavor you most desire for your recipe:

Flavor characteristics of paprika:
- Semisweet – has a very light and almost matte color. It is mildly hot and spicy.
- Sweet – a rich color that is mild and coarse in texture.
- Mild – has an airy red color, fragrant and mildly hot.
- Delicatess – a powdery red that releases a delicious aroma when heated.
- Rose paprika – a Hungarian specialty that is packed with flavor (slightly hot) and has a very lovely rosy color.
- Hot – from a sandy brownish-red to a sun-lit yellow you can expect a very hot flavor.

Culinary applications:
- Barbecue seasoning, raw chili, raw burgers, taco meat

Paprika blends well with:
- Allspice, caraway, cardamom, garlic, ginger, oregano, parsley, pepper, rosemary, thyme.

Medicinal benefits:
- Salivation aid
- Regulates blood pressure
- Antibacterial
- Stimulant
- Improves circulation
- Digestive aid
- Rich in vitamin C

PARSLEY

Parsley is one of the more universal herbs that is used in almost every cultural cuisine on the planet. It flavors sauces, soups, salads, and our raw VEgg salad! Parsley's fresh and delicate flavor allows the leaves to be added at the end of the cooking process. Parsley stems are also used for recipes, requiring longer cooking periods, such as in soups and stews. Medicinally, parsley is a vitamin and mineral powerhouse, and as such should be part of every naturopathic garden. Parsley teas or fresh parsley juice treats kidney stones, bladder infections, or jaundice, as well as digestive aids. The root appears to be more effective than the leaves, but leaves can also be used. Leaves can be dried, pulverized into a powder, and inserted in capsule form. Parsley is a natural deodorizer and has the ability (through chlorophyll) to absorb foul odor. It was put to good use in the stinky Middle Ages where it was placed about tables and people. It was also taken as an antidote to various poisons as well as a form of hangover prevention because of its detoxifying properties.

There are two types of parsley:
- **Curly** – holds a more subdued flavor and is utilized more for garnishes and decoration.
- **Flat** – contains the best aroma and flavor for cooking (also called Italian or French parsley)

Flavor characteristics of parsley:
- Parsley has a light and subtly spicy aroma of anise. The taste is slightly peppery with a cleansing flavor.

Culinary applications:
- Used to flavor soups, spreads, raw mashed potatoes, nut meats, as well as all sauces.

Parsley blends well with:
- Basil, bay, chervil, chives, cumin, garlic, marjoram, mint, oregano, rosemary, and tarragon.

Medicinal benefits:
- Digestive aid
- Heals urinary tract infections
- Jaundice
- Aids with kidney stones
- Breath freshener
- Detoxifier
- High in chlorophyll
- Rich in vitamins & minerals

PEPPERCORNS

Peppercorns or pepper is often used with savory foods, but can be used in flavoring fruits, salads, vegetables, and even baked goods. Pepper has a fruity and pungent aroma with a biting taste and a penetrating aftertaste. There are a variety of peppercorns that have a variety of distinct features which are preferred for different culinary uses:

Here are the flavor characteristics of peppercorns:
- The pink peppercorn is a ripe fruit with a sweet taste and softer outer shell.
- The green peppercorn is not overly hot and is used in pates and brines and combines well with sweeter spices such as cinnamon and ginger.
- Tellicherry (black) peppercorns are highly regarded for their size and clean, flavorful bite.
- White peppercorns (Muntok) are used to make cream sauces and soups to retain a more attractive appearance.

Flavor characteristics of peppercorns:
- Soups and sauces, vegetables, nut meats, sausages, and spice blends.

Culinary applications:
- Used to season soups and sauces, vegetables, nut meats, sausages, and spice blends.

Peppercorns blend well with:
- Basil, bay, chervil, chives, cumin, garlic, marjoram, mint, oregano, parsley, rosemary, and tarragon.

Medicinal benefits:
- Antispasmodic
- Anti-toxic
- Carminative
- Jaundice
- Diuretic
- Antioxidant
- Digestive aid
- Laxative
- Stimulant
- Circulation
- Muscle Relaxant
- Respiratory

POPPY SEEDS

Poppy Seeds (also known as Khus khus in many eastern countries). For the most part, poppy seeds are used throughout the Western world in baked goods such as bagels, breads, and cakes, but for the rest of the planet, the seeds are ground up or incorporated whole in everything from desserts to kormas (korma is one of the best known and appreciated Indian curries worldwide. Creamy and fragrant, this dish inherited from the Mughal influence consists of meat marinated in a mixture of spices and then braised in yoghurt and coconut milk) and curries. Poppy seeds are also used extensively in Middle Eastern and Asian cuisine, especially Indian, Moghlai, and Northwest Indian cuisine. Since they are regarded to have powerful cooling properties, their use is believed to relieve digestive disorders, and the husk, when ground with the seeds, is a great cleanser for the system as well. The poppy seed contains extensive quantities of calcium, almost 1584 percent along with 432 phosphorus grams percent. All this nutrition makes for an amazing food for lactating and pregnant mothers. In addition, it also contains a very high percentage of protein in the form of globulin which has an amino acid makeup similar to whole seed protein. As if that wasn't enough, these seeds contain 50% edible oil, and many cultures (including ancient Egyptians) extract it for usage.

There are two types of poppy seeds:
- Dark poppy seeds – have a sweet and nutty aroma with an almond-like flavor.
- White poppy seeds – have a lighter aroma and more mellow flavor.

Culinary applications:
- Raw bread, any unbaked goods, salad dressing, raw crackers, raw tostadas, etc.

Poppy seeds blend well with:
- Allspice, cardamom, cinnamon, fennel seed, ginger, and vanilla.

Medicinal benefits:
- Digestive aid
- Abdominal
- Diarrhea
- Insomnia
- Sciatica pain
- Blemishes

ROSEMARY

Rosemary is a dense, woodsy perennial that is strongly aromatic, peppery, and outside being a flavor-enhancer for culinary cuisine and its use in cosmetics, rosemary extract has a lengthy historical archive of medicinal uses as well. It has been used to treat a wide range of ailments, including stomach upsets, digestive disorders, and headaches. Rosemary has long been respected as the herb for reminiscence. It strengthens the heart as well as the memory. Dehydrated rosemary leaves also contain a multitude of acids and other chemical substances. They possess antioxidant properties that have been isolated from leaves and its oil. Here are some of the other characteristics and medicinal benefits of rosemary:

Flavor characteristics of rosemary:
- Rosemary has a peppery aroma with hints of pine. Its taste is also peppery with undertones of nutmeg and camphor. The aftertaste is balsamic and slightly bitter.

Culinary applications:
- Baked breads, dehydrated vegetables, soups, dressings, and marinades. Essential to Herbes de Provence and Italian Herb Seasoning.

Rosemary blends well with:
- Bay leaf, garlic, lavender, mint, oregano, sage, savory, and thyme.

Medicinal benefits:
- Digestive aid
- Respiratory
- Flatulence
- Antibacterial
- Antioxidant
- Cardiac stimulant
- Cold / flu aid
- Mental fatigue
- Rheumatism
- Anti-cancer
- Hormone imbalances

CHAPTER 4 THE SCIENCE OF HERBOMETRY & SPICEOLOGY

SAFFRON

Known as the world's most expensive spice, saffron threads are the stigmas of the dried crocus flower. Saffron is mostly used as a food coloring. It is often infused with liquid to make broths to flavor bouillabaisse and stews. Saffron threads are also dried and ground for use in rice dishes, pilafs, sauces, and biryanis. It contains an essential oil which consists of terpenes, terpene alcohols, and esters. Its other constituents are crocin and picrocrocin. Saffron is useful in aiding and balancing menstrual periods. It also has been known to alleviate lumbar back pain which is often a side effect of menstruation. Saffron is also an effective remedy for a multitude of other health disorders for women such as leucorrhea and hysteria. Pessaries of saffron are used to treat painful ailments of the uterus. One way it does this is by strengthening the abdomen and its functionality. As a result it is helpful in the healing of several digestive disorders, specifically flatulence and colic. Saffron also holds many valuable properties as a remedy for skin disorders. You can make a paste of the herb that can be utilized for healing bruises and superficial sores.

Flavor characteristics of saffron:
- Saffron has a rich and musky, floral aroma. Its taste is warm and earthy with a slight bitterness that lingers.

Culinary applications:
- Raw bread, unbaked goods, soups, sauces, mushrooms, and vegetables.

Saffron blends well with:
- Anise, cardamom, cinnamon, fennel seeds, ginger, nutmeg, paprika, and pepper.

Medicinal benefits:
- Digestive aid
- Bruises
- Menstrual cycle
- Skin disorders
- Uterus
- Memory boosting
- Hysteria
- Flatulence
- Colic
- Bruises
- Leucorrhea

SAGE

Of all the culinary herbs in the world, sage is perhaps the one with the broadest range of medicinal uses. To start with, sage is anti-hypertensive, anti-diabetic, anti-inflammatory, and anti-microbial, as well as helps cleanse your blood and may even prevent Alzheimer's disease. Sage is also an herb that aids in the digestion of oily foods. It is used in making our Italian nut sausage and burgers. In Greek cuisine, sage is used as a flavoring for tea. Of course, there is the classic use of sage as a spiritual tool for cleansing spaces in a process called 'smudging'. There is a wide variety of different species of sage which include Greek, variegated, pineapple, and black currant. Since sage has a strong presence, it should be used sparingly.

Flavor characteristics of sage:
- Sage carries a subtle, but musky aroma. It has a warming taste with hints of a spicy camphorous undertone. The variegated species of sage is the milder of the bunch. Dried sage is known to be muskier and pungent, so be conscious when using.

Culinary applications:
- Crackers, cookies, sauces, soups, and nut meats.

Sage blends well with:
- Bay, caraway, ginger, lovage, marjoram, parsley, savory, and thyme.

Medicinal benefits:
- Blood sugar
- Respiratory
- Astringent
- Stimulant
- Antioxidant
- Stimulant
- Joint pain
- Mental fatigue
- Antimicrobial
- Anti-cancer
- Sore throat
- Anti-inflammatory
- Swelling
- Cuts / sprains
- Menopausal symptoms
- Diuretic
- Anxiolytic
- Expectorant

SAVORY

Although savory is primarily a culinary herb, it holds oils and tannins that have mild astringent and antiseptic properties that can be useful in medicines. Ther are two types of savory: winter and summer. Winter savory is the more pungent of the two as it has a more accentuated zest and flavor. Winter savory is primarily utilized in Mediterranean cuisines to flavor soups, stews, and sauces. Summer savory is milder and can be used to flavor vegetables, mushrooms, and salads. Summer savory is the type most often used for medicinal purposes.

Flavor characteristics of savory:
- Both winter and summer savories have a peppery flavor.
- Summer savory has a milder aromatic experience with tones of thyme, mint, and marjoram.
- Winter savory is the stronger variety and has a more expressive flavor and aroma with camphorous tones with accents of pine and sage.

Culinary applications:
- Raw bread, unbaked goods, soups, sauces, dressings, marinades, mushrooms, and vegetables.

Savory blends well with:
- Basil, bay leaf, cumin, garlic, lavender, marjoram, oregano, parsley, rosemary, sage, and thyme.

Medicinal benefits:
- Indigestion
- Diarrhea
- Colic
- Flatulence
- Sore throat
- Expectorant
- Insect bites
- Skin disorders
- Sex drive

SESAME SEED

Also known as Sesamum indicum, this annual plant sprouts oblong leaves and seed pods that produce what we know as sesame seeds. Going back as far as 3,000 B.C., sesame seeds have been cultivated and utilized by ancient civilizations. The Assyrians are on record to be the first to use them as the first seasoning in human history. Their seeds and oils have been used for not just culinary purposes though. Their uses range from medicinal to health and beauty practices as well. These little seeds add a nutty robust taste to many Asian dishes and are the fundamental ingredient in tahini. There are two type of sesame seeds: white and black. The white seeds are the most frequently used in breads, dressings, and seasoning oils. Black sesame seeds are used in Chinese and Japanese recipes as garnishes for pastries, salads, soup, etc. Sesame seeds possess two distinct substances: sesamin and sesamolin. Both of these substances belong to a group of useful fibers called lignans which have demonstrated to have the ability to lower cholesterol. In addition, sesamin has been proven to protect the liver from damage due to oxidation.

Flavor characteristics of sesame seeds:
- Sesame seeds have a light aromatic smell, but a robust earthy flavor. This taste can be extenuated by processing the sesame seeds into a paste.

Culinary applications:
- Raw breads, crackers, baked goods, dressings, and sauces.

Sesame seeds blend well with:
- Cardamom, cinnamon, cloves, coriander, ginger, nutmeg, pepper, sumac, and thyme.

Medicinal benefits:
- Bones / joints
- Source of iron
- Immune response
- Blood vessels
- Anti-inflammatory
- Lowers cholesterol
- Anti-cancer
- Skin
- Source of protein

TAMARIND

Tamarind possesses a multitude of health benefits and has been used in India and South America for centuries. It contains a substantial source of vitamins, potassium, fiber, magnesium, and other nutritional properties. Tamarind is also a significant source of antioxidants, therefore making it effective in fighting cancer. It is utilized in many Indian and Southeast Asian dishes due to its acidic properties for curries, sambals, chutneys, marinades, as well as pickling preserves. Tamarind is very rich in vitamin C and also aids in alleviating digestive disorders. In addition, tamarind lowers cholesterol which supports a healthy heart. The fruit itself has sour flavor when young but gets sweeter as it ripens. The pulp, leaves, and flowers of tamarind in specific variations are used to treat swollen joints to reduce the swelling and, subsequently, the pain. Here are some additional characteristics and uses:

Flavor characteristics of tamarind:
- Tamarind gives off almost no aroma, but its taste is quite the opposite. It is sour in taste due to its tartaric acid.

Culinary applications:
- Chutneys, curries, fruit drinks, elixirs, marinades, and sauces.

Tamarind blends well with:
- Chilies, cilantro, cumin, galangal, garlic, ginger, and turmeric.

Medicinal benefits:
- Bones / joints
- Antioxidant
- Vitamin rich
- Digestive aid
- Anti-inflammatory
- Fever / cold
- Mineral rich
- Skin inflammation
- Sore throats

TARRAGON

The history of tarragon dates back to 500 B.C. where it is believed to have its origins in Southern Russia and Siberia. The name "tarragon" is believed to have been taken from the Arabic word for "dragon", drawing ties to tarragon's snake-like roots. In the present day, there are two species of tarragon cultivated in the world: Russian and French. French tarragon has leaves that are shinier and more potent than the species of Russian tarragon. The most commonly used tarragon for multiple purposes is from the French tarragon. Tarragon is primarily used as an herb for culinary purposes but also holds an ancient record of medicinal uses. One of the reasons for this is its numbing ability, especially for the mouth and gums. In fact, it was an ancient toothache remedy for the Greeks who used to chew in the leaves of the tarragon plant. Tarragon was utilized to remedy poisonous snakebites during the Middle Ages. The list goes on and on for this ancient herb as you'll see below, but here's a few others benefits to give you an understanding of its versatility. It has been known to act as a moderate sedative, a digestive aid, and has shown signs of aiding in the prevention of heart disease.

Flavor characteristics of tarragon:
- Tarragon leaves give off a sweet aroma with hints of licorice. Its taste, although potent, is majestic with tones of spicy basil and star of anise.

Culinary applications:
- Raw breads, crackers, vinaigrettes, flavored raw butter, raw cheeses, dressings, and sauces.

Tarragon blends well with:
- Basil, bay leaf, chervil, chives, dill, parsley, and thyme.

Medicinal benefits:
- Toothache
- Sleep aid
- Immune response
- Digestive aid
- Stomach cramps
- Anti-inflammatory
- Anti-anxiety
- Heart disease
- High blood pressure

CHAPTER 4 THE SCIENCE OF HERBOMETRY & SPICEOLOGY

THYME

Thyme is an evergreen shrub with small leaves that has always been a foundation to many Western and Middle Eastern cuisines. The name thyme was derived from the Greek word meaning 'to fumigate'. It is recorded that the ancient Greeks used thyme as incense that represented grace as well as elegance. Other sources derive the name from the Greek word "thumus" which signifies courage. A real plus with thyme is that it can withstand long and slow dehydration periods (crackers and breads). Another advantage with thyme is the ability to accentuate other herbs in a dish without overpowering them. It is wonderful in soups, marinades, and even salads.

Medicinal benefits:
- Cuts / wounds
- Source of iron
- Antiviral
- Antiseptic
- Anti-inflammatory
- Antibacterial
- Digestive aid
- Cold remedy
- Menstruation

Flavor characteristics of thyme:
- Thyme gives off a hearty pepper zest and has a spicy warming taste with undertones of cloves and mint.

Culinary applications:
- Raw breads, crackers, baked goods, dressings, and sauces.

Thyme blends well with:
- Thyme really blends well with allspice, basil, garlic, lavender, marjoram, oregano, parsley, and rosemary.

TURMERIC

This ancient yogic root is one of my favorites and is the secret blood cleansing ingredient to the ancient golden milk recipe. Turmeric is a perennial shrub that thrives throughout India and other tropical areas of Asia. It is a popular hot yellow spice to flavor Indian cuisine such as curry powders, masalas, and various spice pastes. It is common in the Moroccan spice blend ras al hanout. In our menu, turmeric is utilized to impart a yellowish color to nut cheeses, Vegg salad, medicinal elixirs, and so on. Now, on the medicinal end of the spectrum, for instance in Ayurvedic medicine, turmeric is regarded as a whole body cleanser. For everything from digestive disorders to arthritis. Chinese physicians also treat patients with turmeric for disturbances with the liver and gallbladder, a blood cleanser, and to reduce chest congestion as well as menstrual pain. Turmeric's powerful health attributes can be traced to one active substance called curcumin. This mighty ingredient gives turmeric its versatile healing attributes, its yellow color, as well as its potent flavor. To be more specific, curcumin contains a multitude of antioxidants, anti-inflammatory, antibacterial, stomach-soothing, and liver / heart protecting abilities. Below are more characteristics on this power root.

Flavor characteristics of turmeric:
- Fresh turmeric root – (rhizome) has a zesty citrus essence and the flavor of the earth.
- Dried turmeric root – holds more of an earthy aroma accompanied by subtle essences of a woodsy citrus and ginger. The flavor is fairly bitter with a slight sourness to it, but a warming undertone.

Culinary applications:
- Raw breads, crackers, baked goods, dressings, marinades, and sauces.

Turmeric blends well with:
- Chilies, cilantro, cloves, coriander, cumin, galangal, garlic, ginger, paprika, and pepper.

Medicinal benefits:
- Bones / joints
- Decongestant
- Cardiovascular
- Blood cleanser
- Anti-inflammatory
- Lowers cholesterol
- Anti-cancer
- Digestive aid
- Liver disorders

VANILLA

It is the ancient Totonaco Indians of Mexico who were the first keepers of the secrets of vanilla. Today, the vanilla bean comes from four main areas of the world. Each area produces vanilla beans with specific characteristics and attributes. (Madagascar and Indonesia produce 90 percent of the world's vanilla bean crop.) Vanilla is the second most expensive spice in the world, behind saffron, because it requires such a labor intensive process to cultivate it into a usable form. For instance, one fermented vanilla bean will make roughly three teaspoons of vanilla extract. The extract is generally what is used for cooking, but it has several medicinal uses from being an antioxidant to aphrodisiac.

Flavor characteristics of vanilla:
- Madagascar – an island off the coast of Africa, is the largest producer of vanilla beans in the world. It is the highest quality pure vanilla available, described as having a creamy, sweet, smooth, mellow flavor.
- Indonesia – which is the second largest producer of vanilla – this vanilla has more of a woodsy astringent and phenolic property to it.
- Mexico – Mexico, where the vanilla orchid originated, now produces only a small percentage of the harvest. Mexican vanilla is described as creamy, sweet, smooth, and spicy.
- Tahiti – the last of the four major vanilla-producing regions is Tahiti. Tahitian vanilla, grown from a different genus of vanilla orchid, is flowery and fruity, anisic, and smooth.

Culinary applications:
- Baked goods, ice cream, candy, cakes, cookies, and desserts.

Vanilla blends well with:
- Cardamom, cinnamon, cloves, and saffron to name a few.

Medicinal benefits:
- Antioxidant
- Aphrodisiac
- Sedative
- Antibacterial
- Anti-inflammatory
- Circulatory
- Respiratory digestive aid
- Anti-depressant

WASABI

Wasabi, also known as Japanese horseradish, is a potently spicy condiment used in many Japanese dishes—traditionally with raw fish (sushi and sashimi) and noodle (soba) dishes as a little green blob of a condiment. This delectable spice is processed from the wasabi plant, Wasabi japonica, a Japanese evergreen. Its natural habitat is in cool mountain river valleys, along stream beds and on river sand bars in Japan. The medicinal attributes of wasabi have extensively been recorded throughout Japan's history. In fact, the first Japanese medicinal literature documenting it was some time in the 10th century. Since then, it has been the focus of many modern scientific reports and studies as the chemicals that make up wasabi have been documented to have antibacterial and antifungal characteristics that retard platelet aggregation and protect against cancer.

Flavor characteristics of wasabi:
- Fresh wasabi has a pungent, acrid aroma with a burning, spicy flavor. Dried wasabi powder must be mixed with H20 to activate its essence of a powerful, sharp bite.

Culinary applications:
- Raw sushi, dressings, and sauces.

Wasabi blends well with:
- Garlic, ginger, and pepper.

Medicinal benefits:
- Antibacterial
- Food poisoning
- Immune response
- Antifungal
- Allergies
- Tumors
- Anti-cancer
- Detoxifier
- Anti-inflammatory

CHAPTER 4 THE SCIENCE OF HERBOMETRY & SPICEOLOGY

I've never said I had all the answers or a comprehensive list of all of the herbs. This index of herbs and spices is not finite. They are far from all of the magic of spice in this great wide world of wonder. That is what these pages are for—to add to your Herb & Spice guide—to customize it to you the practioner. These are just the herbs, roots, and spices I've been led to so far on my journey, and it will continue to grow. In fact, by the time you even read this, I guarantee you that I will have discovered more to add to my Herbometry and Spiceology. I trust you'll choose to do the same. Enjoy, and safe journey on your exploration of the science of spices!

NOTES

SUPERFOOD
DICTIONARY

OF
LIVING FOODS

THE ART & SCIENCE OF LIVING FOODS

When you are here the phrase 'Superfoods' today, it has a subjective meaning to the person using it. Everyone is throwing the phrase around because it has become synonymous with some aspect of healing or rejuvenation, which is unfortunately why a lot of companies are throwing this 'trendy' phrase around to sell their products. Now, I think of raw food as a medicine, so when I think of superfoods, I just think of a more potent medicine. In fact, many of the elements in the multitude of recipes to come in this book could be considered 'superfoods', but that's why I say the phrase is subjective. Nonetheless, in this chapter, we're going to explore the true essence of what makes a food "super" and how we can use them to heal ourselves both body and mind.

The general definition of a *superfood* is a term that is sometimes used to describe food with a high phytonutrient content that is subjectively believed to create health benefits as a result. For example, acai berries are often considered a superfood (or superfruit) because they contain a significant amount of antioxidants, and several substances called anthocyanins and flavonoids.

CHAPTER 4 THE SCIENCE OF HERBOMETRY & SPICEOLOGY

The language of superfoods can be confusing because many of the terms for nutrients overlap. So that we can truly understand what makes a superfood 'super', here is a basic glossary:

1. **ANTIOXIDANTS** – An antioxidant is a molecule with the ability to slow or prevent the oxidation of other molecules. Oxidation is a chemical reaction that transfers electrons from a substance to an oxidizing agent. These chemical reactions can produce free radicals that create chain reactions which damage cells. Antioxidants eliminate this domino effect of chemical reactions by removing free radical intermediates and inhibit other oxidation reactions by being oxidized themselves. As a result, antioxidants are often reducing agents such as thiols, ascorbic acid, or polyphenols. Digestion releases free radicals from food. Antioxidants help prevent this and also are thought to destroy free radicals and slow oxidation, reducing allergies, heart disease, cancer, and aging effects. Dozens of antioxidant nutrients have been identified thus far, and there are most likely several more. Many vitamins have antioxidant effects, including vitamins A (which is a carotene), C, and E.

2. **FLAVONOIDS** – These are the best-known antioxidants—two known examples are green tea and cacao—among a variety called polyphenols. You'll also notice the word *flavonol*, which is a subcategory of flavonoids. Some cousins of the flavonoids are anthocyanins (which give blueberries their now notorious reputation as an antioxidant).

3. **CAROTENOIDS** – These are a class of natural fat-soluble pigments found fundamentally in plants, algae, and photosynthetic bacteria where they play a crucial role in the photosynthetic process. They also occur in some non-photosynthetic bacteria, yeasts, and molds where they perform a protective function against damage by light and oxygen. In short, they are the pigments that protect dark green, yellow, orange, and red fruits and vegetables from sun damage. They also act as antioxidants in humans as well. Beta carotene is a well-known example. It's also called vitamin A. There are dozens of other famous carotenoids such as lycopene and lutein, to name a few.

4. **VITAMINS** – Vitamins need no introduction, but on a physiological level, they are organic compounds needed in controlled amounts by a specific organism. These compounds are called vitamins when they cannot be synthesized in significant enough quantities by an organism, thus must be acquired externally from consumption.

Basically, your body needs them to function properly so your body grows and develops at an optimal level. When it comes to vitamins and minerals, each one has a special part to play in this process. That's why a lack of vitamins can create health problems in the body's vitality and longevity.

5. **DIETARY MINERALS** – These are biochemical elements required by living organisms outside of the four foundational elements that make up common organic molecules. They are carbon, hydrogen, nitrogen, and oxygen. The term "mineral" is anachronistic, as the intention of the definition is to describe ions, not chemical compounds or actual minerals themselves.

6. **ENZYMES** – Enzymes are the electric spark of life. I include them in my criteria for superfoods because of the fact that they initiate every biochemical reaction in the human body, illuminating that all "RAW" food is a "SUPER" food. Enzymes that are naturally abundant in raw, uncooked food activate the digestion of that food when we eat it. Baking, cooking, or any processing of food at temperatures over 115 degrees destroy vital enzymes which then must be compensated for by the pancreas. Now, the pancreas must use the body's metabolic enzyme reservoir to make digestive enzymes to compensate for the lack of enzymes in heat-processed food. Humans are the only species on the planet that deplete the enzyme production of the pancreas and bodily tissues by cooking their food. We also affect other species (i.e., our pets) by feeding them cooked food, and so their fate eventually lies in suffering from the same degenerative diseases as their owners. This is a truly tragic cycle that has to change. Again, you eat life, you add to the life of the cells. You eat death, you add to the death of the cells.

7. **PROBIOTICS** – Well, the word, "probiotic" simply means, "for life" which explains why these nutrients are so necessary for your body's life. Since we are exploring the depth of the sacred geometry of raw food, the proper scientific definition of a probiotic is: A living microbial feed supplement which positively affects the host by improving its intestinal microbial balance. Simply put, A probiotic is a good bacterial organism which contributes to the health and equilibrium of the intestinal tract. Did you know that there are 20 times more bacteria than cells in your body? In fact, at any given moment, you have more bacteria in your body than the total number of people who have ever lived on this earth. Probiotics also adaptagenic, which means they adapt to the host that they live in. This means if I consume a probiotic

CHAPTER 4 THE SCIENCE OF HERBOMETRY & SPICEOLOGY

and my liver needs support, they will aid in that process. At the same time, if you ingested the same bacteria and your digestive system was taxed, they would "adapt" to harmonize that imbalance. It is this ability that makes them very effective in helping to fight illness and disease. New research is establishing the necessary role of probiotics as supplementation in the body for everything from enhancing the immune system to balancing the body's alkalinity. It is for a multitude of these reasons that it goes into our guidelines for superfoods.

All of these elements make up the variety of superfoods we're going to explore as the chapter continues. I really wanted to create a mini superfood dictionary as a reference guide to go back to either to supplement or modify recipes to "up the medicinal value," or be able to understand the medicinal content of the recipe in its integrity. Remember, there is no box or confine that contains us or our sacred geometry of nutrition. Let your intuition guide you always. As a great teacher once said...

> "The master can share the knowledge, but the experiences belong to the students. Therefore, we do not claim any result or effect or guarantee, any result or achievement because the experience belongs to the individual student individually, his or her consciousness, and his or her power to practice."
>
> - Yogi Bhajan, PhD

CHAPTER 5
DICTIONARY

CHAPTER 5 DICTIONARY

ACAI BERRIES

The acai (ah-sigh-ee) berry, Euterpe oleracea, is commonly called Açaí Palm, after the European adaptation of the Tupian word ïwasa'I which translates as, 'fruit that cries or expels H20.' It was first used by the Amazon Indians as treatment for a variety of ailments. This majestic berry has been found to possess immense healing characteristics. It was discovered to have natural antioxidants, as well as also being a natural cholesterol regulator. Acai has also been found to build the immune system, fight infection, protect the heart, and control prostate enlargement. It is thought to have natural antibiotic properties. It is also a natural energy booster. It helps promote health in the cardiovascular system and digestive tract. It is an almost perfect essential amino acid complex in conjunction with valuable trace minerals, which is vital to proper muscle contraction and regeneration. It has the vibrant taste of berries with just a hint of chocolate. It is rich in vitamin E, protein, fiber, and omega-3 fatty acids. It also contains similar properties of red wine. Açaí palms are fast-growing and are cultivated for both their fruit and for their superior hearts of palm.

5 BENEFITS OF ACAI BERRIES

1. Nutrient Dense - contain vitsmin A, calcium, and some other trace minerals, including chromium, zinc, iron, copper, manganese, magnesium, potassium and phosphorus. Most notable is the plant compound anthocyanin, which give acai berries their deep purple color and act as antioxidants in the body.

2. High in Antioxidants - Acai berries have an incredibly high amount of antioxidants, edging out other antioxidant-rich fruits like blueberries and cranberries.

3. Improve cholesterol levels - studies have suggested that acai could help improve cholesterol levels by decreasing total and LDL cholesterol.

4. Anti-cancerous - some foods are known to stop cancer cells from forming and spreading. Some studies have shown this sort of anti-cancer effect in acai pulp reducing the incidence of colon and bladder cancer.

5. Boost brain function - antioxidants in acai counteract the damaging effects of inflammation and oxidation in brain cells, which can negatively affect memory and learning

AGAVE

Agave syrup, also called agave nectar, is a nectar commonly produced in Mexico and is made from Agave americana plant (also called Century Plant). Agave syrup is similar to honey in color and texture, but it is not as dense and flows easier. This nectar is available in light or dark shades, the lighter shades being more filtered. One of the most health-promoting properties of agave nectar is its favorable glycemic profile. Its sweetness comes primarily from a complex form of fructose called inulin. Fructose is the sugar that occurs naturally in fruits and vegetables. The carbohydrate in agave nectar has a low glycemic index which provides a 'sweetness' without the notorious "sugar rush", which is an unbalancing spike in blood sugar caused by many of the processed sugars today. Agave nectar is a delicious natural sweetener that can be used to replace high-glycemic and refined sugars. Agave was cultivated for centuries by the Native American population for fibers, food, and drinks. The Aztecs used a balm / paste of agave nectar and salt for wounds and skin infections, and agave's use as a folk remedy still continues today. This medicinal nectar began appearing in health food stores in the early 2000s as the western diet was increasingly dominated by processed sweeteners such as chemically treated sugars and high fructose corn syrup. The danger with these substances is their extremely high glycemic – index and glycemic load. Both are serious reflections of the parallel impact that food has on the blood sugar of the human body. Processed sugars that heighten blood sugar rapidly activate the release of the hormone insulin. Excessive releases of insulin result in chronically high blood sugar and are linked to Metabolic Syndrome, which is a complex of health disorders connected to such ailments as insulin resistance, type II diabetes, obesity (specifically abdominal weight gain), complications with blood lipids (raised triglycerides and cholesterol), as well as high blood pressure.

CHAPTER 5 DICTIONARY

ALOE VERA

The aloe vera plant manufactures at least 6 antiseptic agents: Lupeol, salicylic acid, urea, nitrogen, cinnamonic acid, phenols, and sulfur. They kill or control mold, bacteria, fungus, and viruses, reflecting why this 'medicine' plant has the ability to terminate many internal and external infections. The Lupeol and salicylic acid in the juice explain why it is a very effective as a natural painkiller.

Also, aloe vera contains at least three anti-inflammatory fatty acids, cholesterol, campersterol, and B-sitosterol (plant sterols) which explains why it is a highly effective treatment for burns, cuts, scrapes, abrasions, allergic reactions, rheumatoid arthritis, rheumatic fever, acid indigestion, ulcers, plus many inflammatory conditions of the digestive system and other internal organs, including the stomach, small intestine, colon, liver, kidney, and pancreas. B-sitosterol is also a powerful anti-cholestromatic which helps to lower harmful cholesterol levels, thereby helping to elaborate on its many benefits for heart patients.

If we add that aloe contains at least 23 polypeptids (immune stimulators), then we understand why aloe vera juice helps control a broad spectrum of immune system diseases and disorders, including HIV and AIDS. The polypeptids, plus the anti-tumor agents aloe emodin and aloe lectins, explains its ability to control cancer. It's this synergy between the elements found in the sap, gel, and throughout the entire plant that explains why whole leaf aloe works! This also explains why this ancient plant has transcended through the ages from cultures to culture, leaving the imprint on people and healers alike who have professed that aloe has the ability to heal, alleviate, eliminate, and even cure a vast list of human diseases and disorders. Therefore, it has truly earned itself the name, "Medicine man plant".

MANDALA LIVING FOODS

BEE POLLEN

Bee pollen is basically the male seed from flowers. It is necessary for the pollination of the plant. These finite particles are made up of 50 / 1,000-millimeter corpuscles, formed at the free end of the stamen in the heart of the blossom. Every species of flower on the planet releases a dusting of pollen, including a multitude of orchard fruits and agricultural food crops as well.

Bee pollen is actually the nutritional supply (food) of the young bee. It is made up of about 40% protein. It is understood to be one of nature's most complete superfoods on a variety of levels. It contains almost every nutrient required by the human body. Around half of its protein comes in the configuration of free amino acids that are ready to be synthesized by the body. Such highly absorbable proteins can significantly supply one's protein needs.

Human consumption of bee pollen is praised throughout the ancient texts, from the Bible to the ancient Egyptian and Chinese texts. It has truly been a time-honored prescription advocated by many health practitioners through the ages, including the fathers of Western medicine: Hippocrates, Pythagoras, and Pliny the Elder because of its immense healing effects. Bee pollen revitalizes your body, rejuvenates your organs and glands, enhances vitality, and creates an awakening in the body, therefore leading to a longer life. Bee pollen's capability to distinctly increase levels of energy in the body makes it a primary superfood among many top rated athletes and those interested in maintaining and amplifying quality performance.

CHAPTER 5 DICTIONARY

BLUEBERRIES

We now arrive at the trendiest superfood to the mainstream public to date, and with good reason as you're about to see. When we discussed the characteristics of what makes a superfood "super", there are some superfoods that possess a multitude of those characteristics. The blueberry is one of those. It contains antioxidants, anthocyanins, flavonoids, and proanthycyanins in its composition which distinctly individualizes it as a superfood.

One cup of blueberries contains 14 mg of vitamin C and 0.8 mg vitamin E. Blueberries are among the fruits with the highest antioxidant activity, and the anthocyanins as well as tannins have been linked to prevention, even reversal, of age-related mental decline and the effects from cancer.

7 BENEFITS OF BLUEBERRIES

1. Low in caloeries, rich in nutrients - blueberries are among the most nutrient dense fruits full of antioxidents, fiber, vitamin K, vitamin A, and magnesium.

2. One of the top antioxidnat fruits - is known to be one of the highest antioxidant rich foods with one of main ones in the polyphenol family called flavenoids, in particular anthocyanins.

3. Anti-aging - blueberries reduce DNA damage which helps protect against the aging process and cancer development.

4. Protect against cholesterol - antioxidants in blueberries are strongly linked to reduced levels of oxidized LDL. This makes blueberries very good for your heart

5. Lowers blood pressure - have significant benefits for people with high blood pressure, which is a major risk factor for heart disease.

6. Support brain function & memory - the antioxidants in blueberries may affect areas of your brain that are essential for intelligence and benefit aging neurons, leading to improvements in cell signaling.

7. Anti-diabetes - Research suggests that anthocyanins in blueberries have beneficial effects on insulin sensitivity and glucose metabolism. These anti-diabetes effects have been observed with both fresh and freeze-dried berries

BLUE GREEN ALGAE

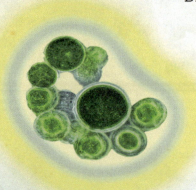

Blue green algae, or in Latin (Aphanizomenon flos-aquae – meaning "invisible H20 flower"), is one of the most nutrient rich foods on the planet. They best way to get it is from a source that harvests and dries it using the latest technology to preserve the enzymes and phyto-nutrients of the algae. What's interesting about algae is that it really is in a category all by itself as it demonstrates the properties and traits of both botanicals and mammals. This blue green superfood also possesses the widest range of phyto-nutrients of any known algae in the ocean. This includes very rare biologically active enzymes, trace elements, amino acids, essential fatty acids, B12, chlorophyll, phenylethylamine (PEA), glycol-proteins, complex sugars, vitamins, and minerals. Even more amazing is the fact that on a cellular level, algae's nutritious cell wall is so soft that all of these nutrients contained in it are ready to be synthesized right into the body. It is for all of these reasons that blue green algae has truly earned the name "Superfood."

Algae's elevated mineral content is a result of the algae feeding in nutrient-rich H20s, which is why it's important to know where your algae comes from. The chlorophyll alone in algae aids in detoxifying the body and maintaining a harmonious immune system. A multitude of recent research confirms this superfood stimulates the immune system to remove unhealthy cells with more efficiency. In reflection, algae has been consumed in some form or another for several thousand years. It is biological power house of active enzymes, vitamins, neuropeptide precursors, B-12, minerals, beta-carotene, chlorophyll, trace elements, and essential fatty acids. Below is a general list of the benefits of blue green algae:

1. Healthy immune system
2. Healthy brain and nervous system
3. Balanced metabolism
4. Increased energy, stamina, and mental clarity
5. Increased stress tolerance

CHAPTER 5 DICTIONARY

CACAO

Cacao, (Theobroma cacao) (Mayan: kakaw, Nahuatl: Cacahuatl), or the cocoa plant, is a small evergreen tree that is in the Sterculiaceae family and is native to the deep tropical region of the Americas. The seeds of the cacao plant are what is used to make what the world has known as cocoa and chocolate. Unfortunately, it was usually contaminated with the congestive mucus of the cow and was overly processed that most of the medicinal content was lost. Which brings us to the pure power of cacao in its natural state. It contains some of the most powerful antioxidants in existence. The synergetic harmony of a multitude of antioxidants, vitamins, minerals, etc., is just beginning to be recognized as mandatory to our health and longevity.

Incorporating cacao as part of a balanced diet along with a balanced foundation of physical and spiritual exercise will not only enhance your quality of life, but your lifespan as well. The combination of various superfoods such as cacao activate the body on a multitude of levels to bring it back into a state of equilibrium from its slumber. Our vehicles require these natural 'power' foods to operate at an optimal level of functionality, as opposed to some processed supplement. The research on cacao is constant, but here is what some studies have shown one may experience from incorporating cacao into their diet:

- Decreases cardiovascular disease by stopping bad cholesterol from forming on vessel walls and narrowing the passage, and lowers cholesterol levels
- Prevents the formation of blood clots which can lead to heart attacks and strokes
- Increases the flexibility of blood vessels in order to lower blood pressure and decrease the stress on the heart
- Helps the body utilize sugars better, thus preventing diabetes as well as decreasing the complications of diabetes – vision problems, amputations, as well as kidney problems
- Prevents dental caries and gum disease
- Improves memory and slows down dementia
- Prevents certain types of cancer
- Improves breathing problems.
- Improves the quality of the skin
- Decreases the inflammation associated with arthritis, fibromyalgia, or any inflammatory disease

- Decreases the size of the prostate and prevents urinary tract infections
- Provides energy
- Improves liver fuction
- Improves depression
- Helps with weight gain and decreased appetites

Cacao is one of my most beloved superfoods. I incorporate it into dishes whenever I can, which you will see in the recipes of this guide. It is great in smoothies, desserts, and even some salads. Some of my raw teachers got by just eating it raw, exploring the chemical reactions as it hit the, and then as it began to be absorbed into the blood. This food is truly a medicine... Hallelujah, Cacao.

CHAGA MUSHROOM

Chaga, (Inonotus obliquus), also bearing the name cinder conk, is a fungus in family of Hymenochaetaceae and is the Northwestern brother of the reishi mushroom which we will be covering further along in this chapter. Its origins are vast, growing on birch trees in Russia, Korea, Eastern Europe, northern areas of the United States, as well as Siberia. It is the first of a few parasitic fungi that are highly medicinal for the human body. This one feeds on birch and other trees until they are completely dead, upon which the sterile conk is irregularly formed and has the appearance of burnt charcoal. After the chaga is harvested, the host tree is completely dead. Like reishi, it has a woody fibrous body and a powerful array of health benefits which we're going to explore now.

Dating back to the 16th century, there are accounts of the chaga mushroom being utilized in folk medicine and homeopathic medicine throughout the Eastern European countries as a treatment and cure for cancer, gastritis, ulcers, and tuberculosis of the bones, to list a few. A number of subsequent studies out of Finland and Russia reported that the chaga mushroom made a monumental mark in treating breast cancer, liver cancer, uterine cancer, and gastric cancer, as well as in hypertension and diabetes. Herbalists and naturopaths alike have deemed it the most powerful anti-cancer medicinal mushroom in existence. One of the reasons why is the anti-mutagenic activity of the molecules found in the white part of the bark of the birch tree where the chaga feeds which hinders free-radical oxidation and also activates the production of interferons, which helps initiate the repair of DNA. The materials that the white part of birch bark are made up of help to decrease hypoxia and to increase the strength of the organism to the deficiency of oxygen, thus correcting the metabolism of cells. Another property of birch trees is the anti-cancer properties of betulin or betulinic acid. It is an isolated chemical from the birch tree of which the chaga hold large amounts. This betulinic acid is in a format that can be consumed directly. In addition, it is comprised of a wide variety of immune-boosting phytochemicals that are also found in other mushrooms known to have immense medicinal properties, such as maitake and shiitake mushrooms.

CHLORELLA

Chlorella is a type of single-cell green algae that contains a high amount of chlorophyll, vitamins, and nutrients. It grows naturally but is also harvested in artificial ponds. I suggest not purchasing chlorella that has been pasteurized or freeze dried as these processes can deplete the chlorella of its natural enzymes that help to promote digestion in the body. When dried, chlorella is generally composed of 10% minerals and vitamins, 5% fiber, 20% fat, 20% carbohydrates, and 45% protein. Chlorella contains calcium, zinc, iron, magnesium, phosphorus, pantothenic acid, and tryptophan, as well as vitamins E, A, C, and the B spectrum, among other nutrients. Chlorella is an extremely efficient detoxification tool. It secures itself to heavy metals and pesticides and removes these harmful substances from the body. Chlorella also activates the immune system's ability to react to foreign bacteria, viruses, and chemicals by increasing interferon levels. During the food shortages in the World War II era, researchers at Stanford University, the Carnegie Institute, and elsewhere explored the possibility of cultivated chlorella as a solution to the problem. Momentum for this quickly faded as researchers calculated that cultivation of chlorella was not economically possible.

CHAPTER 5 DICTIONARY

COCONUT OIL / BUTTER

The definition of coconut oil truly pales in comparison to its highly medicinal properties. It is a pale yellow to colorless oil or a white semisolid fat obtained from the flesh of the coconut. It is widely used in raw food products and in the recipes of this book, especially the desserts. In its purest form (extra virgin, unrefined), it truly is a superfood in its own right. Now, the oil varies from the butter as the butter has an accumulation of meat and oil, and has more of a girth to it. It is more of a food. Both hold a significant place in a well-rounded raw foodist's diet. On the following pages, we are going to explore the vast spectrum of healing benefits of this godly food. So strap on your seat belts as this superfood deserves at least a page and a half. It can be used as everything from a butter to a base for desserts or salad dressings, and so much more!!!

Interesting facts about coconut oil:

1. Coconut oil that has been kept at room temperature for a year was tested, and showed no evidence of rancidity.

2. In animal studies, feeding unprocessed coconut and coconut oils prevented tumor development, both malignant and benign.

3. It lowers cholesterol if it is high and raises it if it is low.

4. Coconut oil is anti-viral, anti-bacterial, and anti-fungal in the originating plant, in our gut, and in our blood. Reducing seed oil consumption and using coconut milk or coconut oil as the dietary staple reverses viral loads in HIV, eliminates all types of the herpes virus, and reduces or prevents other viral diseases, including the yearly 'flus' and measles. The antiviral effect seems to combat lipid-enveloped viruses which is due to the presence of lauric acid in coconut oil.

5. It has been reported that coconut oil helps prevent weight gain by stimulating the metabolism; but further evidence needs to be presented to support this claim. It is quickly metabolized, and functions in some ways as an antioxidant.

MANDALA LIVING FOODS

6. Every study using natural, unprocessed coconut oil found a normalizing of cholesterol, blood sugar, and blood pressure. This is also true of extra virgin olive oil, peanut oil, and avocado oil.

7. Within a week, abnormal cortisol levels show improvement, indicating adrenal restoration using vitamin B1, B complex, and coconut milk. Patients seem more awake, their mood, energy, and memory improves, and sleep becomes normalized.

There are a large amount of misunderstandings based off of research and data declaring the harmfulness of coconut oil. Let me clear the air on this matter by clarifying that this "research" has been compiled from studies using hydrogenated oils. The conclusions drawn from these studies cannot factually be applied to the use of unprocessed tropical oils. It's as simple as that. As for all the other hydrogenated fats, which include margarine, shortening, and all other hydrogenated and partially hydrogenated vegetable oils found in everything from most restaurant foods contribute to such degenerative diseases as diabetes, obesity, stroke, heart disease, depression, hypoglycemia, thyroid disorders, cancer, and the list goes on. Now, I know you're thinking, *how can this rich decadent ingredient be good for me?* Welcome to the future...You can have your cake and eat it too!!!

CHAPTER 5 DICTIONARY

COLLOIDAL GOLD

Certain rare trace elements like gold, silver, titanium, as well as other platinum group metals are now being examined for their capability to nutritionally assist in higher potentials of mental, emotional, and physical well-being. Some minerals are very specific in their action and others, like gold, have a vast spectrum of explorative effects and seem to synergize the dynamic of the mind / body paradigm in extremely constructive ways. In this day and age, there is a major depletion of minerals in the soil, which in accompaniment with the disconnectedness of the average human being to their food chain and connection to this planet, there is far less vital minerals and nutrients in our daily intake of food. The problem lies in that the human body requires a whole supply of trace minerals and nutrients to function at a peak mental, emotional, and physical state of well-being. The following page lists the effects felt by individuals who have taken colloidal gold.

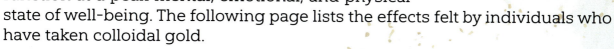

These experiences are subjective as to each individual, but there are some interesting commonalities from a number of different subjects' experiences from different sources. Now keep in mind that everybody has a different chemistry, a different genealogy, a different lifestyle, etc. For that reason, the explorer of colloidal gold is bound to experience a uniquely individualized array of physiological effects that will vary in degrees of intensity.

An individual may experience the following from consuming colloidal gold over a period of time:

1. Elevated sense of optimism and motivation

2. Heightened wholistic sensation of well-being

3. Focus, concentration, and memory increased

4. Deep-rooted, more rejuvenating sleep, and greater dream recall

5. Sense of elevated creativity and imagination

MANDALA LIVING FOODS

6. Sense of heightened mental clarity and awareness

7. Mood support through mood-affected seasonal change

8. Alleviation of addictions or cravings

9. Sensation of energy, with a calm centered awareness

10. Evolved capability to deal with or release stress

Known to date back to ancient times as the "Elixir of life," the fusion of colloidal gold was originally used as a method of staining glass in the Ancient Roman times. During the 16th century, the alchemist Paracelsus declared that he created a potion called Aurum Potabile. Modern scientific evaluation of colloidal gold did not begin until Michael Faraday's work of the 1850s. The unique optical, electronic, and molecular-recognition properties of gold nanoparticles merit the focus of substantial research with applications in a wide spectrum of fields. For many, its focus is on electronics and nanotechnology, but my focus is more on the physiological and energetic effects to the body, mind, and spirit. Once again, all I can do is speak from my own preferences, and I love to use it to make desserts. It adds a whole other level of mind expansion to your raw cheesecake, fruit tart, etc.

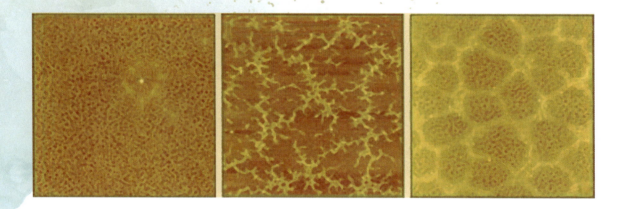

COLLOIDAL SILVER

Colloidal silver (CS) is a organic antibiotic which has been used throughout the world for hundreds of years with a multitude of purposes. The most important being to destroy viruses, bacteria, and microbes of all kinds as well as healing many health problems. It was withdrawn from public usage in the U.S. in the 1920s and 1930s by the ever-controlling western medical profession as an ongoing attempt to eradicate natural health remedies from the marketplace. As late as August 1998, the FDA ordered all colloidal silver withdrawn from U.S. health stores; but due to public resistance, this attempt has been presently halted. In the present day, colloidal silver and its uses are spreading like wildfire through the wholistic and medical communities. A primary use is on burn victims.

Silver works as reinforcement to the immune system in the human body by eliminating bacteria and viruses of all varieties. It is deadly to bacteria, viruses, yeasts, fungi (molds), protozoa, and parasites in their egg stage. In that respect, colloidal silver will kill the more rampant bacteria / viruses like staph and strep bacteria which are spreading across the country because of unhealthy ill-equipped individuals with no true understanding of the food-medicine paradigm. In the research on colloidal silver, there is a list of over 650 diseases and health problems that silver in colloidal form will affect in very constructive ways. The mechanics of *why* is based on the frequency of silver. It has a higher frequency than almost all of the known harmful crystal-headed viruses. Even viruses such as AIDS, Ebola, West Nile, and SARS. Therefore, it destroys their existence. Now a lot of times viruses such as these are no problem to a person who has a strong immune system and a solid foundation of nutrition. Unfortunately, like predators in the wild, these viruses prey on the weak, and in this case they would have neither of the previous mentioned to protect them.

There are three basic properties that colloidal silver users attempt to harness by its use:

1. Silver has biocidal properties that fight infection.

2. Silver has tissue healing properties that are demonstrated by altered cell morphology, resulting in increased (and healthy) cell reproduction.

3. Silver has electrical stimulation properties. The theory is that with an increased zeta potential, colloidal silver can aid the body to reclaim health through numerous means which are not yet fully understood, including catalyst reactions in the body with substances like minute amounts of hydrogen peroxide.

Exploring and overstanding these three properties is a vital role in calculating both when and how colloidal silver might be effective for use as a health-preserving rejuvenating substance in the human body.

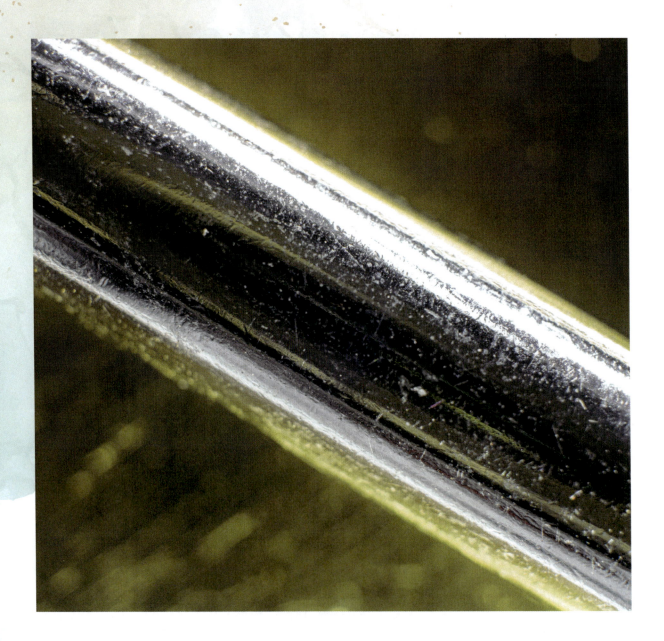

CHAPTER 5 DICTIONARY

CORDYCEPS

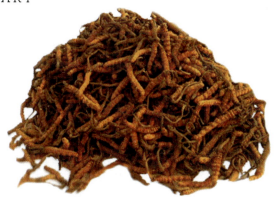

Known as the Chinese longevity mushroom, cordyceps are a very unique fungus in both methodology of cultivation and their immense healing benefits. It is a parasitic fungus and cultivates itself by infiltrating various types of worms or insects, in which it grows inside of, eventually consuming it from the inside out. Sound appetizing? That's why most companies don't reveal its origins. Nonetheless, it is completely vegan, raw, and a powerhouse superfood. I say powerhouse because it is literally used to remarkably increase stamina and virility. This amazing superfood came to the spotlight of the western world in 1993 when the Chinese national running team blew away all their competitors by a sizeable margin. That year, they set nine new world records. Obviously being tested for steroids, it was after the testing that it was revealed that their trainer was supplementing their diets with this little powerhouse mushroom!

Here's a broad list of known effects on the physiology of the human body:

1. Strengthens the immune system
2. Increases libido and sexual performance
3. Supports a healthy, strong heart and cardiovascular system
4. Radically increases cellular energy
5. Dramatically increases stamina and endurance
6. Supports healthy lungs and respiratory system
7. Cellular detoxification
8. Improves memory
9. Increases nutrient absorption
10. Being an adaptogen, they build resistance to stress and anxiety
11. Promotes restful, productive sleep

MANDALA LIVING FOODS

DURIAN FRUIT

Durian, known as the "King of Fruits" in Southeast Asian countries where it is widely abundant, is a deceptive food of great stature. People who only see it or smell it are instantly put off by its strong, pungent odor; but for the more courageous and explorative who manage to taste the fruit itself, the pungency of the smell quickly fades away. Those who taste this sacred fruit usually become lifelong addicts. If not for the rich, creamy taste, then for the medicinal properties and nutritional girth. Durian is not plucked off the tree but rather allowed to naturally fall. This is when they are perfect for eating. In many rural areas of Asia, villagers clear the earth beneath the durian trees, build grass huts nearby at the time of harvest, and camp there for six to eight weeks in order to be prepared to gather each fruit as it falls.

Fruit Description: The fruit's shape is an elongated ovalular shape with five or less compartments containing creamy-white or yellowish edible pulp with custard-like consistency. It is a delicacy. The rind is thick and yellow-greenish in color with a wood-like density covered with stout, sharply pointed spikes.

The health benefits of durian:

1. Durian is extremely nutritious because it is rich in vitamins B, C, and E and a high iron content. Eating durian is alleged to restore the health of ailing humans and animals.
2. A preparation from its roots and leaves is prescribed by traditional doctors for fevers and jaundice.
3. Decoctions of the leaves and fruits are applied to swellings and skin diseases.
4. Durian fruit helps lower cholesterol.
5. Durian is a strong blood cleanser.
6. The ash of the burned rind is taken after childbirth.
7. Durian contains high levels of the amino acid tryptophan, known to alleviate anxiety, depression, and insomnia, and create feelings of happiness, by raising levels of serotonin in the brain.
8. Durian contains high levels of soft protein which makes it a good muscle builder.
9. Durian has a reputation as a powerful aphrodisiac.
10. Durian is recommended as a good source of raw fats.

ELDERBERRY

Elderberry (Sambucus nigra) has been an ancient folk remedy over the centuries in Europe, North America, Western Asia, as well as North Africa. For this reason, the healing benefits of elderberry is now presently being researched and rediscovered. The elderberry is rich in antioxidants, which results in lowering cholesterol, improving vision, replenishing the immune system, and improving the functionality of the heart. Some other conditions that this medicinal berry aids in the healing of are coughs, colds, flus, bacterial and viral infections, as well as tonsillitis. This is done through the bioflavonoids and other proteins in the juice that terminate the ability of cold and flu viruses to contaminate the body's cells. In 1995, elderberry juice was used to heal a flu pandemic in Panama. Remedies of this fruit are said to be helpful for nerve disorders as well as back pain. It has also been used to relieve inflammation in the urinary tract and bladder.

Listed attributes of elderberry are:

Properties:
- Antioxidant, diaphoretic, diuretic, laxative, immune-boosting, anti-inflammatory

Uses:
- Immune system boost, coughs, colds, flu, bacterial infections, viral infections, tonsillitis, lower cholesterol, enhanced vision, and promotion of a healthy heart

Indicated for:
- Cancer, HIV, asthma and bronchitis, reduces inflammation of the urinary tract and bladder

FLAX SEEDS

Flax is an oil seed that has been used as a food product for thousands of years. Flax, also known as linseed, is an ancient crop that has its origin traced back to 3,000 B.C. when cultivated by the Babylonians. It has been grown all over the world, with its higher production as a field crop noted in fertile river valleys. Around 650 B.C., Hippocrates wrote about the soothing nature of eating flax to relieve abdominal pains. There are three components to flax seeds that make flax seeds such a nutritional force: Omega-3 oils (also known as alpha-linolenic acid or ALA), Lgnans, and fiber-both soluble and insoluble.

The National Cancer Institute has classified golden flax seeds as a food that has earned further research and observation in light of its prospective cancer fighting attributes and various nutritional benefits. In accordance to the U.S. Department of Agriculture, golden flax seeds contain 27 detectable cancer preventing agents. The National Heart, Lung, and Blood Institute also recommends integrating flaxseeds to your daily nutritional regiment to improve overall health. There are two types: golden flax seed and brown flax seed. As we get into a more detailed breakdown of this ancient seed, we'll explore the full regiment of potential health benefits that have been reported over the years, none of which, by the way, is confirmed by the FDA, of course. Explore for yourself; your body will tell you what is truth.

CHAPTER 5 DICTIONARY

Health benefits of flax seeds:

1. Lowers blood cholesterol levels
2. Lowers high blood pressure
3. Increases IN energy, stamina, and vitality
4. Lowers of the threat of blood clots
5. Protects against cancers, particularly hormone sensitive cancers such as breast and prostate
6. Increases a sense of calm and center under stress
7. Better regulation of blood sugar levels
8. Eases inflammatory tissue conditions, including arthritis
9. Alleviates dry skin, eczema, and psoriasis
10. Enhances the immune system
11. Increases the metabolic rate with a positive impact on weight management
12. Aids with Attention Deficit Disorder (ADD)
13. Acts as natural laxative

The list actually goes on and on... you'll notice that we use this medicine seed in a lot of our recipes, from the cheese to the tostadas – even the bread! I say what's bread without a little medicine?...

GOJI BERRIES

(Symphoricarpos occidentalis). Also known as lycium berries or "wolf berries," they are native to Southeastern Europe and Asia. They produce a bright orange-red, elliptical berry 1–2 cm long. They can contain anywhere between 10-60 little yellow seeds that are compressed with a curved embryo. They are sweet and salty in taste, but their nutritional value makes them taste even sweeter. It's not just the berries of this tree that are medicinal, the leaves are used to make an age old tea, and the root bark of the lycium tree is used to treat inflammatory and certain types of skin diseases. This is because glucopyranoside and phenolic amides that have been isolated and identified from the root bark of the goji tree demonstrate preventative attributes in vitro against human pathogenic bacteria and fungi. The goji berry is also known as the happy berry for its capability to generate a feeling of welfare and positivity. It just so happens that this extraordinary berry is also one of the world's most nutrient-rich berries, placing it rightfully in our superfood dictionary. A general list of benefits below elaborates a little more on what this little berry has to offer.

Benefits of goji berries:
1. Boosts the immune system
2. Creates energy and relieves fatigue
3. As an antioxidant, it lowers the effects of free radicals in the body
4. Creates a sensation of welfare and positivity
5. Acts as a regulator to control appetite and excessive eating compulsions

Overall, the goji berry is one, if not the "super berry" in circulation today. It is definitely a superfood to have in your collection and utilize whenever possible. In salads, smoothies, and especially desserts!

CHAPTER 5 DICTIONARY

HEMP SEEDS

Also known the seeds of the plant cannabis sativa, hemp seeds hold all the essential amino acids and essential fatty acids necessary to maintain a healthy body. There isn't another single plant source in the world that has the essential amino acids in such an effortlessly digestible form. In addition, no other single source has the essential fatty acids as divine a ratio to meet the human body's demand for nutrition sustenance. Truly the characteristics of a "superfood," and we're just getting warmed up. Now, the true importance of the hemp seed's nutritional value to humanity can't be completely recognized without some greater 'overstanding' of the biochemistry that makes up this life.

Let's start with the fact that are eight amino acids that the human body cannot create and two more that the body cannot supply an adequate amount of. These amino acids are so vital to proper health and homeostasis in the body. Significant time without any one of them will eventually cause degeneration and disease. These key amino acids, as well as the other eleven that the body can produce from them, are sequenced together according to various genetic criterion. It is through the RNA configuration via DNA blueprints that they are organized into structural proteins that give the body life, as well as into enzymes (globular proteins) that carry out the mechanics of living. Virtually three fourths of body solids are proteins. In all actuality, the body is composed of and sustained by a limitlessly intricate system that basically constructs proteins from amino acid sub components. This takes place every time an amino acid consists of an amine and a carboxyl that are attached to the same carbon atom. Everyone except the smallest amino acid has one, complex, carbon composed side sequence that is connected to the carbon atom and shared by the amine and carboxyl groups. The AMINE GROUP, ND is rather basic, with the CARBOXYL GROUP, COOH being a mild acid. The amine group of one amino acid joins with the carboxyl group of another forming a peptide link. Proteins are made of amino acid peptide chains in specific sequential arrangements. The number of possible amino acid peptide variations are endless.

Hemp seeds, like flax and many other seeds, possess all the essential amino acids in their embryonic seed. The distinctive property of the hemp seed is that its protein is made up of 65% globulin edistin, which is the most superior in

MANDALA LIVING FOODS

the botanical kingdom. These specific proteins are called antibodies and are remarkable in that they are programmed to destroy antigens (any substance provoking a response from lymphocytes, which include bacteria, viruses, toxins, living and dead tissue, internal debris, etc.) They move about in blood plasma like floating explosive charges floating through your ocean. These antibodies are on alert, ready to make contact with any intruders, and upon contact they unleash a barrage of corrosive enzymes that eat away the surface of the antigen, causing it to break down.

With the latest statistics showing one out of every two Americans dying from cardiovascular disease (CVD) and one out of every four Americans dying from cancer, it's time to explore what is at the root of this degeneration. Well, many scientists believe cancers develop when the immune system's responsiveness is debilitated. Many modern day trailblazers in the fields of biochemistry and nutrition now believe CVD and the majority of cancers are fat degeneration-based diseases that are the result of prolonged over-consumption of saturated fats and refined vegetable oils that transform essential fatty acids into carcinogenic killers.

As if that isn't disturbing enough, more Americans are falling to immune deficiency diseases than ever before. Sadly, it is the pure ignorance of our species in our lack of knowledge on (a) how to operate the biological vehicles (the human body) in the true intended manner with which it was created, and (b) what it requires nutritionally to run as it was divinely intended. That is the core truth of this country's sickness, and tragically it will be the catalyst of an inordinate amount of Americans dying slowly from these tribulations. It is for this reason that I dedicated over two pages to this magical seed that is a fighting force against the "American Tragedy."

CHAPTER 5 DICTIONARY

HIMALAYAN HUNZA RAISINS

In the scientific study of aging, it is a well known fact that the Hunza People, who live in the high Himalayan mountain regions, are not only the healthiest, but the longest-living people in the world. Based on the research performed by several medical doctors who observed the Hunzas in their natural habitat throughout the 1950s and 1960s, 100% of the Hunza populace had 20/20 vision, no high blood pressure, no cancers, no heart diseases, and no cases of high cholesterol. These people of all ages are highly active, energetic, and full of vim and vigor well into their 90s. What is it that they are doing that is giving them, who live in a so-called third world country, the opposite results of our 'advanced' culture with all its technology and resources? What is producing such strength, vigor, and health at the age of 100+ years old?

Well, their diet is bountiful year round in fresh or dried fruits and nuts. Fruits are grown at high altitudes and are completely organic. In addition, their ancient Himalayan mountain orchards were irrigated for hundreds of years with the purest glacial-melt waters. Cultivated at 6,000 to 9,000 feet above sea level, Hunza raisins are enriched with highly mineral-rich glacial H20s containing iron, calcium, copper, and gold. Himalayan Hunza raisins are hand-picked, sun-dried, unsulfured, and acclaimed throughout the world. An interesting fact about these ancient raisins is that they contain one of t

he highest forms of the bone-enhancing trace mineral called boron. Raisins, in general, rank among the top antioxidant-containing foods in existence. Recognized health authorities all concur that the regulated consumption of antioxidant containing fruits and vegetables will help to prevent heart disease and cancer as well as hinder the effects of aging and degeneration in the body.

MANDALA LIVING FOODS

THE ARTS & SCIENCE OF LIVING FOODS

INCA BERRIES

Golden Inca berries are quickly becoming known as one of the most intensely flavorful berries on earth. The taste experience is a tart, and sometimes sour one, with an undertone of sweetness. Now, what makes them taste even better is knowing that they pack quite a punch of nutritional value. These unique berries originating in Peru contain a vast array of B-vitamins and are thought to be one of the only known plant-based sources of B12 in the world. This fact makes this special berry an integral energy generator that is necessary to maintain a healthy cellular metabolism. Jam-packed with a vast spectrum of nutrients, these energizing super berries should truly become a pillar to your raw food diet.

5 BENFITS IF INCA OR GOLDEN BERRIES:

1. Increase metabolism

2. Improve digestion

3. Helps control diabetes by regulating insulin levels

4. Cleanses the blood

5. Supports prostate health

JACKFRUIT

Well where do I begin with this interesting life food? I say life food because it is one of those fruits that if you were trapped on a deserted island with just one type of fruit, this would be the one you want. Jackfruit, artocarpus heterophyllus, originates out of Southeast Asian countries, but has migrated to other countries like Jamaica, Hawaii, Trinidad, and others. The appearance of this unique fruit (shown on the opposite page), is similar in many respects to durian which we previously explored. A large spikey fruit measuring anywhere from 12 to 20 inches long and 8 to 10 inches in width, depending on the individual fruit, they can weigh up to around 40 pounds and more! Jackfruit is a very fragrant fruit. Once opened, you'll discover the bright yellow flesh (when ripe) can be eaten raw, pureed in a sauce, or even dehydrated. When the flesh is unripe its green, and it can be made into a variety of vegetable dishes. Inside the fleshy part are the seeds (nut) which are very similar to chestnuts and can be flavored and dehydrated. Now that we know a little about the taste, let's explore the substance of this strange fruit on the following page.

Nutritional Values: per a 100 gram serving:

- Vitamin A: none
- Vitamin B:
    - Thiamine .03 mg
    - Riboflavin: none
    - Niacin: .4 mg
- Potassium: 303 mg
- Vitamin C: .8 mg
- Fat: .3 g
- Carbohydrates: 25.4 g
- Protein: 1.3 g
- Calories: 98

Health Benefits:

1. An amazing energy food with only a minuscule amount of fat.

2. Helps prevent and treats tension and nervousness.

3. Helps with obesity.

4. Aids in the prevention of constipation.

5. Aids in the cure of ulcers and indigestion.

6. Lowers blood pressure as a result of its high potassium content.

7. Contains high amounts of phytonutrients that fight cancer and regress the degeneration of cells that can lead to various diseases.

8. Is a good source of vitamin C.

9. The root of the jackfruit tree is a remedy for skin diseases as well as asthma, and an extract of the root can be taken to treat fever and diarrhea.

10. Overall, jackfruit provides a healthy supply of proteins, carbohydrates and vitamins, thus earning a spot in our superfood dictionary.

CHAPTER 5 DICTIONARY

KAMUT

Now, I found out recently that kamut is a trademark owned by Kamut International, Ltd. I had originally learned it was an ancient Egyptian grain that was discovered in an excavated tomb and was sprouted and brought back to life into the modern day. I have more recently learned that this cannot be truly confirmed. What can be confirmed is that kamut is higher in protein and many minerals, especially selenium, zinc, and magnesium, than other wheat products. It is also rich in vitamins B, C, and E, calcium, iron, pantothenic acid, phosphorus, and amino acids. The word kamut now refers to a variety of khorasan wheat with certain confirmed characteristics. These include being certified organic in production, preservation of the variety in its ancient, non-GMO form. My first yogic recipe was a sprouted cereal mix that my yogi gave me upon our first meeting which you will see later in the breakfast recipes. This was my first introduction to kamut, and it has impressed me ever since.

7 Benefits of Kamut:

1. Maintains healthy tissue.

2. Lowers cholesterol

3. Protects against free radicals

4. Supports hormone balance

5. Boosts immune system

6. Aids in bone health

7. Nutrient dense

KOMBUCHA

Kombucha is the Westernized name for sweetened tea that has been fermented using a macroscopically proportioned solidified masses of microorganisms referred to as a "kombucha colony". Its use dates back to the Qin Dynasty in China (around 250 BC). The Chinese regarded it as an "Immortal Health Elixir." They understood that kombucha balances the Middle Qi (spleen and stomach) and supports in digestion, which allows the body to focus on healing. The culture itself is made up of a symbiosis of Acetobacter (acetic acid bacteria) and yeast, mostly Brettanomyces bruxellensis, Lactobacillus Bacterium, S. Boulardii, Candida stellata, Schizosaccharomyces pombe, Torulaspora delbrueckii, and Zygosaccharomyces bailii. In addition, on an acidic level, it contains the antioxidants and organic acids EGCG, glucuronic acid, lactic acid, and acetic acid. On a nutrient basis, it contains vitamins B1, B2, B3, B6, B12, as well as folic acid. This formula of active enzymes, usable probiotics, amino acids, antioxidants, and polyphenols combine to create an elixir that instantly works with the body to restore both energetic harmony and vigor. On the following page is the top ten list of the most significant benefits form this magical ancient life tonic:

CHAPTER 5 DICTIONARY

Top 10 benefits of drinking kombucha tea daily:

1. Balances acidity and prevents acid reflux
2. Burns body fat, aiding in weight loss
3. Supports the digestion of heavy meals
4. Strengthens and restores hair
5. Enhances your energy through the day
6. Helps with sleep disorders
7. Relieves constipation
8. Rejuvenates the body with electrolytes for pre- and post-workout (cardiovascular and resistance training)
9. Rejuvenates and detoxes the body after a "late night"
10. Enhances skin complexion and healing

I've always enjoyed the fizzy effervescent experience of sodas, but the processed sugars (specifically high fructose corn syrup) and artificial carbonation are one of the most corrosive and detoxifying pollutants in the contemporary diet of the average human being. High fructose corn syrup is one of the most toxic substances on the planet. Then spirit guided me to this magically ancient tonic...and I share it with you...

LONGAN BERRIES

The delightfully sweet longan berry is renowned for its dramatic restorative properties. In the ancestral tradition, longan berries were used as a tonic herb, revealing that this age old berry has a strengthening quality that rejuvenates specific organs, systems, or general weakness in the body. The longan berry nourishes particularly the spleen, stomach, and heart. It also immensely regenerates qi, vital energy – both physical kinetic strength as well as intellectual functionality. The longan berry is also renowned for enhancing beauty from the inside out. The longan was initially consumed daily by the ancients to restore vitality and youth.

Now on a temporal / spiritual level, this spirit berry communicates to the intellect and integrates a sense of centered oneness. The berry itself tastes sweet and juicy and is beloved by both adults and children alike. In that respect, longan berries actually make a great snack for children as it cultivates both intelligence and creativity. In this multi-dimensional matrix of consciousness that we are all experiencing simultaneously, the spleen is said to facilitate the intellect and the heart. This berry creates a balance between heart and mind that is the true evolution of the human into the being. By nourishing these organs through proper use of this earth's medicine, we nourish the associated esoteric embodiments as well. The fact that it is a delicious experience to do so is even better! Here's a basic evaluation of the values of the longan berry:

Longan berries may help with:
- Neurosis
- Insomnia
- Anxiety
- Hyperactivity
- Anemia
- Exhaustion
- Heart palpitations
- Fatigue

Supports organs and systems:
- Heart disorders
- Spleen
- Pancreas
- Strengthens the reproductive
- organs of women

MACA

Raw maca powder is high-powered superfood for enhancing your physical, mental, and emotional experience in life. It not only raises your day-to-day energy level and self-realization of well being, but replenishes and rejuvenates your core energy supply by integrating nourishment to the depths of your endocrine system. This extraordinary and powerful superfood comes in a few different forms, either in tonic of the roots' extract or in a dried powder that tastes kind of malty with undertones of a woodsy earthy vibe. It can be integrated creatively in smoothies, desserts, drinks, or straight into the mouth with a squirt of raw milk or coconut oil! Here's a few benefits to get your brain buzzing about this powerful root...

- Increases physical energy and daily staminaKey nutrients to support libido and peak sexual functioning
- Helps promote physical and emotional well-being by providing key nutrients for hormonal balance for men and women of all ages
- Nutritional support for healthy menopause transition
- Increases mental clarity and focus

This superfood can safely be eaten in large quantities and used over long periods of time without harmful effects. Use a minimum of 1 tablespoon of dried root powder per day to experience the best results. You can increase the dosage considerably without any adverse side effects. This is one ancient medicine that you will feel different after taking. It's that powerful. Woman who are pregnant should consult their naturopathic physician before exploring.

MAITKE MUSHROOMS

Grifola frondosa is a polypore mushroom that grows in groups at the bottom of trees, specifically oaks. Commonly known among English speakers as Sheep's Head mushroom, in Japan they are known as "Maitakes," which translates to "dancing mushroom." Maitakes are native to the northeastern part of Japan and North America and are renowned in traditional Chinese and Japanese herbology as an adaptogen that assists in balancing out unharmonious bodily systems to a state of equilibrium.

- The main ability of maitake mushrooms that was utilized in the ancient time and now in the present day is cancer prevention. It does this by activating various effector cells, such as macrophages, natural killer cells, T cells, interleukin-1, and superoxide anions which initiate an anti-cancer activity throughout the body.
- It also contains grifolan, an important beta-glucan polysaccharide (molecule composed of many sugar molecules linked together). Grifolan has been reported to activate macrophages, a type of cell that has proved itself to be the "heavy artillery" of the immune system. As if that wasn't enough, maitakes also contain a polysaccharide called D-fraction, known to energize both the innate immune system and adaptive immune system.
- Maiktakes have also been shown to help people with type 2 diabetes from a specific, high-molecular polysaccharide in maitake called the X-fraction. This polysaccharide can hinder insulin resistance, resulting in an increase in insulin sensitivity.
- Maitake mushrooms lower blood pressure and blood lipids – two key risk factors in cardiovascular disease.
- Maitake mushrooms help with stomach ailments, aids in digestion by regulating the stomach and intestines, and helps eliminate food stagnation.

Maitakes other uses:
- Antifungal, anti-infective, antitumorigenic, antiviral, arthritis, bacterial infection, diagnostic agent, high blood pressure, high cholesterol, HIV, liver inflammation (hepatitis), and weight loss.

CHAPTER 5 DICTIONARY

MANGOSTEEN

The purple mangosteen (Garcinia mangostana) is a tropical evergreen tree, understood to have originated in the Sunda Islands and the Moluccas of Indonesia. The meat is a whitish cream color and can be described as tangy and sweet with hints of a citrusy peach flavor as well as consistency. In my opinion, the taste is one of the most decadent of all the super fruits out there...but the nutritional content, well, is a whole other level of decadent. Here is a breakdown of the kind of power packed roster of nutrients I'm talking about:

1. Anti-fatigue (energy booster)

2. Powerful anti-inflammatory (stops inflammation)

3. Analgesic (prevents pain)

4. Anti-ulcer (stomach)Mouth and bowel ulcersAnti-depressant (low to moderate)

5. Anxyolytic (anti-anxiety effect)

6. Anti-alzheimerian (helps prevent dementia)

7. Anti-tumor and cancer prevention / shown to be capable of killing cancer cells

8. Immunomodulator (helps the immune system)

9. Anti-aging

10. Antioxidant

11. Anti-viral

12. Anti-biotic (modulates bacterial infections)

13. Anti-fungal (prevents fungal infections)

14. Anti-seborrheaic (prevents skin disorders)

MANDALA LIVING FOODS

15. Anti-lipidemic (blood fat lowering, LDL)
16. Anti-atherosclerotic (prevents the hardening of arteries)
17. Cardioprotective (protects the heart)
18. Hypotensive (blood pressure lowering)
19. Hypoglycemic (anti-diabetic effect, helps lower blood sugar)
20. Anti-obesity (helps with weight loss)
21. Anti-arthritic (prevention of arthritis)
22. Anti-osteoporosis (helps prevent the loss of bone mass)
23. Anti-periodontic (prevents gum disease)
24. Anti-allergenic (prevents allergic reaction)
25. Anti-calculitic (prevents kidney stones)
26. Anti-pyretic (fever lowering)
27. Anti-parkinson
28. Anti-diarrheal
29. Anti-neuralgic (reduces nerve pain)
30. Anti-vertigo (prevents dizziness)
31. Anti-glaucomic (prevents glaucoma)
32. Anti-cataract (prevents cataracts)
33. Has a synergistic effect on the whole body

Even though it's true that most young people are healthy, age has nothing to do with the fact that you are being exposed to free radicals by the millions each day. They have calculated that every human cell is subject to ten thousand strikes from free radicals every single day. This, in turn, causes degeneration to cell proteins, DNA, fat lipids, as well as membranes through oxidation. The end result is a cycle of malfunctioning molecules that create conditions of degeneration responsible for everything from cancers to cardiovascular disease.

MARINE PHYTOPLANKTON

Out of the 40,000 species of phytoplankton in the ocean, a team of scientists and researchers calculated the most suitable species in each category to use for everything from biofuel to human consumption. There were only four species of marine phytoplankton that were found to be valuable for human ingestion. After exploring their nutritional compositions, there was one species with invaluable super attributes that was chosen for production. Marine phytoplankton supplies a rare and complete food that nourishes the body with literally all of the raw components that it requires to create healthy new cells as well as neurochemicals for the brain. These chemicals range from serotonin to dopamine. It seems to be able to stifle a number of diseases and imbalances because it operates at the core level of the cells. It has quite a reputation with an extremely high success rate with overpowering a number of diseases and health conditions. This is because of a few different elements. One, it is completely raw, therefore alive with enzymes and nutrients ready to be synthesized and utilized in the body. Two, marine phytoplankton contains over 65 nutritional resources including all of the amino acids, essential fats, vitamins, key minerals and trace elements, rare antioxidants, phospholipids, electrolytes, nucleic acids, enzymes, and coenzymes. It's not only the nutritional content that makes this such a superfood, but this living food also holds an electrical frequency that syncs with the intelligence of the human vehicle. Many believe that it's the fusion and exact quantities of each element and nutrient that allow phytoplankton to be so effective at initiating cellular regeneration and thus 'true' healing. Its composition is almost specifically designed for the human body.

MARINE MAGNESIUM

Magnesium, a metal, is the ninth most abundant element in the universe. It is named after a region in Greece called Magnesia where magnesium ores were first discovered. Magnesium is an essential mineral nutrient which plays a role in energy metabolism, mineral homeostasis, neuromuscular, and endocrine functions. Many compounds can be used in health supplements to provide magnesium in a biologically available form. These compounds may also provide additional benefits specific to each compounds. Magnesium compounds commonly used for these purposes include magnesium taurinate, magnesium ascorbate, magnesium citrate, magnesium oxide, and magnesium trisilicate. Magnesium is an essential nutrient for all life forms and is especially beneficial for supporting heart and bone health. Magnesium also helps regulate neurotransmitters that are directly related to sleep. Some studies have shown that taking magnesium supplements can support healthy sleep patterns and improve the quality of sleep. You specifically want a marine magnesium that is processed without solvents and from a purer source with higher mineral content. It's a more premium form of magnesium because it can contain up to 70 trace minerals and electrolytes in addition to the main active ingredient—magnesium chloride. These trace minerals have been found to positively affect overall health, such as better bone density and improved cardiovascular health.

Health benefits

1. Powerful anti-inflammatory (stops inflammation)

2. Bone health

3. Neuralogical regulator

4. Anti-fatigue (energy booster)

5. Detoxifier (Cesium 137 specifically)

6. Improves sleep

CHAPTER 5 DICTIONARY

MATCHA GREEN TEA POWDER

Matcha is a type of finely-powdered green tea used specifically with the Japanese for tea ceremonies. They would also use it to season and color foods like soba noodles or cakes. The most well-known regions in Japan, Uji in Kyoto, Nishio in Aichi, Shizuoka, and northern Kyūshū were most known to yield the matcha powder. Matcha is more costly than other forms of tea as it is usually a higher quality leaf, and matcha uses the whole leaf in the powder, thereby giving it more potency in nutritional and medicinal substance. The health benefits of matcha tea exceed those of green tea because when you drink matcha, you ingest the whole leaf, not just the brewed H20. One cup of matcha is equal to 10 glasses of green tea in equivalence to its nutritional substance and antioxidants.

Matcha tea:
- Is rich in antioxidants and chlorophyll
- Contains catechins - EGCG
- Is naturally mood enhancing
- Is zero on the glycemic index
- Is sugar-free and high in fiber

Health benefits:
1. For antioxidants – exponentially higher in antioxidants than both blueberries and spinach

2. Known for cancer fighting catechin EGCG – found only in green tea

3. For cleansing the body of toxins – rich in chlorophyll, a renowned detoxifying agent

4. Amino acids – naturally mood enhancing

5. Suited for meditative practice – create your own ceremony and relieve stress

NATTOKINASE

Nattokinase is an enzyme that comes from a Japanese food called natto. Natto is made from boiled soybeans that have been fermented with a type of bacteria. Nattokinase may thin the blood and help break up blood clots. This might protect against heart disease and conditions caused by blood clots such as stroke, heart attack, and others. Nattokinase is produced by the bacterium Bacillus subtilis during the fermentation of soybeans to produce natto. Nattokinse has been extensively studied in Japan, Korea, and China. According to a Japanese legend, about a thousand years ago a man put warm, cooked soybeans in a rice-straw sack on the back of his horse and rode off. He didn't realize that as the sun beat down, the soybeans would ferment into a pungent, gooey paste that tasted great with white rice. And thus, natto was born, a staple of the Japanese diet reputed to contribute to longevity and health. There are two sides to the blood clotting cascade. There's the formation of blood clots on one side, and on the other is how our body breaks down blood clots once they're created. Unlike other blood thinners like aspirin that only decreases the tendency to form blood clots, nattokinase affects both sides of the clotting cascade. Fibrinogen is a blood protein that increases the risk of forming blood clots. Nattokinase decreases levels of fibrinogen in our blood. Nattokinase also supports healthy blood clotting by activating our body's own natural enzymes that break apart blood clots after they're already formed. Nattokinase has been compared to our clot-dissolving enzyme, plasmin. Nattokinase enhances our body's production of plasmin and another clot-dissolving enzyme, urokinase. Nattokinase has been shown to increase tissue plasminogen activator (tPA), a protein that activates plasmin so it can do its job of breaking down blood clots. As tPA goes up, so does plasmin, and so does the ability to dissolve blood clots. By all these means, nattokinase helps decrease blood viscosity, or thick, sludgy blood, and supports healthy blood flow. Nattokinase activity has been demonstrated to last as long as eight hours, providing more lasting benefits than many other naturally based molecules.

Health benefits:
- Natural blood thinner
- Breaks down spiked proteins
- Contributes to longevity and health
- Breaks down blood clots
- Enhances digestion
- Increases bone health
- Aides in weight loss
- Great source of amino acids

CHAPTER 5 DICTIONARY

NONI FRUIT

Morinda citrifolia, also referred to as great morinda, Indian mulberry, Tahitian noni, cheese fruit, or noni, is a fruit in the botanical family of the coffee plant. Noni originates out of Southeast Asia but has been increasingly circulated throughout the Pacific islands, French Polynesia, the Indian subcontinent, Puerto Rico, as well as the Dominican Republic. Tahiti continues to be the most renowned location for growing noni. The appearance of this fruit at first glance could seem quite alien as it is covered with what look to be a matrix of eyes on the outside of the skin. If the sight doesn't throw you, then getting within five feet of a ripe one will as noni is notorious for its pungent stinky cheese-like smell. The flesh of the fruit is a whitish cream color, with a texture that's a cross between a slime and a paste-like consistency.
It is interlaced with several seeds throughout it to keep in mind upon raw consumption of the fruit. Speaking of the flesh actually has a numbing quality that takes effect upon eating it raw which I personally find invigorating, but you should definitely know this going into the experience. It is one of the most intense fruits I have ever crossed paths with. As are the health benefits of noni, in fact, they continue to still be discovered by modern science as more and more research has directed to focus on this strange, stinky fruit. Noni, a traditional element of Polynesian / Hawaiian medicine, is regarded to have the ability to heal a wide variety of long-term chronic diseases. Many approach noni as a last effort, while others utilize it as an integral part of their diet / lifestyle. Either way, after understanding the power of the noni, you will agree that there truly are some health benefits of this strange super fruit. In Hawaiian history, it is known that noni juice, when taken as a daily supplement, allows the body to counteract degenerative developments within the body that could ultimately lead to chronic disease.

MANDALA LIVING FOODS

There are basically 7 health benefits of noni juice:

1. Noni boosts the immune system – A variety of its nutrients they're discovering act to activate the immune system.

2. Noni activates digestion – traditionally, Noni juice has always been used as a laxative.

3. Noni is rich in antioxidants – many reports are coming out showing that noni juice demonstrates greater antioxidant activity than grape seed extract and pycnogenol.

4. Noni works as a natural analgesic – the noni tree was traditionally called the 'Painkiller or Headache tree.' Noni has been discovered to be 75% as effective as morphine sulphate in relieving pain without the toxic side effects.

5. Noni has antibacterial, antifungal, and antiparasitic properties. With the presence of active compounds like anthraquinones, scopoletin, and terpenes, noni is effective against bacteria and fungus.

6. Noni has anti-inflammatory properties. Noni juice has shown similar results to the newer over-the-counter anti-inflammatory drugs called non-steroidal anti-inflammatory drugs (NSAIDs).

7. Noni has shown to be anti-tumor / anti-cancerous. Noni juice contains noni-ppt, which has shown anti-tumor activity.

CHAPTER 5 DICTIONARY

POMEGRANATE

Have you EVER eaten a pomegranate, the notorious fruit Greek mythology in the story of Persephone, daughter of the harvest goddess Demeter? Well the modern tales, or reports I should say, are not quite as fantastical and dramatic as the myth…or are they? There's a lot of talk lately about this ancient and exotic fruit. Let's explore… many researchers have been studying the health benefits of pomegranates and pomegranate juice for the last several years, and I've compiled this data to breakdown 11 benefits of pomegranate:

1. Fights breast cancer
2. Inhibits the development of lung cancer
3. Regresses prostate cancer
4. Keeps PSA levels stable
5. Protects the neonatal brain
6. Maternal supplementation helps protect neonatal brain damage after injuryAids in the prevention of osteoarthritis
7. Prevents plaque build up in the arteries
8. Helps in the prevention / regression of Alzheimer's disease
9. Lowers LDL cholesterol
10. Lowers blood pressure
11. Protects against plaque build up on teeth

REISHI MUSHROOMS

Reishi mushrooms, Ganoderma lucidum, or its Chinese name Lingzhi (which means "spiritual potency"), have been honored and utilized by Chinese practitioners for over 2,000 years as a valuable remedy. Reishi mushrooms have been long praised by the Chinese people as the "Medicine of Kings". Though there are six varieties of reishi, all categorized by color, practitioners usually call red Reishi the most powerful and healing of the species. This is why the most commonly integrated form of reishi in North America, Japan, China, Taiwan, and Korea is the red reishi. In its natural habitat, the reishi mushroom grows on deciduous trees in the extremely dense forest areas of China and Japan.

It was generally respected that the prolonged supplementation of Reishi will create a strong, healthy body and ensure a long-lasting life. Reishi mushrooms specifically treat the nervous system and were originally used by herbalists to treat insomnia due to their ability to aid in the promotion of Theta wave sleep. These master mushrooms are used to treat a variety of other psychiatric and neurological afflictions, including diseases that deal with the muscles, anorexia, and the loss of physical ability following lengthy illnesses.

Now as for the reishi mushroom's composition, it's more than 90% indigestible fiber, giving it an intensely wood-like consistency as well as a pungently bitter taste. Despite the flavor, several devotees of the reishi grind the mushroom up to make teas or soups. The more conventional forms of reishi are capsules, tablets, and extracts. Some research has shown taking vitamin C along with the reishi mushroom may amplify the reishi's healing effects. The next question is, how much reishi should you take? Some say an average dose of 100 milligrams daily to enhance your immune system, relieve inflammation, and alleviate joint pain, and some recommend up to three 1,000-milligram tablets up to three times a day. It really depends on the individual. I recommend starting out with a smaller dose and exploring it from there. The tincture or tonic has been said to have more of a spiritual or esoteric effect on the consciousness, where the capsules or tablets are more about integrating the physiological healing effects against the following:

CHAPTER 5 DICTIONARY

- It has been proven to have an anti-tumor effect.
- Reishi also has an anti-allergy effect that significantly inhibits all four types of allergic reactions, including positive effects against asthma and contact dermatitis.
- Reishi can be effectively used in treating stiff necks, stiff shoulders, conjunctivitis (inflammation of the fine membrane lining the eyes and eyelids), bronchitis, rheumatism, and improving the overall ability of the immune system without any notable side-effects. The major reason behind the anti-inflammatory effects of reishi could be tied to its free radical scavenging ability. The reishi extract significantly elevates the free radical scavenging ability of the blood, especially against the particularly harmful hydroxyl radicals. The hydroxyl radical scavenging ability of reishi is so powerful that even after the reishi extract is assimilated and metabolized, the scavenging action continues.
- Aids in the treatment of chronic hepatitis by promoting regeneration of the liver.
- Lowers LDL (Low density lipo protein – the harmful cholesterol)

MANDALA LIVING FOODS

THE ART & SCIENCE OF LIVING FOODS

SCHZINDRA BERRIES

The schizandra plant is part of the magnoliaceae family and is a prized Chinese fruit / herbal extract. These medicinal berries are thought to be a subtle sedative and sexual amplifier. Many consider it a youth tonic to preserve beauty. Here is a breakdown of the health benefits and nutrients of the schizandra berry:

Health benefits:
- Speeds recovery
- Increases stamina
- Strengthens immune system
- Increases eye acuity
- Improves adrenal health
- Protects against motion sickness
- Increases lung health
- Sexual enhancer
- Protects the liver
- Helps balance body functions

Nutrients:
The extract from schizandra comes from the little red berries on the plant. Their nutritional content is more potent than the leaves. One the main reasons the berries are more potent is because they contain lignans. Lignans are known for containing regenerative health benefits for the liver. They actually regenerate the cells. Where this is extremely helpful is after a heightened level of toxification to the liver from alcohol consumption which destroys the liver's cells.

CHAPTER 5 DICTIONARY

SEA VEGETABLES

Sea vegetables, which encompass a broad category of superfoods, are in short... Seaweeds, not that long ago, was all they were dismissed as. In the present day, now recognized for the nutritional significance, they can be found in any health or specialty store on the planet. One of the reasons why is that sea vegetables are low in caloric content and rich in vitamins and minerals which, with the depletion of nutrients in the soil from commercial farming, can't be said about land derived foods. Here are some of the more renowned sea vegetables being utilized in the world today:

- From the East Coast – Dulse, Kelp, Alaria, LaverFrom the West Coast – Sea Palm
- From Asia - Nori, Hiziki, Arame, Kombu, and Wakame

Health Benefits of sea vegetables:
- Sea vegetables reduce the risk of breast cancer.
- They empower the immune system to function and have been credited with increasing energy, improving general well-being, and accelerating wound healing.
- These also maximize the body's metabolism and anti-aging defenses.
- They have anti-inflammatory effects and help in the treatment of certain skin conditions.
- Seafood has minerals like zinc, boron, tin, selenium, chromium, antimony, and bismuth, which are missing in modern food.
- An unusual amount of full spectrum vitamins, including E, A, C, and B12 are also present in seafood.
- Certain enzymes and the full range of essential amino acids are found in the vegetables.

Incorporating these "super" veggies into your diet is fairly easy. All you need to do is just start adding small amounts to your favorite soups, salads, sandwiches, and stir-fries. You will start naturally acclimating to the taste. Some of them are stronger in taste than others, but they are too high in vital nutrients to pass up! Just keep an open mind and an open palette when exploring these veggies of the sea!

MANDALA LIVING FOODS

SHUNGITE

Shungite (it's also called shungit, schungit, or shieldite) is unique in the world as a natural mineral containing fullerenes (opened in 1985). It's a special type of molecular form of carbon. The importance of the finding of fullerenes is spoken about at the Royal Swedish Academy of Sciences.

MINERAL CONTENT:

- Carbon: 20 – 95 %
- Silicon: 5 – 60
- Aluminium: up to 4 %
- Iron: 3.5 %
- Magnesium: up to 3.5 %
- Kaliy: up to 12 %
- Sulfur: up to 1.2 %
- Calcium: up to 0.58 %
- Phosphorus: up to 0.34 %, and many other macroelements as well as other types of trace elements.

Scientists who have investigated shungite have declared unanimously that it is a miracle mineral! This stone eliminates and absorbs all that imposes a hazard on people, and living beings, but concentrates and restores to the human body. The shungite H20 helps the body's struggle with various illnesses: the general conditions improve, nervous pressure is removed, and the inflow of energy is regulated. It can be applied in different ways to obtain a steady remission of some chronic diseases from gastrointestinal tract, liver, kidneys, and metabolic processes. With the help of the shungit H20, skin diseases are cured much easier and H20 sprinkled on the head decreases the loss of hair. Your hair can look resilient and healthy looking. The most common ways of using shungite as a supplement is mineralizing H20 with the stone form, ingesting small amounts of the powder. You can also use it externally as an EMF protection with wearables such as pendants, bracelets, and necklaces as well as structural pieces in your home or even mixing the powder in paint and applying it as an EMF protection system for your house.

CHAPTER 5 DICTIONARY

SILICA

Silica, also known as silicon dioxide, is an oxide of silicon with the chemical formula SiO_2. It is commonly found in nature as quartz and is the major constituent of sand in many parts of the world. Silica is a complex and abundant family of materials, existing as a compound of several minerals and as a synthetic product. Crystalline silica is a common mineral found in the earth's crust and is used to make products such as glass, pottery, ceramics, bricks, and artificial stone. Silica has widespread industrial applications, including use as a food additive, anti-caking agent, and an excipient in drugs and vitamins. It is generally colorless to white and insoluble in H_2O. Silica helps your body produce its own collagen for healthy hair, skin, nails, teeth, and bones. This essential mineral element also helps our body internally by supporting gastrointestinal health, strong cartilage, and joint function. Eidon Silica may be applied topically to soothe the skin.

Health benefits:

- Promotes healthy skin, hair, and nails
- Supports bio-electric conductivity
- Promotes gastrointestinal health
- Assists the body's collagen production
- Aids in dental & skeletal regeneration
- Heathy joints & cartilage

MANDALA LIVING FOODS

SPIRULINA

Spirulina is a fresh H20 algae–correction, a form bacteria that is one of the most nutritionally rich superfoods on the planet to date. Just on a protein level alone it knocks both red meat, at 27%, and soy, at 34%, out of the H20, literally, with a whopping 60% protein content in terms of muscle-building potential. With that 60% protein, a powerful combination of minerals, including iron, calcium, and magnesium, as well as all the vitamins that make up the first five letters of the alphabet. If only this little H20-loving organism were a little bigger, it quite possibly could've been able to fit all the vitamins in existence in it.

The key features of spirulina are:
- Rich in antioxidants
- Boosts energy and cellular health
- More than 60% easy-to-digest all-vegetable protein
- Rare food source of the essential fatty acid GLA
- High in B-12 and easy-to-absorb iron
- Spirulina is an excellent source for RNA

Spirulina Contains:
- vitamin A, B1 (thiamine), B2 (riboflavin), B3 (niacin), B6 (pyridoxine), B12 (cobalamin), vitamin C, vitamin D, vitamin E, folate, vitamin K, biotin, pantothenic acid, beta carotene (source of vitamin A), and inositol.
- calcium, manganese, iron, chromium, phosphorus, molybdenum, iodine, chloride, magnesium, sodium, zinc, potassium, selenium, germanium, copper, boron.
- phycocyanin, chlorophyll, carotenoids. myxoxanthophyll, zeaxanthin, cryptoxanthin, echinenone and other xanthophylls, gamma linolenic acid, glycolipids, sulfolipids, polysaccharides.
- isoleucine, phenylalanine, leucine, threonine, lysine, tryptophan, methionine, valine, alanine, glycine, arginine, histidine, aspartic acid, proline, cystine, serine, glutamic acid, tyrosine.

The only conscious awareness when integrating spirulina to your diet is the possibility that, according to the Hong Kong Dietitian Association, its high protein, vitamin, and mineral content could cause kidney and liver problems of not moderated. Excessive protein intake can overload the kidneys, too many vitamins and minerals, the liver. It is so powerful in its content that you can get too much of a good thing, but it would really take a lot to do so.... and I've never known a case myself of spirulina overdose. I present this information more to create awareness toward the power of this superfood... it is to be respected.

CHAPTER 5 DICTIONARY

SHIMBAVU-URINE THERAPY-GOLDEN FOUNTAIN

It would not be an authentic superfood dictionary without including this powerful, free, and all around wholistic customized superfood in the archives. There is so much to share about this ancient superfood that there are entire medical books written on it. In fact, many of the present day top doctors have compiled all the science and research onto one website (which I urge you to go explore) called www. Urine therapy or urotherapy (also called urinotherapy, Shivambu, uropathy, or auto-urine therapy) in alternative medicine is the application of human urine for medicinal or cosmetic purposes, including drinking of one's own urine and massaging one's skin, or gums, with one's own urine. In short, your body is such an amazing piece of technology that it produces its own bio-chemically customized medicine that has all the antibodies for anything that's compromising your system, all the nutrients that you couldn't absorb from your food is fully synthesized to be absorbed, and a concentration of your own stem cells. It also has all 13 mineral salts that your body requires for true hydration and remineralization. So amazing, but there's more. It also holds the morphogentics code for your DNA and can restore any damage to your genetic coding. That's the basics for injection, but there's a whole entire spectrum of health benefits for its topical use as well. Most of the expensive beauty products on the market for skin and hair use urea from animals – read the label. The urea and stem cells in urine regenerate the skin and hair when topically applied daily. It can be applied to cuts and wounds, as well as for removing scars. I have been a urotherapy practitioner for over almost two decades and it is one of my foundational health and wellness regiments. I have done entire radio shows and podcasts on the Golden Fountain, and I encourage you to wake up to the divinity of our organics supercomputer that we call our body. We make the perfect medicine which is one of the first books on the subject I suggest you start with, *Our Own Perfect Medicine*. It was written...

Health benefits:
- Rich in antioxidants
- Boosts energy and cellular health
- Hydrates the body with 13 vital mineral salts
- High in stem cells
- Full of antibodies
- Full of bio-available vitamins & nutrients

MANDALA LIVING FOODS

WALNUTS

Walnuts are one of the most significant sources of botanical protein. They are full of fiber, vitamin B, magnesium, and antioxidants such as Vitamin E. All nuts for the most part high in plant sterols and fat, with the majority being in monounsaturated and polyunsaturated fats (omega 3 fatty acids – the healthy fats) that have the ability to lower LDL cholesterol. Walnuts specifically have exponentially higher amounts of omega 3 fatty acids in comparison to its relatives in the nut family.

More than a decade of scientific research over the last decade revealed that integrating walnuts into a healthy diet lowers the risk of heart disease by improving blood vessel elasticity and plaque accumulation. Walnuts have also been proven to help in lowering LDL cholesterol (the degenerative cholesterol) as well as the C-Reactive Protein (CRP) which not long ago was shown to be an independent sign / precursor to heart disease. Now you're going to see these nut heavyweights in a variety of recipes in the chapters to come. What's nice about them is that they are versatile in their practicality for creating certain elements in our dishes, especially as a meat substitute for burgers, lasagna, tacos, etc.Aids in your brain function – your brain is more than 60% structural fat. For your brain cells to function properly, this structural fat needs to be primarily the omega-3 fats. This is because the membranes of all our cells, including our brain cells or neurons, are primarily composed of fats. Cell membranes are the gatekeepers of the cell.

- A significant source of melatonin – a hormone produced by the pineal gland, which is involved in inducing and regulating sleep and is also a powerful antioxidant, has been discovered in walnuts in bio-available form, making them the perfect evening food for a natural good night's sleep.
- Alpha linolenic acid, the omega-3 fat found in walnuts, promotes bone health by helping to prevent excessive bone turnover.
- Helps prevent gallstones
- Lowers risk of weight gain

CHAPTER 5 DICTIONARY

In closing this chapter, I would like to explore some reflections. First and foremost, this superfood dictionary is not finite nor iron-clad in its context, nor does it have limits that have been set to where it can be expanded upon to. It is the collection of medicinal super foods that I have discovered in my studies up to this point in time, and every day there are more and more discoveries. These are the fundamental elements that have healed my body and helped me to undo all that our society, our government, and the controlling powers that control it so diligently work to do…toxify and poison our mind, body, and soul. From fluoride and pharmaceuticals in the H20 to *codex alimentarius* (and if you don't know what that is, please look it up). In this day and age, we must more than ever utilize everything this ancient mother organism (earth) has to offer in preparation for the great changes that lay ahead. I will not speak of them as that is your destiny and truth to discover, but I will say that whatever your destiny is…you will always be able to manifest it better with a body, mind, and spirit that is resonating at the highest levels. We can achieve this through the trinity of health and wellness.

Spiritual practices / sciences – temporal, energetic, and physical; they are all just as important for a well-rounded self-realization. From tai-chi to kundalini yoga, these esoteric arts channeled through the first to walk this earth for a reason… to evolve the human being from the human to the being… to activate the other 95% of your brain and DNA… to awaken the true power that we have fallen into a state of forgetting its existence. Our SAT NAM (TRUE IDENTITY), which has been lost in this five sense reality. A state that you must go in search of within. These sciences are a structured strategic series of applications…a map, so to speak, to lead us to a lost treasure deep within us.

Touch—it's as simple as that and yet can be so scientific and intricate in its depth of release. There are some many healing sciences that have come into this world, into humanity; from shiatsu to Swedish, Thai to reflexology, and the list goes on…your body is designed to be touched. When it is not stimulated to release its memory (neurochemicals), it becomes heavy and weighted down. Have you heard the term, "The weight of the world is on your shoulders"? This literally becomes the case. We must release as we go along accumulating in life.

Last but by far the least, the food. There are so many spiritual practices I have trained in, and the food is always left out as a part of the training. That is when I knew I had found the right sciences… they were conscious that the food is the foundational, biochemical spiritual practice, and must be honored as such.

It is this trinity that I have witnessed heal a number of human beings who were suffering from a variety of health disorders, disharmonies, and diseases—

everything from cancer to rheumatoid arthritis—all healed with this trinity, their commitment to healing thyself, and their power of will. The power of the will is the greatest gift given to man, but no one has truly shown us its power or how to use it. So it gets buried away, and we become lost in the ego and the monotonous routine orchestrated by the past versions of our self that first became lost in the illusion of this world... asleep in the dream. It is to them that I dedicate this piece!

A FLaMe of TRUTH.

Sometimes I find myself trying to write,
Trying to fill space on a page,
You can bring a pen to paper, but you can't force it write,
Squeezing one last drop of creativity out of an endless
flow that I find myself temporarily restricted from,
What is this place?
Ahhh...I'm in the think zone,
A 3rd dimensional creator's worst nightmare,
The grey area between the purity of creation, and the
earthly embodiment of its beauty,
My ego,
When this ego becomes a lonely place,
I long to swim again in the tide pools of what once saturated
my eyes, my heart, and my soul,
It's this trinity of elements that invokes the pure white flame
in the lantern of my heart,
A flame of FAITH, LOVE, and TRUTH,
How have I strayed from these grains of consciousness
that so engrain my being,
Lost in this illusion, I closed my eyes and brought
darkness to my room,
Asleep in the darkness,
Asleep in the dream,
But I am awake now,
My eyes are open in the darkness,
And I see a light switch on the wall beside me,
The LIGHT SWITCH on the wall beside me!
Is it really that easy,
Was it always really that easy...
Darkness can't exist where there is light,
I guess I just needed to know where the light switch is...

-- Micah Skye

TONIC ALCHEMY

OF LIVING FOODS

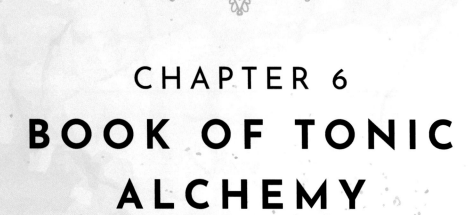

CHAPTER 6
BOOK OF TONIC ALCHEMY

CHAPTER 6 BOOK OF TONIC ALCHEMY

TONIC BAR - ESSENCES

Rose Essence – 64 oz
- 15 drops rose extract
- 64 oz H20

Mugwort Essence – 64 oz
- 20 drops mugwort extract
- 64 oz H20

Geranium Essence – 64 oz
- 18 drops geranium extract
- 64 oz H20

Vanilla Essence – 32 oz
- 3 tbsp vanilla extract
- 10 droppers vanilla stevia
- 32 oz H20

Lavender Essence – 64 oz
- 20 drops lavender extract
- 64 oz H20

Sage Essence – 64 oz
- 14 drops white sage extract
- 14 drops clary sage
- 64 oz H20

Ylang Ylang Essence – 64 oz
- 20 drops ylang ylang extract
- 64 oz H20

Violet Essence – 64 oz
- 17 drops violet extract
- 64 oz H20

Instructions:
Mix plant extracts in H20, evenly shaking for at least a minute, and refrigerate.

Be mindful that extracts pour fast depending on individual plant essences.

TINCTURES

Tinctures are individual organic superfood concentrates that are in both the tincshots, tonics, and can be added to evolve any beverage.

- Lasts 1–2 weeks
- Used for the base of our tincshots, tonics, and smoothies

Reishi Tincture – 32 oz
- 5 droppers Reishi extract
- 3 tbsp Reishi powder
- 32 oz Reishi tea base

Shilajit Tincture – 32 oz
- 3 tbsp Shilajit
- 32 oz H20

Iodine Tincture – 2 oz
Individual dosing from concentrate bottle. Ask the customer how many drops they see without thinking, and dose accordingly.
- 2 oz H20

Chaga Tincture – 32 oz
- 5 droppers Chaga extract
- 3 tbsp Chaga powder
- 32 oz Chaga tea base

Detox Tincture – 64 oz
- ½ cup shungite stones
- 3 tbsp shungite powder
- 3 tbsp charcoal powder
- 64 oz H20

Immunity Warrior – 2 oz
Individual dosing from concentrate bottle.
- 1 dropper
- 2 oz H20

Hawaii Chili Pepper – 64 oz
- 1 cup ACV
- 6 tsp sea salt
- 30 Hawaiian chili peppers
- 7 cups H20
- 4 cloves garlic

Instructions:
Mix elements with H20 in Vitamix on low to medium speed, then add to a 32 oz or 64 oz jar and refrigerate.

CHAPTER 6 BOOK OF TONIC ALCHEMY

TEA BASES

The art of tea and making tea bases for tonics and fermented brews is ancient, and these are some of the formulas we've collected to support your exploration into this age old art & science.

Chaga Tea Base
- 60 - 80 grams
- 1 gallon of H20

P'Darco Tea Base
- 16 - 20 grams
- 1 gallon of H20

Mamaki Tea Base
- ½ cup mamaki tea
- 1 gallon of H20

Reishi Tea Base
- 60 - 80 grams of dried reishi
- 1 gallon H20

Instructions: Boil less than half the gallon of H20 with tea, allow to steep for 8 minutes; strain if it's loose tea, and add the remaining half gallon plus of H20 so that the finished tea is room temperature. Refrigerate.

MLF BREWERY RECIPES

Kombucha / Jun Tea Base

- 8 tea bags - 2 tbsp or 12 - 16 grams loose black tea
- 2 tea bags brown rice green tea
- 1 cup cane sugar
- 1 gallon H20

BULK RECIPE
- 5 gallons
- 30 tea bags 80+ grams black tea
- 10 tea bags brown rice green tea
- 5 cups cane sugar
- 5 gallons H20

Instructions:
Boil less than half the gallon of H20 with tea, allow to steep for 8 minutes; strain if it's loose tea and add the cane sugar, stirring until completely dissolved. Then add the remaining half gallon plus of H20 so that the finished tea is room temperature. Remove scobey from the brewing container and add the fresh brewed tea to the 10% of previously brewed kombucha. Then place scobey on top, cover and place in 1st stage brew area.

Stage 2 Double Fermentation
5 Gallon Recipe

Recipe 1
- 96 oz juice of choice
- 15 - 20 drops of extract of choice

Recipe 2
- 96 oz herb/sugar concentrate of choice
- 15 - 20 drops of extract of choice

Instructions:
Transfer 90% of 1st stage kombucha brew to kegs and add to recipe 1 or recipe 2, seal kegs and place in Stage 2 brew area. Double fermentation is at least a week + before it's ready to tap.

TINCSHOTS

Tincshots are generally made from a cold tea base with essences, herbal powders, and tincture liquid extracts in a single supplemental shot.
- Lasts 1–2 weeks
- Used for the base of our potions (6 oz)

Reishakti Cacao – 6 oz
- 2 oz shakti cacao mix
- 2 oz coffee fix mix
- 1 oz shilijit tincture
- 1 oz chaga mix

Super C Shot – 6 oz
- 3 tsp camu camu
- 20 oz cold-pressed citrus juice
- 12 oz H20
- 3 drops Mexican Lime extract
- 1 tsp papaya powder
- 1 tbsp goji berry

Root Awakening – 6 oz
- 2 oz shakti cacao tincture
- 1 tsp cordyceps
- 1 tsp vitality mix
- 1 drop sandalwood
- 1 tsp he shou wa
- 1 tsp MSM mix
- 1 tbl maca (gelatinized)

Vanillajit Temple – 32 oz
- 2 tsp shilajit powder
- 32 oz H20
- 2 droppers vanilla stevia
- 1 tbs vanilla extract

Green Goddess – 6 oz
- 2 ½ tbsp Moringa
- 2 tbsp blue algae
- 2 tbsp spirulina
- 12 oz cold pressed lemon juice
- 4 oz chlorophyll
- 20 oz H20
- ¼ cup matcha powder
- 4 drops mugwort

Earth & Sea
Single serving
- 2 oz shungite
- 2 oz sage tincture
- 1-5 drops nascent iodine

Rose Pearl – 32oz
- 4 tsp pearl
- 4 oz Rose essence
- 6 tsp schizandra powder
- 3 tsp goji berry paste
- 28 oz cloud kefir
- 3 tsp camu camu powder

Brain Booster – 32 oz
- 2 tsp pearl
- 6 tsp schizandra powder
- 6 tsp goji berry paste
- 32 oz cloud kefir
- 3 tsp camu camu powder

Instructions:
Mix elements with H20 in Vitamix on low to medium speed, then add to gallon jug, mixing evenly and refrigerate. Multiply measurements to make a larger batch to have throughout the week.

NOTES

THE ARTS & SCIENCE OF LIVING FOODS

CHAPTER 6 BOOK OF TONIC ALCHEMY

TONICS

Tonics are generally made from a tea base or premixed tonic base combined with tichshots, essences, herbal powders, and tincture liquid extracts in a 12 or 16 oz beverage served hot, cold, or blended with ice.

- Lasts 1–2 weeks
- Makes bulk batches for multiple servings

(BULK RECIPES)

Roots Brew 64 oz
- 8 tbsp dandelion / burdock powder or coffee fix
- 5 tbsp cacao powder
- 2 drops of cade extract
- 64 oz H20

Spring Cleaning Tonic 1 Gallon
- 16 oz lemon juice
- 8 oz ACV
- 6 drops Mexican lime extract
- 1/8 cup Hawaiian chili pepper H20
- 1 cup grade A maple syrup
- 1 tbsp charcoal
- 1 tbsp shungite powder
- 4 oz colloidal silver
- 96 oz H20

COLDPRESSO – 64 oz
- 4 cups of organic French roast whole coffee beans
- 64 H20

  - Instructions: Pulse in 3–4 rounds just breaking the beans in half to quarter size; but not too fine as it will be pulsed again on a second brew cycle & combined with first brew cycle. Let steep for 48, strain into jug and refrigerate.

MANDALA LIVING FOODS

Hot Macacao Milk – 64 oz
- 32 oz nut milk
- 32 oz hot H20
- 6 tbsp cacao powder
- 2 tbsp maca powder
- 2 droppers stevia
- ¼ tsp sea salt
- 1 tsp cinnamon
- 2 tsp MCT oil
- 1 tsp cacao butter
- 5 tbsp maple syrup
- 2 droppers vanilla stevia

Golden Milk – 64 oz
- 20 oz turmeric juice
- 20 oz ginger juice
- 1/3 cup honey
- 1 tsp black pepper
- 2 tbsp cinnamon
- 24 oz H20

- Instructions: Boil H20 with cinnamon and black pepper, strain into jar. Let cool. Then add honey, fresh ginger juice, and turmeric juice. Serve 4 oz with 8–12 oz of live milk of choice for Golden Yogi.

Poichata – 64 oz
- 1 ¾ cup fresh poi - 2 cups for thicker
- 2 tbsp cinnamon
- 1 ½ tbsp vanilla extract
- ½ tsp sea salt
- 1.2 cup maple syrup
- 62 oz H20

CHAPTER 6 BOOK OF TONIC ALCHEMY

(SINGLE SERVING FORMULAS)

Roots Brew / Coffee Fix
- 12 or 16 oz Roots Brew (hot or cold)

Shaman's Detox
- 8 or 12 oz of tonic
- 4 oz live milk of choice

Single Serving Formula 16 oz:
- 14 oz PDA tea
- 1 tbsp colloidal silver
- 1 tbsp colloidal gold
- 1 tsp cordyceps
- 1 oz vanilla essence
- 1 oz sage essence
- 1 oz chaga tincture
- 1 oz shilajit tincture
- 1 oz reishi tincture
- 1 tsp ho shu Wu
- 1 drop palo santo
- 1 drop sandalwood

Krishiva Tonic
- 12 or 16 oz Krishiva Tonic (hot or cold)

Single Serving Formula 16 oz:
- 6 oz mamaki or blue lotus tea concentrate (fresh mint, 3-6 leaves)
- 8 oz hot H20
- 1 kefir lime (if available)
- 2 oz green goddess
- 1 tbsp raw honey
- 2 tsp nano colloidal silver
- 1 tbsp colloidal gold
- 2 tbsp bag of tricks
- 3 tsp MSM Mix

Latte Fix
- 12 or 16 oz Roots Brew (hot or cold)
- 4 oz live milk of choice
- Essence of choice (optional)

Golden Yogi
- 8 or 12 oz Golden milk tonic (hot or cold)
- 4 oz live milk of choice

Single Serving Formula 16 oz:
- 1 oz turmeric juice
- 1 oz ginger juice
- ½ tsp cinnamon
- 1 tbsp colloidal gold
- 1 tsp raw honey or maple syrup
- 8 oz hot H20
- 4 oz live milk of choice

Spring Cleaning Tonic
Single Serving Formula 16 oz:
- 1 oz lemon juice
- 1 drop Mexican lime
- 1 oz ACV
- 1/8 tsp chili pepper H20
- 1 oz turmeric juice
- 2 super C shots
- 1 dropper (1 mil) minerals
- ½ tbsp colloidal silver
- 1 oz maple syrup
- 1 oz detox tincture

Instructions:
Mix elements with H20 in Vitamix on low to medium speed, and then add to gallon jug and mix evenly and refrigerate.

GOURMET COOKBOOK

OF
LIVING FOODS

THE ARTS & SCIENCE OF LIVING FOODS

MICAH SKYE

CHAPTER 6: SMOOTHIE ALCHEMY

SMOOTHIES

VANILLA CLOUD

16 oz

Smoothies are generally made from a live milk base or coconut H20, frozen fruit, and dates, but can have premixed tonic bases combined with tichshots, essences, herbal powders and tincture liquid extracts in a 12 or 16 oz beverage blended with ice. This is one of our most beloved smoothie formulas, and when done properly tastes like vanilla whip cream magic that will have you coming back for seconds.

- Lasts 1–2 days refrigerated

Ingredients:

- 10-12 oz live milk vanilla
- ¾ cup coconut meat
- 1 tsp vanilla
- 1 bananas (frozen)
- 2 oz vanilla cloud (fresh or frozen)
- 1/8 cup dates
- 1/8 cup almonds
- 2-3 oz vanilla pea protein powder
- 1/8 tsp sea salt

Instructions:

Mix elements with H20 in Vitamix on low to medium speed, then add to gallon jug and mix evenly and refrigerate.

MANDALA LIVING FOODS

THE ART & SCIENCE OF LIVING FOODS

GARDEN OF EDEN

16 oz

This smoothie embodies everything about its title and is nothing short of divine. Filled with greens to awaken the light within and nourish you down to a cellular level while tasting delicious at the same time. With a medicinal serving of greens and chlorophyll, balanced with a wholistic serving of protein, fiber, and fruit, this is truly the smoothie of eden.

- Lasts 1–2 days refrigerated

Ingredients:

- 6 oz coco H20
- 1 banana (frozen or fresh)
- 4 oz live milk (vanilla)
- ½ cup coconut meat
- 1 tsp spirulina
- 1 tsp blue green algae
- 1 tsp chlorophyll
- 1 tsp chlorella
- ¼ cup dates
- ½ cup papaya (fresh or frozen)
- ¼ cup mac nuts (raw)
- 2 oz ginger juice
- 1 tsp raw honey
- ¼ tsp sea salt
- 2 tbsp bag of tricks (optional)

Instructions:

Mix elements with H20 in Vitamix on low to medium speed, then add to gallon jug and mix evenly and refrigerate.

CHAPTER 6: SMOOTHIE ALCHEMY

MANDALA EFFECT

16 oz

This is one of my personal favorites in terms of a well-rounded smoothie formula. Its flavor is wholistically reflective to its nutritional content, showing that healthy food medicine can also be profoundly delicious. With layers of citrus, creamy coconut, mango, and vanilla, this smoothie takes you into a vortex we call the Mandala Effect.

- Lasts 1–2 days refrigerated

Ingredients:

- 6-8 oz live milk: vanilla
- 4 oz fresh orange juice¼ cup coconut meat
- Seasonal: 2 oz (¼ Cup) Lilikoi
- 4 oz papaya (fresh or frozen)
- 1 tbsp MCT Oil
- 1 banana (fresh or frozen)
- 1–2 dates
- 1 tsp three treasures or He shu wu
- 4–5 drops vanilla stevia
- 1/8 cup mac nuts
- 1 tbsp bee pollen
- 1/8 cup 2oz goji berries
- 1/8 cup 2oz dried mango
- tiny pinch sea salt

Instructions:
- Mix elements with H20 in Vitamix on low to medium speed, then finishing on high speed. Serve and enjoy!

MANDALA LIVING FOODS

THE ART & SCIENCE OF LIVING FOODS

SLEEPING GIANT

16 oz

Another green smoothie nutritional giant, this hearty smoothie lives up to its name which comes from one of the mountains here on the island of Kauai. As filling as it is refreshing, it's sure to awaken the sleeping giant within you after a workout or hike. Amazing on a hot day with the cool undertone of peppermint.

- Lasts 1–2 days refrigerated

Ingredients:

- 6 oz coconut water
- 1 frozen banana
- 2 oz live milk vanilla
- 2 oz cloud shot
- 2 oz green goddess
- ¼ cup massaged kale
- ¼ tsp cosmic blue algae
- 1 tsp matcha powder
- 4–5 mint leaves
- ½ cup coconut meat
- 1–2 pitted dates
- ½ cup papaya (fresh or frozen)
- ¼ cup mac nuts
- ½ cup ice
- 1 drop peppermint oil (optional)
- 1 tsp raw honey
- tiny pinch of sea salt

Instructions:

Mix elements with H20 in Vitamix on low to medium speed, then finishing on high speed. Serve and enjoy!

CHAPTER 6: SMOOTHIE ALCHEMY

LAVA FLOW

16 oz

This is your smoothie if you're feeling called to both nourish and detox. With a healthy serving of charcoal, probiotics, protein, vitamin C, and minerals, this is a regenrative detox journey you want to take. On top of it, it tastes amazing.

- Lasts 1–2 days refrigerated

Ingredients:

- 6 oz cloud milk vanilla
- 2 oz cloud shot
- ¼ cup coconut meat
- or 1/8 cup coconut cream
- 1 tbsp raw coconut butter
- 1 frozen banana
- 3oz frozen papaya
- 2 oz shot super C
- 1/2 cup of ice
- 1 tbsp MCT
- ¼ cup mac nuts
- 1–2 dates
- 1–2 oz detox tincture
- 5 drops vanilla stevia

Instructions:

Mix elements with H20 in Vitamix on low to medium speed, then finish on high speed. Serve and enjoy! Dress with strawberry or raspberry sauce on top like a lava flow and serve.

MANDALA LIVING FOODS

DATE WITH DESTINY

16 oz

If you are a lover of dates and destiny, this is your smoothie of choice. Fashioned after one of my favorite local smoothies I had when I first came to the island, it is the perfect fusion of banana, dates, nuts, and so much more, including an accent of ginger that brings it all together in perfect harmony.

- Lasts 1–2 days refrigerated

Ingredients:

- 8-10 oz live milk of choice
- 1 banana frozen or fresh
- ¼ cup dates
- ½ papaya (fresh or frozen)
- 1/8 cup mac nuts
- 1 tsp raw honey
- 1 tsp fresh ginger (minced)
- ¼ tsp sea salt
- ¼ cup coco meat
- 1 tsp MCT oil
- 2 tsp bee pollen
- EVOLVE Bag of tricks
- or pea protein

Instructions:

- Mix elements with H20 in Vitamix on low to medium speed, then finish on high speed. Serve and enjoy!

CHAPTER 7
RAWVELATIONS OF DAIRY

There are three general definitions for milk and cheese in most dictionaries to date: (1) A whitish liquid containing proteins, fats, lactose, and various vitamins and minerals that is produced by the mammary glands of all mature female mammals after they have given birth and serves as nourishment for their young, (2) the milk of cows, goats, or other animals, used as food by humans, and (3) a liquid, such as coconut milk, milkweed sap, plant latex, or various medical emulsions that is similar to milk in appearance. For cheese, it is similar; (1) a solid food prepared from the pressed curd of milk, often seasoned and aged, (2) a molded mass of this substance, or something resembling this substance in shape or consistency. Well it's time now to expand our definition of dairy... to have a Rawvelation so to speak on the concept of milk and cheese.

You see, milk can be acquired from so much more than the mucus membrane of an animal. In this chapter we're going to explore our options, and what we can do with those options, which are truly limitless. We're going to explore a variety of nuts, as well as seed milks and cheeses. It is up to you to find which ones really taste right and digest the best for you as it is all about preference, and there is only one way to find out what you like... experiment!First and foremost, let's explore 10 facts about cow dairy:

THE ART & SCIENCE OF LIVING FOODS

CHAPTER 7 RAWVELATIONS OF DAIRY

1. Milk is not an essential component of the human diet. We're actually the only species on the planet to consume another species' mucus membrane (milk). Once more, milk of any kind is only a necessary dietary requirement for baby mammals, in which they should be feeding off the milk of their own species. In fact, humans between the ages of two and five years old no longer require milk in any form and have in fact lost the ability to digest it properly.

2. Cows' milk is not digestible to human beings. All mammals produce a mucus membrane (milk) that is specifically engineered to nourish the young of their species, and their species alone. In the case of a cow, it is essential for a calf to develop ten times its weight within the first year of its life cycle. Thus, cow's milk is rich in all the vitamins, minerals, proteins, and especially fats needed for this level of growth. How does this fit into a human baby's growth cycle? It does not. A human baby doesn't need to increase its weight by anything close to this. The fat globules in cow dairy are so massive that they cannot be digested by a human being—baby or adult. They merely overwhelm the digestive system and then eventually create an array of problems from obesity to osteoporosis. Thus, the term 'lactose intolerant' comes in. You see, all human beings are lactose intolerant to a certain degree. Some may have a genealogy that has allowed them to adapt better, but no human being was designed to handle digesting another species' milk.

3. Milk consumption has many adverse side effects in humans. To elaborate more on how indigestible cow milk is, we come to number three. It is simply not created to be broken down and synthesized by the human digestive system. Unfortunately, as a result of this, it can cause variety of health afflictions such as bloating, stomach cramps, and flatulence. In addition to gastrointestinal conflictions, the body also reacts by raising its mucus development, creating excessive congestion, chronic coughs, and sinus blockage. In fact, the human body produces excess mucus as an allergic reaction to this foreign substance. Also to be addressed is the very contested connection to certain variances of cancer due to the hormone- and antibiotic-treated cows in order to increase excess milk production. This milk is now saturated with hormones and antibiotics and is shared with whomever consumes it.

4. Drink milk for healthy teeth and strong bones… it's quite the opposite. When the human body reaches high levels of protein from an excessive protein diet, the result is an increase in the body's natural pH levels. This creates a high acidity level in the body, which is balanced by the body's amazing adaptagenic abilities. As a result of this balancing act

to raise the PH to a safe level of alkalinity, the body requires calcium, so it takes calcium from your own bones supply to counteract the acidity. This is calcium that you can never reabsorb which is later excreted by the kidneys. The end result is a highly acidic body full of excess protein with weak bones from a depleted calcium supply. Is it any surprise that the U.S. is the largest country in the world to consume dairy products, and also the largest country in the world to suffer from osteoporosis? Not really.

5. Milk is NOT a source of calcium. Contrary to the barrage of celebrity-endorsed campaigns riddled with false information about how dairy products are an 'essential' foundation of calcium, and for this reason should be methodically consumed—especially by our growing children. In all actuality, milk is a completely illegitimate source of dietary calcium. The illusion projected is that milk contains high levels of calcium, but what many do not know is that this calcium is in a form that is indigestible to the human body. This is because the calcium is bonded to a protein called casein. In order for this calcium to be digested, it has to be isolated from the casein which requires the use of two digestive enzymes: rennin and lactase. A baby mammal creates these enzymes in order to be able to digest this calcium and synthesize it, but once they mature to an age where they no longer require this nourishment as part of their diet, their system naturally stops the production of these enzymes as they are no longer needed.

6. There are plenty of sources for calcium in a RAW food diet: Leafy green vegetables, beans, nuts, and seeds are the richest in dietary sources of calcium and, specifically, the nuts and seeds are going to be the foundation for our rawvelation of the concept of what 'dairy' is. You know, when you think that cows get all their calcium from a green, leafy vegetable, it makes sense that we should too.

7. Adult human beings are lactose intolerant. All through adaptation, some blood types are more tolerant; 75% of the world's population is unable to digest lactose. More specifically, Caucasians have a genetic mutation that allows their bodies to keep producing lactase beyond young childhood, therefore enabling them to more successfully digest lactose. Around 15% of the Caucasian populace is lactose intolerant. However, in other races, Africans and Asians in particular, the percentage of lactose tolerance is extremely lower, as low as between 10% to 30%. Making almost 90% of the population lactose intolerant. Lactose intolerance is also much higher in Mediterranean regions and indigenous peoples such as the Native Americans. Simply from these statistics, lactose intolerance should be

considered normal for adult humans, and with good reason, as there is no logical use for us to continue struggling to digest a substance that we gain little to no nutritional content form.

8. Milk = junk food. As with any junk food, they are designed to taste great and be less filling. Rich, creamy, and saturated with false emotional fulfillment, dairy plays on a void most humans have for maternal nurturing. You've heard of the term 'comfort food'. Where did this concept come from? Comfort foods or not, these toxic delicacies are nutritionally equivalent to junk food and should most definitely not be considered an essential part of your diet.

9. When you eat dairy, you become a part of the cruel cycle of dairy farming. Commercially-farmed dairy cows have anything but happy lives. Besides being impregnated regularly as to guarantee that their milk yield does not lessen, they get plugged into giant milking machines which frequently creates a condition called mastitis, which is basically an udder infection that is a result of excessive milking; and to top it all off, as soon they stop producing enough milk, they are butchered for their meat.

10. All milk has a certain amount of pus in it! That's right, the number 10 fact about dairy to be shared is revolting, but tragically the truth. The modern methodology of mass dairy farming has no allowance in its production schedule to separate milk from infected udders and healthy ones. The FDA thus allows a certain percentage of pus into the supply of processable milk. I guess that explains why they pasteurize it—you know, to kill all the excess bacteria. Drink up if you dare!

So this concludes 10 reasons to explore your options on the concept of what dairy is and can be. On what you can make milk, or cheese from. How about something your body can actually digest and synthesize? What a concept. In this chapter, we're going to explore all the alternatives available to create a lot of the 'comfort foods' that were probably introduced to you from the generations before you, and some new comfort foods that will excite the palette and nourish the body. We can really replicate anything from mayonnaise to ricotta cheese. The sky is the limit once you understand the structural mechanics of how to make raw cheeses from nuts and seeds. Some work better for one type of dairy replacement than another, and some you will prefer the taste to that of others. This is again where exploring and experimenting come in. Keep an open mind, an ambitious heart, and an empty stomach in hand because you're going to need it. Enjoy your Rawvelations in dairy!

THE ART & SCIENCE OF LIVING FOODS

THE CASHEW CONSPIRACY

I write this next passage fully prepared to trigger, offend, and disrupt many of you who read it. Sadly, that's what the truth usually does in a world of deception. I want to state that my intention is to educate and share this knowledge and truth without bias, but the purest intention of learning, evolving, and ultimately growing. In many respects, I truly believe it's one of the divine reasons I didn't publish this book over a decade ago. Like many living food chefs, I not only used cashews in so many of my recipes, but I also created some of the most amazing recreations of your favorite creamy dairy delights with them. From the ultimate cream cheese to cheesecakes, cashews were a foundation of my developing living food culinary artistry. Then I found out what no one wants to talk about. It's truly the vegan & vegan raw community's dirty little hypocritical secret, and once I found out, I could never look at cashews the same way again. We are going to explore the biochemistry and science behind this nut, the physiology of its effects on the digestion and human body, and the sociological trend within the vegetarian community that's created a huge industry of capitalism around this toxic nut. Let's begin this discussion with an initial question to stir the pot. Why is 80% of the "raw or living foods" being produced is being made from a nut that's not only pasteurized, but poisonous to eat, unless pasteurized. Do you really think this nut is that good on your digestion either way?

CHAPTER 7 RAWVELATIONS OF DAIRY

AN EXPLORATION INTO CASHEWS

Cashews are now one of the most popular tree nuts consumed worldwide and has greatly expanded from its surge in the vegetarian or non-dairy alternative communities. Although considered to be nutritious and offers numerous health benefits such as improving blood sugar control among people with type 2 diabetes and reducing total and LDL (bad) cholesterol, many people are unaware that eating cashews in certain forms can be harmful as they contain a dangerous toxin called urushiol.

With the booming market of alternative dairy products that has risen from the vegan diet trends over the last several decades riding off the coat tails of the 'soy trend', that has clearly been exposed a non-dairy alternative that's not all it's cracked up to be, cashews are the next wave. Although some people enjoy eating cashews on their own, most of the cashew industry that's expanded along with its commercial farming industry invesstment is for an explosion of vegan non-dairy products where cashews are puréed into a dairy-free cream alternative that's being integrated into everything from soups, sauces, and ice creams, to milks and cheeses. Although it seems great to have these alternatives and so many people have now incorporated them into their diet with a very indentified passion, is it just another soy wolf in sheeps clothing?

Well, let's examine what makes cashews poisonous, what it does to your health and digestion, and whether there's a way to eat these tree nuts without risk of toxicity. What are the alternatives to this pasteurized nut we can use for a cream alternative?

Cashews (Anacardium occidentale) grow on cashew trees. As such, they're classified as a type of tree nut. Mature cashew trees grow red or yellow pear-shaped drupes called cashew apples. The actual cashew nut grows inside of gray shells on the ends of those fruits. When the cashews are ready for harvesting, the cashew apples begin to fall from the tree. The cashew apples, which are edible and can be pressed into cashew juice which is delicious but can only be consumed in smaller amounts, are collected and the nuts are harvested. The raw cashew nuts that are still in their shell are removed from the ends of the fruits and must be pasteurized depending on the manufacturer's process. Why? These actual raw cashews are full of urushiol and cannot be sold due to a risk of exposure. The raw toxic cashews are then roasted at high heat, either by steaming them in a large rotating drum or vat of boiling oil, to remove urushiol remnants (only removing around 70%) before they can be shelled, thoroughly dried, and peeled. At this stage, the initial marketing deception comes in as these cashews are still often labeled as raw since they're free of added flavorings. Many cashews may be roasted a second time for the purpose of flavoring if being sold as "roasted cashews". This second round of roasting also helps to ensure any remaining urushiol residue is removed before sale. Next, commercial cashews are then ready for quality checks, packaging, and sale.

So for the vegan raw foodies, your "raw cashews" have higher levels of this toxin. Urushiol, which is toxic and can even be deadly in high enough amounts if ingested, is actually so toxic it can cause rashes or burns if it contacts the skin. The anacardic acid present in the fruit that cashew nuts grow from is caustic and burns the skin. Urushiol fools your own cells into thinking there is something foreign in the body. This causes a violent immune system response. In Vietnam, drug addicts in forced-labor 'rehabilitation' camps were engaged in the production and processing of cashew nuts, and those who refused to work were beaten with truncheons, given electric shocks, locked in isolation, deprived of food and H20, and obliged to work even longer hours. That's the whole darker side to the industry that you unconsciously support when you purchase ALL of these products, but that's its own exposing in and of itself, and I hope you will look into it more on your own as you should know what you're supporting with the companies your funding as the source is important.

SOLUTIONS?!

So, what are the alternatives to this pasteurized nut that we can use for a cream alternative? Well, I've spent the last decade reinventing all of my recipes with the most bio-available food source I know of and love on the planet—the coconut. Obviously, living on a tropical island in the Pacific, I have access to an abundance of coconuts, and we are currently building the first processing facility here on our island to get coconut creams and milks all over the world. Creams, milks, cheeses, yogurts—even cheesecakes will be accessible in the U.S. and abroad. It's the most unutilized natural resource on our island and we are doing something about it, and in the process giving the world a healthy alternative to cashews. Remember, dairy is a concept, and can be created from other things besides the pasteurized milk from a cow or a toxic nut. Until we are fully launched, find a source for coconut meat locally at a health food store or use any other nut that's actually raw and not poisonous, and keep an eye out for The Cloud Coconut Creamery as we're coming to a store near you!

THE ART & SCIENCE OF LIVING FOODS

TOOLS OF TECHNOLOGY

 CUTLERY

 COFFEE GRINDER

 SPROUTING DEVICE

 BLENDER

 FOOD PROCESSOR

 DEHYDRATOR

MICAH SKYE

CHAPTER 7 RAWVELATIONS OF DAIRY

SPICY CHOCOLATE MILK

Creation time: 8 hours - sprouting / 20 mins - preparation
Serves 1-3
Ingredients:
- 2 cups almonds (soaked)
- 4 cups spring H20
- 1 tsp sea salt (or to taste)
- ¼ raw honey
- ½ cup cacao powder
- 1 tsp cayenne pepper powder

Add the almonds into the blender with the H2O and sea salt. Next, blend until the almonds are finely ground and the liquid becomes white in color. The next step is to filter the almond pulp through a cheesecloth. Get a glass pitcher, place a cheesecloth over the top, and secure the cloth to the pitcher allowing for it to dip down into it. Begin to pour the almond milk into the cheesecloth until it fills the cloth. Allow it to drain through, stirring it slightly until it drains enough to pour again. Once the cloth fills with enough pulp that it inhibits the flow of filtration, carefully remove the cheesecloth with the pulp in it, squeeze any excess milk out, and place the pulp in a separate bowl (which can be used for a number of different recipes to be explored later in the book). Return the cloth to the pitcher, secure it, and continue filtering the remainder of the milk.

To make your spicy cacao milk, combine the cayenne and cacao with the agave in the coffee grinder or in a measuring cup with a spoon. Then either pour the filtered milk back into the blender to mix the remaining ingredients or mix the spicy cacao mix with the filtered milk in the glass container you're going to store it in. You may want to make it sweeter, spicier, or more chocolatey... this is just a foundation to build from. Enjoy!

Maintains freshness for 3-5 days in refrigeration.

MANDALA LIVING FOODS

THE ART & SCIENCE OF LIVING FOODS

VANILLA DREAM MILK

Creation time: 8 hours - sprouting / 20 mins - preparation
Serves 1-3
Ingredients:
- 3 cups almonds (soaked)
- 5 + cups spring H20
- ¼ tsp sea salt (or to taste)
- 1 tsp vanilla extract
- 1/8 cup raw honey or maple syrup or 1 dropper stevia

Add the almonds into the blender, the H2O, and sea salt. Next, blend until the almonds are finely ground and the liquid becomes white in color. The next step is to filter the almond pulp through a cheesecloth. Get a glass pitcher, place a cheesecloth over the top, and secure the cloth to the pitcher, allowing for it to dip down into it. Begin to pour the almond milk into the cheesecloth until it fills the cloth. Allow it to drain through, stirring it slightly until it drains enough to pour again. Once the cloth fills with enough pulp that it inhibits the flow of filtration, carefully remove the cheesecloth with the pulp in it, squeeze any excess milk out, and place the pulp in a separate bowl (which can be used for a number of different recipes to be explored later in the book). Return the cloth to the pitcher, secure it, and continue filtering the remainder of the milk.

To make your vanilla dream, combine the honey, maple syrup, or stevia and vanilla with the filtered milk in the glass container you're going to store it in and shake until evenly mixed. You may want to make it sweeter or add more vanilla... this is just a foundation to build from. Enjoy!

Maintains freshness for 3-5 days in refrigeration.

MICAH SKYE

CHAPTER 7 RAWVELATIONS OF DAIRY

SPIRULINA DREAM MILK

Creation time: 8 hours - sprouting / 20 mins - preparation
Serves 1–3
Ingredients:
- 2 cups almonds (soaked)
- 4 cups spring H20
- ½ tsp sea salt (or to taste)
- ¼ raw honey
- 1/8 cup cacao
- 2 tbsp spirulina powder

Add the almonds into the blender, the H2O, and sea salt. Next, blend until the almonds are finely ground and the liquid becomes white in color. The next step is to filter the almond pulp through a cheesecloth. Get a glass pitcher, place a cheesecloth over the top, and secure the cloth to the pitcher, allowing for it to dip down into it. Begin to pour the almond milk into the cheesecloth until it fills the cloth. Allow it to drain through, stirring it slightly until it drains enough to pour again. Once the cloth fills with enough pulp that it inhibits the flow of filtration, carefully remove the cheesecloth with the pulp in it, squeeze any excess milk out and place the pulp in a separate bowl (which can be used for a number of different recipes to be explored later in the book). Return the cloth to the pitcher, secure it, and continue filtering the remainder of the milk.

To make your spirulina dream, combine the spirulina and cacao with the agave in the blender. Then either pour the filtered milk back into the blender to mix the remaining ingredients or mix the green mix with the filtered milk in the glass container your storing it in and shake until evenly mixed. You may want to make it sweeter, greener, or more chocolatey... this is just a foundation to build from. Enjoy!

Maintains freshness for 3-5 days in refrigeration.

MANDALA LIVING FOODS

THE ART & SCIENCE OF LIVING FOODS

VANILLA ROSE MILK

Creation time: 8 hours - sprouting / 20 mins - preparation
Serves 1-3
Ingredients:
- 2 cups any raw nuts or seeds (e.g., soaked almonds, sunflowers, or hazelnuts)
- 4-5 cups spring H20
- 1 tsp sea salt (or to taste)
- 1/8 raw honey (optional)
- 1 tsp rose H20
- 1 ½ teaspoons vanilla extract

Begin by adding the almonds into the blender with the H2O and sea salt. Next, blend until the almonds are finely ground and the liquid becomes white in color. The next step is to filter the almond pulp through a cheesecloth. Get a glass pitcher, place a cheesecloth over the top, and secure the cloth to the pitcher, allowing for it to dip down into it. Begin to pour the almond milk into the cheesecloth until it fills the cloth. Allow it to drain through, stirring it slightly until it drains enough to pour again. Once the cloth fills with enough pulp that it inhibits the flow of filtration, carefully remove the cheesecloth with the pulp in it, squeeze any excess milk out, and place the pulp in a separate bowl (which can be used for a number of different recipes to be explored later in the book). Return the cloth to the pitcher, secure it, and continue filtering the remainder of the milk.

To make your vanilla rose milk, combine the agave, rose, and vanilla with the filtered milk in the glass container you're going to store it in and shake until evenly mixed. You may want to make it sweeter or add more vanilla... this is just a foundation to build from. Enjoy!

Maintains freshness for 3-5 days in refrigeration.

MICAH SKYE

CHAPTER 7 RAWVELATIONS OF DAIRY

RAW HORCHATA

Creation time: 8 hours - sprouting / 20 mins - preparation
Serves 3-10
Ingredients:
- 4-5 cups raw almonds (soaked)
- 8 ½ cups spring H20
- ½ tsp sea salt (or to taste)
- 2/3 cup raw white long-grain rice (soaked overnight preferably)
- ½ tbsp vanilla extract
- 2 sticks cinnamon
- ½ tbsp ground cinnamon
- 1/3 cup raw honey (or to taste) or 1-2 droppers stevia

Also known as Horchata de Arroz, Horchata (or-CHA-tah) is a sweet rice infused milk beverage that was introduced to Spain by the Moors. The original Spanish version was prepared with ground tiger nuts and is still very popular in Valencia. In Latin America, where the tiger nut is not commonly accessible, they pulverize rice and use it. In Mexico, horchata is one of the most common aguas frescas and is ladled from a big glass jar placed on ice.

Begin by making a batch of richer raw almond milk using the extra almonds allotted in the ingredients (4 cups almonds to 3 cups H20). Place the 2/3 cup soaked rice in a blender along with the 2 ½ cups of H20 and 2 cinnamon sticks. Blend until the rice and cinnamon are roughly ground. Add the remaining cup of H20 and blend thoroughly. Then pour the mixture into a glass container and place it in the refrigerator to soak (overnight is best), at the very least 4-5 hours. Strain the mixture through a sieve. To complete your horchata, Stir the raw almond milk, vanilla, and agave into the rice H20. Allow to chill and stir before serving over ice. Ole!

Maintains freshness for 3-5 days in refrigeration.

MANDALA LIVING FOODS

THE ART & SCIENCE OF LIVING FOODS

YOGI GOLDEN MILK

Creation time: 8 hours - sprouting / 20 mins - preparation
Serves 2
Ingredients:

- ½ -2/3 tsp turmeric powder or 1/8 cup fresh turmeric juice
- 1/8 cup ginger juice
- 2 cups raw almonds milk
- 2/3 cup spring H20
- 1 tbsp raw almond oil
- 1 pinch sea salt (or to taste)
- Honey to taste

In accordance with the Yogic science of nutrition, it is best to drink golden milk within one hour before or after eating as to allow the digestive enzymes in the stomach to break down the food in the intestine without diluting the excess liquids. Turmeric is best known for its blood cleansing abilities as well as its benefits in lubricating the joints. Many current studies have also shown it to have a preventative effect on cancer and diabetes.

Begin by heating the turmeric in the H20 on low (under 115 degrees) for 8–10 minutes. Next, add the raw almond oil and milk, stirring them into the turmeric H20. Continue heating below 115 degrees for another 5–10 minutes or until the ingredients are mixed evenly. Finally, remove from the heat, stir in the agave to taste, and zen out into a blissful state! Golden milk is a great drink before bed or on a cold night to warm you up. Please enjoy, Sat nam.

Maintains freshness for 3-5 days in refrigeration.

MICAH SKYE

CHAPTER 7 RAWVELATIONS OF DAIRY

YOGI'S RAW CHAI TEA

Creation time: 8 hours - sprouting / 20 mins - preparation
Serves 1-8
Ingredients:

- 2 quarts raw almonds milk
- 7 ½ whole cloves
- 10 green cardamom pods (crushed slightly)
- 7 black peppercorns
- 2 ½ 2-inch sticks of cinnamon
- 4 slices ginger root
- ¼ tsp black tea (optional)
- ¼ cup raw honey (or to taste)

In this Yogic recipe, milk plays a vital role in the assimilation of these five medicinal spices. I feel a brief profile of the herbs in this ancient brew is necessary, and they are the following: Black pepper - purifies the blood, cardamom - aids the digestion, cinnamon - strengthens the bones, and ginger root - heals colds, flus and increases energy. When diluted with milk or H20, it is also really good for young children teething.

Heat all of the herbs in one quart of the raw milk at just under 115 degrees for 15-20 minutes. Next, add the other quart of raw almond milk and agave, stirring it evenly into the chai brew. Continue heating below 115 degrees for another 5-10 minutes or until the ingredients are mixed evenly. Finally, remove from heat, strain, and serve. Yogi chai tea is rejuvenating, soothing, and a great coffee substitute. Please enjoy this Yogic family recipe that takes me back to my childhood, now recreated within the realm of raw diet. Let it transport to another world! To make chai concentrate, follow the same instructions, but use only 3 cups of H20 instead.

Maintains freshness in the fridge for 4-6 days in refrigeration.

MANDALA LIVING FOODS

THE ART & SCIENCE OF LIVING FOODS

YOGI'S JALAPENO MILK

Creation time: 8 hours - sprouting / 20 mins - preparation
Serves 1-2
Ingredients:

- 2 cups raw almond milk
- 4-8 fresh jalapenos (chopped)
- 1 tsp lime juice
- 1 pinch sea salt

This Yogi flu formula packs a punch. Use It at the first sign of a cold or flu; it is the remedy to activate your immune system. I warn you though that hot it is! I suggest beginning with the minimum amount of jalapenos and build from there. There's been a few techniques to dealing with the fire that have been passed along: (1) you can freeze jalapenos as it lessens their odor and their juice won't burn your fingers, and (2) if you drink this fiery mile through a straw, it's not as hot going down. Good Luck!

In a blender, combine the jalapenos, lime juice, sea salt, and almond milk. Blend until they are evenly fused, strap on your seat belt, and drink up!

Maintains freshness for 1-2 days in refrigeration.

MICAH SKYE

CHAPTER 7 RAWVELATIONS OF DAIRY

SESAME GINGER MILK

Creation time: 8 hours - sprouting / 20 mins - preparation
Serves 2-4
Ingredients:

- ½ cup sesame seeds
- 4 tablespoons ginger root (chopped)
- 3 cups raw almond milk
- 4 teaspoons raw honey

This creamy milk magic is not only nourishing to the nervous system, but specifically stimulates the production of healthy sexual fluids to the male sex organs. It is a simple, but powerful drink that is great for the morning time.

Simply soak the sesame seeds for 30 minutes or more, then combine all the ingredients in a blender and blend at high speed until it reaches a smooth, frothy consistency. Strain if desired, and drink cold or heat for a warm tasty version.

Maintains freshness for 3-5 days in refrigeration.

THE ART & SCIENCE OF LIVING FOODS

DESTINY'S DATE MILK

Creation time: 8 hours - sprouting / 20 mins - preparation
Serves 1-3
Ingredients:

- 3 cups raw almond milk
- 12 dates
- 1 pinch sea salt

This date with destiny is one not to miss out on. It is highly nutritious but is also known to maintain a youthful vigor. Date milk has such a nourishing quality that it can even be used to wean babies from breast-feeding. It gives the body energy and helps aid the body in everything from prevention to recovery from a cold and flu.

There are two methods to making date milk: One is a little thicker and richer than the other. The first allows the dates to simmer in the almond milk at around 100 degrees for about 20 minutes, or until the milks starts to turn pink in color. You want to stir occasionally before straining, and then serve. The second method makes a thicker, heartier milk by following the same steps, but instead of straining the dissolving dates, you pour the mixture into the blender and blend it to a smooth consistency. Either way, you have a date with destiny.

Maintains freshness for 3-5 days in refrigeration.

MICAH SKYE

RAW BUTTER

Creation time: 20 mins - preparation
Serves...?
Ingredients:

- 1 ½ cups raw coconut oil
- ½ cup raw cream
- ½ tbsp sea salt

Nature creates magical alternatives to all of the rich and congestive elements that have been the 'norm' for so long. Raw coconut oil, butter, and EVOO are no exception to this truth. They are simple, healthy-medicinal, as well as easy to prepare. To prepare coconut butter, just place a small container of coconut oil in the fridge or somewhere cool. It will solidify into a rich, buttery spread in no time! You can add salt or herbs to your liking.

To prepare olive oil, it is somewhat the same. Take a small jar, salt it to taste, and place it in the fridge. You can also accent your olive oil butter with herbs if you choose. It is all up to you to explore. The sky's the limit!

THE ART & SCIENCE OF LIVING FOODS

GARLIC HERB BUTTER

Creation time: 20 mins - preparation
Serves...?
Ingredients:

Option 1
- 1 ½ cups EVOO2 cloves garlic (minced)
- 1/8 cup herbs of choice (chopped)
- ½ tbsp sea salt

Option 2
- 1 ½ cups raw coconut oil
- ½ cup raw cream
- 2 cloves garlic (minced)
- 1/8 cup herbs of choice (chopped)
- ½ tbsp sea salt

This is a classic staple to your fridge whether you're a raw foodist or not as it can be used for all sorts of things as an alternative to all the rich and congestive 'butter' that has been the 'norm' for so long. They are simple, healthy, medicinal even, as well as easy to prepare.

To prepare garlic herb butter, start by placing the garlic, herbs, and olive oil in a small prep food processor or blender. Begin blending, and as it reaches a balanced consistency, add in the sea salt. Pour it in a small jar and place it in the fridge for at least 30 min before usage.

MICAH SKYE

CHAPTER 7 RAWVELATIONS OF DAIRY

BALSAMIC BUTTER

Creation time: 20 mins - preparation
Serves...?
Ingredients:

Option 1
- 1 ½ cups EVOO2 cloves garlic (minced)
- 3/4 cup aged balsamic
- 1/8 cup herbs of choice (chopped)
- ½ tbsp sea salt

Option 2
- 1 ½ cups raw coconut oil
- ½ cup raw cream
- 3/4 cup aged balsamic
- 2 cloves garlic (minced)
- 1/8 cup herbs of choice (chopped)
- ½ tbsp sea salt

This recipe is for those with a sweet spot for the balsamic. It is a nice accent for anything that needs a little zest. This super easy condiment is a nice element to have in your fridge for all occasions.

To prepare balsamic butter, start by placing the garlic, balsamic, and olive oil in a small prep food processor or a blender. Begin blending and as it reaches a balanced consistency, add in the sea salt. Pour it in a small jar and place it in the fridge for at least 30 minutes before usage.

MANDALA LIVING FOODS

THE ART & SCIENCE OF LIVING FOODS

NUT BUTTER

Creation time: 20 mins - preparation
Serves 1-5
Ingredients:

- 2 ½ cups your nuts of choice (soaked and dehydrated)
- ½ cup coconut H20, fresh squeezed orange juice, or just spring H20
- ½ cup raw coconut oil
- 1 tsp sea salt

In a food processor, grind your dehydrated nuts into a fine powder. Then begin integrating your liquid (I prefer coconut H20). Use as little liquid as possible to create a butter consistency, and then add the salt.

You are nuts if you think the only way to get raw nut butters is to pay $12 – $15 in health food stores. This is a simple recipe that gives you the power to get nutty with your own homemade nut butters. Now even though I recommend soaking the nuts and dehydrating them, you can make the recipe with plain raw nuts. There is also a world of nut butter varieties you can experiment with, but we couldn't fit them all in this book. So here are a few ideas: spirulina almond butter, orange ginger butter, cayenne cacao nut butter, and so on. Experiment, go nuts!

Maintains freshness for 35 days in refrigeration.

MICAH SKYE

CHAPTER 7 RAWVELATIONS OF DAIRY

BUTTER FROSTING

Creation time: 20 mins - preparation / 4-6 hours refrigeration
Serves...?
Ingredients:

- ½ cup raw coconut oil
- ½ cup maple syrup
- ½ cup honey
- ½ cup dates
- ½ tsp sea salt
- 1 tbsp cinnamon
- ½ tbsp cardamom
- 1 tsp vanilla extract

Who doesn't love butter? Especially in dessert frostings. This one is specifically used for our cinnabons, and they are not the same without it. You can also use it for other unbaked pastries or really whatever your heart desires.

To prepare coconut butter frosting, just blend all the ingredients in a Vitamix, transfer to a container and place in the fridge. It will solidify into a rich buttery frosting over the next 46 hours or overnight if you can wait that long.

VANILLA CREAM FROSTING

Creation time: 20 mins - preparation / 4-6 hrs refrigeration
Serves…?
Ingredients:

- 1 ½ cup raw coconut oil
- 1 cup coconut cream
- ½ cup maple syrup
- ½ cup honey
- ½ tsp sea salt
- 2 tsp vanilla extract

We can do frosting, and it's a necessity if we're making live cake! This is our base vanilla cream frosting recipe and can be modified with essences and fruit sauces to your liking once you get the feel for making it. You can also use it for other unbaked pastries or really whatever your heart desires.

To prepare the frosting, just blend all the ingredients in a Vitamix, transfer to a container and place in the fridge. It will solidify into a rich buttery frosting over the next 4-6 hours or overnight if you can wait that long.

CHAPTER 7 RAWVELATIONS OF DAIRY

LIVE CREAM CHEESE

Creation time: 20 mins - preparation
Serves...?
Ingredients:

- 2 cup raw coconut meat (younger/soft)
- 1 cup raw coconut oil
- 4 tbsp apple cider vinegar
- 1 tbsp lime juice or lemon juice
- 1 tsp sea salt
- 1 tsp cloud culture or probiotic culture

If you like cream cheese, then you will be in heaven when I tell you that you can still have your cream cheese! It lasts at least a week in the fridge.

Combine ingredients in food processor and blend until it reaches a cream-like texture. I recommend if you don't have a high powered blender like a Vitamix, then blend in a food processor, and then transfer to a blender and continue blending until you achieve that smooth, cream consistency. Pour into a container and refrigerate for at least 30 minutes or until .

Maintains freshness for 5-7 days in refrigeration.

MANDALA LIVING FOODS

THE ART & SCIENCE OF LIVING FOODS

RAWCOTTA CHEESE

Creation time: 20 mins - preparation
Serves 1-3
Ingredients:

- 4 cups raw coconut meat, soaked mac nuts or cashews
- 1/8 cup extra virgin olive oil
- 4 tsp apple cider vinegar
- 1 tbsp lime juice
- 2 tsp sea salt or 2 tbsp umi plum vinegar
- 1/4 cup nutritional yeast
- 1 tsp cloud culture or probiotic culture
- herbs of choice (optional)

For those who love ricotta, take a deep breath as you have to look no further. Your rawcotta is here! It's an essential element to our greek pizza and our old world lasagna, but it's great even as an accent to a salad. Lasts 3-5 days in the fridge.

Combine ingredients in a food processor and blend on pulse until it reaches a crumbly ricotta-like texture. Not too chunky, but not too pureed. Transfer into a container and refrigerate.

Maintains freshness for 3-5 days in refrigeration.

CHAPTER 7 RAWVELATIONS OF DAIRY

RAW COTTAGE CHEESE

Creation time:
15 mins - soaking / 20 mins - preparation / 2-12 hours - fermentation
Serves 2-4
Ingredients:

- 3 cups raw/medium to older coconut meat
- 1 cup raw almonds (soaked)
- 1 cup raw macadamia nuts (soaked)
- 4 tbsp apple cider vinegar
- 1 tbsp lime juice
- 2 tsp sea salt
- 1 cup coconut H20 or
- 1 tsp cloud culture or probiotic culture
- 4 tbsp apple cider vinegar
- 1 tbsp lemon
- 1 tsp sea salt

The cottage cheese revolution will not be televised, but it is on this page. This power packed alternative is great for the morning with honey or maple syrup on top, as well as a final touch to a fruit bowl or salad. Either way, you'll never look back at yesterday's cottage cheese again.

Combine ingredients in a food processor and blend on pulse until it reaches a crumbly texture. You want to get it just like cottage cheese—not too chunky but not too pureed. Transfer it into a glass wide mouth jar, cover the top with a breathable fabric or paper towel, and let it sit for a couple hours to mildly ferment. Finally, remove the cloth, seal with a lid, and refrigerate.

Maintains freshness for 3-5 days in refrigeration.

MANDALA LIVING FOODS

THE ART & SCIENCE OF LIVING FOODS

SOUR CREAM HYBRID 1

Creation time: 20 mins - preparation / 2-12 hours fermentation
Serves 1-5
Ingredients:

- 3 cups raw coconut meat
- 1 cup fresh-squeezed lemon juice
- 2 tbsp apple cider vinegar
- 1 tbsp umi plum vinegar
- ½ cup coconut H20
- ½ cup raw coconut oil
- 1 tsp sea salt
- 1 tsp cloud culture or probiotic culture

Another comfort food that is also cooling to the palette after the fire of spice is our beloved sour cream. There are several variances to this recipe, including the second hybrid recipe on the following page. I encourage you to explore both and even try fusing them together. There is no wrong way to do anything in this life. Enjoy yourself and the sour cream!

Combine ingredients in a food processor or a blender and blend until it reaches a creamy texture. I recommend if you don't have a high powered blender like a Vitamix, then blend it in a food processor, and then transfer it to a blender and continue blending until you achieve that smooth, creamy consistency. Transfer into a container and refrigerate.

Maintains freshness for 3 days in refrigeration.

CHAPTER 7 RAWVELATIONS OF DAIRY

SOUR CREAM HYBRID 2

Creation time: 20 mins - preparation / 2-12 hours fermentation
Serves 1–5
Ingredients:

- 1 cup raw coconut meat
- 1 cup avocado
- ½ cup fresh-squeezed lemon juice
- 2 tbsp apple cider vinegar
- 2 tbsp raw coconut oil
- 1 tsp sea salt
- 1 tsp cloud culture or probiotic culture

In this hybrid recipe, the avocado is the star! You can, in fact, just make a simple raw sour cream by combining avocado and lemon or lime juices, but this is the gourmet formula that I found really takes me back to that sour cream flavor. Enjoy, and don't be afraid to explore customizing it to your liking!

Combine ingredients in a food processor or blender and blend until it reaches a creamy texture. I recommend if you don't have a high powered blender like a Vitamix, then blend it in a food processor, and then transfer it to a blender and continue blending until you achieve that smooth, creamy consistency. Transfer into a container and refrigerate.

Maintains freshness for 3 days in refrigeration.

MANDALA LIVING FOODS

SOUR CREAM HYBRID 3

Creation time: 20 mins - preparation / 2-12 hours fermentation
Serves 1-5
Ingredients:

- 1 cup raw coconut meat
- 1 cup mac nuts (soaked)
- ½ cup fresh-squeezed lemon juice
- 2 tbsp apple cider vinegar
- 1 tbsp raw coconut oil
- 1 tsp sea salt
- 1 tsp cloud culture or probiotic culture

In this hybrid recipe, the avocado is the star! You can, in fact, just make a simple raw sour cream by combining the soaked mac nuts, coconut, and lemon or lime juices, but this is the gourmet formula that I found really takes me back to that sour cream flavor. Enjoy, and don't be afraid to explore customizing it to your liking!

Combine ingredients in a food processor or a blender and blend until it reaches a creamy texture. I recommend if you don't have a high powered blender like a Vitamix, then blend it in a food processor, and then transfer it to a blender and continue blending until you achieve that smooth, creamy consistency. Transfer into a container and refrigerate.

Maintains freshness for 3 days in refrigeration.

CHAPTER 7 RAWVELATIONS OF DAIRY

SOUR WHIPPED CREAM

Creation time: 20 mins - preparation / 2-12 hours fermentation
Serves 5-7
Ingredients:

- 3 cups raw coconut meat
- 3/4 cup raw coconut oil
- 1 tsp vanilla extract
- 1 ½ tbsp lemon juice
- 3/4 cup coconut H20
- 1 pinch sea salt
- ¼ raw honey
- 2 dropper vanilla stevia
- 1 tsp cloud culture or probiotic culture

And on the 6th day, let there be raw sour whipped cream! That's right, you can have your cream and whip it too. This recipe took me a long time to get just right. Enjoy this delicacy with fresh fruit or atop a piece of raw apple pie. I don't think I have to elaborate on the endless possibilities of whipped cream, and don't be afraid to explore or experiment with customizing each batch. I recommend a teaspoon of vanilla or almond extract to accent your cream as well as supplementing a few tablespoons of monk fruit in place of stevia. Play, have fun with it, food is supposed to be fun—especially desserts!

I recommend if you don't have a high powered blender like a Vitamix, then blend in a food processor, and then transfer it to a blender and continue blending until you achieve that smooth, creamy consistency. Transfer it into a container and refrigerate.

Maintains freshness for 3-5 days in refrigeration.

MANDALA LIVING FOODS

WHIPPED CREAM

Creation time: 20 mins - preparation
Serves 1-3
Ingredients:

- 3 cups raw coconut meat
- 3/4 cup raw coconut oil
- 1 tsp vanilla extract
- 1 ½ tbsp lemon juice
- 3/4 cup coconut H20
- 1 pinch sea salt
- ¼ cup raw honey
- 2 dropper vanilla stevia

And on the 6th day, let there be raw whipped cream! That's right you can have your cream and whip it too. This recipe took me a long time to get just right. Enjoy this delicacy with fresh fruit or atop a piece of raw apple pie. I don't think I have to elaborate on the endless possibilities of whipped cream, and don't be afraid to explore or experiment with customizing each batch. I recommend a teaspoon of vanilla or almond extract to accent your cream as well as supplementing a few tablespoons of dates for agave. Play, have fun with it, food is supposed to be fun—especially desserts!

I recommend if you don't have a high powered blender like a Vitamix, then blend it in a food processor, and then transfer it to a blender and continue blending until you achieve that smooth, creamy consistency. Transfer it into a container and refrigerate.

Maintains freshness for 3-5 days in refrigeration.

MICAH SKYE

CHAPTER 7 RAWVELATIONS OF DAIRY

LIVE CREAM

***Creation time:** 20 mins - preparation / 2-12 hours fermentation*
Serves 1-4
Ingredients:

- 3 cups raw coconut meat
- 1 cup raw cocnut H20
- 1 cup spring H20 / H20
- ½ tbsp vanilla extract
- 1 tsp sea salt
- 1 tsp cloud culture or probiotic culture
- 1-2 droppers stevia or monk fruit (optional, depending on what you're using the cream for)

This cream is the perfect alternative in a raw gourmet to a rich cream in a traditional gourmet cuisine. Whether used in a soup base or a dessert, it is an amazing element to richen any dish. Bon appetit!

Combine all ingredients in a blender and puree to a smooth, creamy consistancy. You can also substitute almonds for the cashews, but then you have to filter the almond pulp with a cheesecloth to seperate the cream.

Maintains freshness for 3 days in refrigeration.

MANDALA LIVING FOODS

THE ART & SCIENCE OF LIVING FOODS

LIVE YOGURT

Creation time: 20 mins - preparation / 3 hours – 5 days fermentation
Serves 1-4
Ingredients:

- 6 cups raw coconut meat
- 2 cups raw coconut H20
- 2 cups spring H20 / H20
- 1 tbsp vanilla extract
- 1 tsp sea salt
- 1 tsp cloud culture or probiotic culture
- 1-2 droppers stevia

Got raw yogurt? Now you do, and it is quite a tasty likeness to the real thing and full of nutrients, probiotics, and enzymes. Serve it with some fresh fruit or on top of some groats. Makes the perfect snack or meal for any time of the day.

Grind the nuts and seeds in a food processor or coffee grinder until it becomes a fine powder. Combine the rest of the ingredients in the food processor or a blender and blend until it reaches a creamy texture. I recommend if you don't have a high powered blender like a Vitamix, then blend it in food processor, and then transfer it to a blender and continue blending until you achieve that smooth, creamy consistency. Transfer into a glass canning jar and tightly secure a piece of cheesecloth on the outer ring of the jar's lid. Allow it to ferment for 2-3 hours before sealing it with the full lid and refrigerating. If you want to create a more solid cheese from this, you can keep the cheesecloth on and flip it upside down over a bowl in the fridge which gives the H20 and nut whey a chance to drain. This is a common raw technique to solidify cheeses which we'll explore more in the pages to come.

Maintains freshness for 3 days in refrigeration.

CHAPTER 7 RAWVELATIONS OF DAIRY

LIVE CHEESE

Creation time: 2-3 hours - preparation / 3-7 days fermentation
Serves...?
Ingredients:

- 4 cups coconut meat or soaked nuts
- 3 tbsp apple cider vinegar
- 2 tsp white miso
- 2 tbsp lime juice
- 1 cup coconut H20
- ½ tbs garlic (minced)
- 3 tbsp herbs of choice
- 1 tsp cloud culture or probiotic culture
- 3/4 cup raw coconut oil
- 2 tsp sea salt

Say cheese! You can now say this with pride because you now have the ultimate cheese recipe. Like so many of my recipes, they are foundations to build off of. This is a basic recipe to create a semi-soft to hard cheese. You can accent it with herbs, spices, or whatever comes to mind.

Grind the nuts and seeds in a food processor or blender until it becomes a fine powder. Combine the rest of the ingredients in the food processor or a blender and blend on until it reaches a creamy texture. Transfer into a glass container and tightly secure a piece of cheesecloth over the top. Allow it to ferment for 2-3 hours before flipping it upside down over a bowl in the fridge which gives the H20 and nut whey a chance to drain. As the cheese becomes more solid, you can press it into a block-like shape through the cheesecloth, and then store it in a sealed container.

Maintains freshness for 3 days in refrigeration.

MANDALA LIVING FOODS

CHEDDAR CHEESE

Creation time: 2-3 hours - preparation / 3-7 days fermentation
Serves...?
Ingredients:

- 2 cups coconut meat or soaked nuts
- 1 ¼ cups nutritional yeast
- 3 ½ tsp sea salt
- ¼ tsp fresh ground pepper
- 3 tbsp apple cider vinegar
- ½ white miso
- 2 cups raw coconut or nut milk
- 1 cup agar agar flakes (optional)
- 2 tbsp lime juice
- 1 tsp cloud culture or probiotic culture
- 1 cup coconut H20
- 1 tbsp garlic (crushed)
- 1 cup raw coconut oil

Without sounding cheesey, this recipe will literally leave you cutting the cheese. Whether for raw mac and cheese, pizza, or a cheeseburger, this cheese is very vesatile in its applicability. You will feel content in knowing you can still have your cheese and eat it too.

Grind the coconut, coconut H20, and apple cider vinegar in a food processor until it becomes as finely ground as possible. Add in the nutritional yeast, sea salt, and spices. In a sauce pan, heat the raw almond milk and olive oil to just under 115 degrees. Add the agar agar, and stir until the agar agar is as dissolved as possible. Transfer into a blender and blend the milk and agar agar to a smooth consistency. Combine the agar milk puree in the food processor or a blender and blend on until it reaches a creamy texture. Then add in the miso and lime juice.

For solid cheese to be sliced or grated, pour your cheese into a container and ferment it in a refrigerator until it solidifies to curd, strain, or press. Continue to ferment until it solidifies. Once hard, you can slice, grate, and so on.

For liquid nacho cheese, transfer it from the food processor to a pan and heat to under 100 degrees until smooth and creamy. Pour in a bowl or over chips and serve.

Maintains freshness for 3 days in refrigeration.

CHAPTER 7 RAWVELATIONS OF DAIRY

NACHO CHEESE

***Creation time:** 20 mins - preparation*
Ingredients: *Serves...?*

- 3 cups coconut meat/soaked nuts
- 2 ½ cups nutritional yeast
- 2 tsp sea salt
- 2 tbsp ACV or jalapeno juice
- 2 tbsp white miso
- ¼ tsp cayenne pepper (optional)
- 2 tbsp cumin
- ½ tbsp coriander
- 1 tbsp chili powder
- ½ cup fresh orange juice
- 1 cup coconut H20
- 2 tbsp minced garlic optional
- 1 tsp cloud culture/probiotic culture
- 3 tbsp raw coconut oil

That's nacho cheese! Actually it is, and this recipe makes more than enough for all your amigos and amigas to enjoy. This is a great addition to any party buffet. Whether over chips on a plate of nachos or just in a bowl to be dipped and enjoyed, this nacho cheese disappears quickly.

Blend the coconut, coconut H20, and ACV or jalapeno juice in a food processor until it's pureed. Add in the nutritional yeast, sea salt, and spices. In a sauce pan, heat the coconut H20 and coconut oil to just under 115 degrees. Transfer into a blender and blend the coconut H20 and agar agar to a smooth consistency. Combine the milk puree in the food processor or a blender and blend on until it reaches a creamy texture. Then add in the miso and lime juice.

For liquid nacho cheese, transefer it from the food processor to a pan and heat to under 100 degrees until smooth and creamy. pour in bowl, or over chips and serve. To spice it up a little more, you can add 3 tablespoons of minced jalapenos!

Maintains freshness for 3 days in refrigeration.

MANDALA LIVING FOODS

MOZARAWLLA CHEESE

Creation time: preparation: 3-4 hours / fermentation: 2-12 hours
Serves…?
Ingredients:

- 2 cups coconut meat or soaked nuts
- 3 tbsp apple cider vinegar
- 2 tsp white miso
- 2 tbsp lime juice
- 1 cup coconut H20
- ½ tbsp garlic (minced)
- 3 tbsp herbs of choice (optional)
- 1 tsp cloud culture or probiotic culture
- 3/4 cup raw coconut oil
- 2 tsp sea salt

Combine ingredients in a food processor and blend until it reaches a dough-like consistency. Transfer the raw cheese mix to a mixing bowl and proceed to spread a 1/4 inch thick square of cheese that covers the length of your Teflex sheet / dehydrator tray. You should be able to get at least four cheese sheets. Dehydrate for 4-6 hours at 105 F, and then flip the cheese using another tray by placing the second tray upside down atop the tray holding the cheese. Holding the trays together, flip the trays in unison and remove the original tray. Then peel the Teflex sheet off the cheese, leaving it on the new tray without any Teflex sheet to continue dehydrating for another 3-4 hours or until the cheese reaches desired dehydration. Be conscious of your cheese after the flip as to not let it get crispy.

To make shredded cheese, take a cheese sheet and cut it into thirds, and then stack them on top of each other. Begin cutting thin strips of cheese, and every 6-8 strips gather your 'faux' shredded cheese in a bowl (you can also slice the strips in half once more if you want to make it finer). The beauty of this is that you can 'shred' the cheese how ever thin or thick you want it!

Maintains freshness for at least 2 weeks in a Ziploc bag.

CHAPTER 7 RAWVELATIONS OF DAIRY

RAW CHEESE SLICES

Creation time: 20 mins - preparation

Serves…?

Ingredients:

- 3 cups raw corn kernels
- (fresh or frozen)
- 3/4 cup flax seeds
- (ground in a coffee grinder)
- ½ cup fresh orange juice
- 2 tbsp Nama Shoyu (or to taste)
- 1 ½ tsp paprika
- 1 tsp coriander
- ½ cup nutritional yeast
- 1 ½ tbsp garlic (minced)
- 1/4 cup olive oil
- 1/2 yellow sweet onion
- 1 cup herbs of choice

Combine ingredients in a food processor and blend it until it reaches a dough-like consistency. Transfer the raw cheese mix to a mixing bowl and proceed to make 1/8 inch thick sheets of cheese on your Teflex sheets on top the dehydrator trays. Dehydrate for 4-6 hours at 105 F, and then flip the cheese using another tray by placing the second tray upside down atop the tray holding the cheese. Holding the trays together, flip the trays in unison and remove the original tray. Then peel the Teflex sheet off the cheese, leaving it on the new tray without any Teflex sheet to continue dehydrating for another 3-4 hours or until the cheese reaches desired dehydration. Be conscious of your cheese after the flip as to not let it get crispy.

To make shredded cheese, take a cheese sheet and cut it into thirds, and then stack them on top of each other. Begin cutting thin strips of cheese, and every 6-8 strips gather your 'faux' shredded cheese in a bowl (you can also slice the strips in half once more if you want to make it finer). The beauty of this is that you can 'shred' the cheese how ever thin or thick you want it!

Maintains freshness for at least 2 weeks in a Ziploc bag.

MANDALA LIVING FOODS

THE ART & SCIENCE OF LIVING FOODS

NONI BLUE CHEESE

Creation time: preparation - 30 mins / fermentation - 2-12 hours
Serves...?
Ingredients:

- 3 cups coconut meat or soaked nuts
- 1 cup raw macadamia nuts (soaked)
- 4 tbsp apple cider vinegar
- 1/8 cup raw noni flesh (pulp)
- 1 tbsp lime juice
- 4 tbsp apple cider vinegar
- 1 tbsp lemon juice
- 2 tsp sea salt
- ½ cup raw noni juice or fresh noni
- 1 tsp cloud culture or probiotic culture
- ½ cup coconut H20 or rejuvelac (for recipe see page)

How could I forget blue cheese? Talk about a medicinal alternative, this raw blue cheese is a classic example. If you don't know the medicinal qualities of noni, flip back to the superfood chapter and read up. This not only has that stink that you love, if you love blue cheese, but really brings the taste as well. Great on a burger or even as a spread on your raw crackers.

Combine the noni pulp with the coconut H20 and noni juice in a food processor and evenly blend. Then add the remaining ingredients and blend on pulse until it reaches a crumbly texture. You want to get it just like blue cheese—not too chunky but not too pureed. Transfer into a glass wide mouth jar, cover the top with a breathable fabric or paper towel, and let sit for a couple hours to mildly ferment. Finally remove the cloth, seal with a lid, and refrigerate.

Maintains freshness for 3-5 days in refrigeration.

MICAH SKYE

CHAPTER 8
DRESSINGS, SAUCES, & SIDES

SHITAKE GINGER DRESSING

This is the best of the flavors of the East & Asian cuisine combined into one dressing that checks all the boxes. This dressing is amazing on salads, with sushi, and can also be used as a marinade for your favorite mushrooms and vegetables.

Creation: 15 mins - preparation
- Lasts 1–2 weeks

Ingredients:
- ½ cup nama Shoyu
- ½ cup sesame oil
- 1 tbsp toasted sesame oil
- 1 ½ cups raw shiitakes
- ½ cup H20
- ¼ cup ACV
- 2 tbsp thyme (minced)
- 1 tsp cilantro (minced)
- 1 tbsp raw honey
- 2 tbsp ginger (minced)
- 2 tbsp garlic (minced)
- ½ tsp black pepper

Instructions:
Mix elements in a Vitamix blender on low to medium speed, then transfer to a dressing bottle or a serving jar with pour spout and refrigerate.

CHAPTER 8 DRESSINGS, SAUCES, & SIDES

BALSAMIC FUNGI MARINADE

This is a classic balsamic-based mushrrom marinade that we will use for our Magi Mushroom burger recipe and can also be used as a marinade for your favorite mushrooms and vegetables. With a variety of herbs, spices, and garlic, this marinade has a diveristy of culinary applications, including being used as a wonderful dressing for a salad. Be sure to bottle it and use it as a dressing after you marinate your mushooms as it becomes infused and evolved into a mushroom dressing with more flavor—so don't let it go to waste!

Creation time: 15 mins - preparation
- Lasts 1–2 weeks

Ingredients:
- ½ cup EVOO
- 3 tbsp Nama Shoya
- 3 tbsp Bragg's or Umi Plum Vinegar
- ½ tsp sea salt
- ¼ cup balsamic vinegar
- ¼ fresh herbs (e.g., basil, fennel, dill, cilantro, rosemary)
- 1 tbsp fresh chopped garlic 1 tbsp honey
- 1 tsp black pepper
- 1 tsp paprika
- ½ cup H20

Instructions:
- Mix elements in a Vitamix blender on low to medium speed, then transfer to a dressing bottle or a serving jar with pour spout and refrigerate.

MANDALA LIVING FOODS

THE ART & SCIENCE OF LIVING FOODS

CITRUS AVO DRESSING

One of the best fresh flavor partnerships is citrus and avocado, and this dressing embodies this synthesis in the most beautiful way. This dressing is on the richer spectrum for our dressings with avocado giving a healthy regiment of natural fats. It can also be used as a base for a dip if you want to add more avocado or some nut cheese to the mix.

Creation time: 15 mins - preparation
- Lasts 1-2 weeks

Ingredients:
- ½ cup nama shoyu
- or 1/4 cup umi plum vinegar
- ½ cup EVOO
- 1-2 butter avocados
- 3 tbsp apple cider vinegar
- ¼ cup lemon juice
- ¼ cup fresh orange juice
- 1 tbsp ginger (minced)
- 2 tbsp thyme (minced)
- 1/8 cup raw honey
- 2 tbsp garlic (minced)
- ½ tsp black pepper

Instructions:
Mix elements in Vitamix on low to medium speed, then transfer to a dressing bottle or to serving jar with pour spout and refrigerate.

MICAH SKYE

CHAPTER 8 DRESSINGS, SAUCES, & SIDES

SUN DRIED TOMATO & HERB DRESSING

Another amazing partnership that gives such a rich and refreshing experience taking you to the country side of Italy is sundied tomatoes and herbs. The acidity of the tomatoes and hint of balsamic together with the herbs brings a unique flavor experience all its own. Again, a multi-purpose dressing that can be used for an assortment of other things including a wonderful pizza dressing!

Creation time: 15 mins - preparation
- Lasts 1–2 weeks

Ingredients:
- ½ cup nama shoyu or 1/2 cup umi plum vinegar
- ½ cup EVOO
- 1/3 cup S.D.T
- ¼ cup balsamic Vinegar
- 2 tbsp thyme (minced)
- 2 tbsp oregano (minced)
- 1 tsp rosemary (minced)
- 1 tbsp raw honey
- 2 tbsp garlic (minced)
- ½ tsp black pepper

Instructions:
Mix elements in Vitamix on low to medium speed, then transfer to a dressing bottle or to serving jar with pour spout and refrigerate.

TAHINI TREASURE

Tahini dressings have become one of my favorite dressings over time, and this is our creative expression of this reflected in its name. Tahini is an acquired taste if you haven't been raised culturally with it in your flavor experience but is so nutritious and truly a delcious element in either ssweet or savory dishes. We're going the savory route with this dressing, and it does not disappoint. This treasure is also on the richer spectrum for our dressings as Tahini is made from sesaame seeds giving a healthy regiment of natural protien and nutrients. It can also be used as a base for a dip if you want to add more avocado or some nut cheese to the mix.

Creation time: 15 mins - preparation
- Lasts 1-2 weeks

Ingredients:
- ½ cup tahini (raw)
- ¼ cup EVOO
- ¼ cup lemon juice
- ¼ cup H20cress (chopped)
- ¼ cup cilantro
- 3 tbsp green chives (minced)
- 2 tbsp nama shoyu
- 3 tbsp H20
- 3 tbsp raw honey
- 1 clove garlic (minced)
- 1 tbsp ginger (fresh)

Instructions:
Mix elements in Vitamix on low to medium speed, then transfer to a dressing bottle or to serving jar with pour spout and refrigerate.

CHAPTER 8 DRESSINGS, SAUCES, & SIDES

LIVE RANCH DRESSING

How could we not recreate a ranch dressing? It's such a classic dressing that's used for so many culinary applications these days outside of salad. It was a no brainer, so we took all the magical elements you love and just replaced the heavy dairy with our coco-mayo, and created something magical we trust you'll get as much useage out of as we do!

Creation time: 15 mins - preparation
- Lasts 1-2 weeks

Ingredients:
- 2 tbsp EVOO
- 3 tbsp lemon Juice
- ¾ cup coco mayo
- ¼ cup H20
- 1 ½ tsp real mustard
- ¼ cup red onion
- 1 cloves garlic (minced)
- 3 tbsp chives (minced)
- ½ tsp celery seed
- ½ tsp nutritional yeast
- 1 ½ tsp sea salt
- ¾ tsp black pepper
- ¼ tsp cloud culture

Instructions:
Mix elements in Vitamix on low to medium speed, then transfer to a dressing bottle or to serving jar with pour spout and refrigerate.

MANDALA LIVING FOODS

THE ART & SCIENCE OF LIVING FOODS

CEASAR LIVE

Non dairy cream based dressings have become a fascination for me as a chef, and this ceasar is no exception. With such a classic dressing with a signature flavor profile, we had to be on point when recreating it dairy free and raw. This royal dressing is also on the richer spectrum for our dressings with a coconut cream base, but non of the congestive aspects to a dairy cream base and all of the natural protien and nutrients. It can also be used as a base for a dip if you want to add more avocado or some nut cheese to the mix.

Creation time: 15 mins - preparation
- Lasts 1-2 weeks

Ingredients:
- 1 cup EVOO
- 1 cup lemon juice½ cup H20
- ¾ cup coco cream or avocado
- 5 cloves – garlic (minced)
- 6 tsp capers
- 6 tsp raw white miso
- 1 whole sheet of nori or 1 tsp guise
- 4 ½ tsp nutritional yeast
- 1 ½ tsp sea salt
- ¾ tsp black pepper

Instructions:
Mix elements in Vitamix on low to medium speed, then transfer to a dressing bottle or to serving jar with pour spout and refrigerate.

CHAPTER 8 DRESSINGS, SAUCES, & SIDES

KRAUT VINEAGRETTE

How could we not recreate a ranch dressing? It's such a classic dressing that's used for so culinary applications these days outside of salad. It was a no brainer, so we took all the magical elements you love and just replaced the heavy dairy with our coco-mayo, and created something magical we trust you'll get as much useage out of as we do!

Creation time: 15 mins - preparation
- Lasts 1–2 weeks

Ingredients:
- 24 oz kraut juice
- ¾ cup nama shoyu soy sauce
- 6 tsp ume plum vinegar
- 3 tbsp raw honey
- ½ cup EVOO

Instructions:
After making saurkraut, drain the juice and mix elements with other ingredients in Vitamix on low to medium speed, then add to dressing bottle or serving jar with pour spout, and refrigerate.

THE ART & SCIENCE OF LIVING FOODS

BALSAMIC RAWDUCTION

Balsamic reductions have always been a fan favorite in the culinary arts, and for myself included. I only had one issue which was the excess heating to create the thick rich texture which is so wonderful to dress and garnish plates with. So began teh journey of reverse engineering a live balsamic reduction or aged balsamic vinegar. Magical on savory or sweet dishes, this balsamic will not disappoint.

Creation time: 15 mins - preparation
- Lasts 1–2 weeks

Ingredients:
- 1 ½ cups balsamic vinegar
- ¾ cups pomegranate juice
- 3 tbsp umi plum vinegar
- 1/2 cup raw honey
- 1 tsp garlic (minced)
- ¼ cup agar agar

Instructions:
Mix elements in Vitamix on low to medium speed, then add to sauce bottle or serving jar with pour spout and refrigerate.

MICAH SKYE

CHAPTER 8 DRESSINGS, SAUCES, & SIDES

AGED LIVE BALSAMIC

Enthusiasts pay top dollar for 10 and 20 year aged balsamic vinegars, and search all over the world for them as they have always been a fan favorite in the culinary arts. The only issue is they're so expensive! I completely honor the art of why and love the brilliance of the process. For that reason, I wanted to create a version that could capture the magic of 10 or 20 years of aging. This is what manifested. Magical on savory or sweet dishes, this balsamic will not disappoint.

Creation time: 15 mins - preparation
- Lasts 1-2 weeks

Ingredients:
- ½ cup nama shoyu
- ½ cup EVOO
- ¼ cup balsamic vinegar
- 2 tbsp thyme (minced)
- 2 tbsp oregano (minced)
- 1 tsp rosemary (minced)
- 1 tbsp raw honey
- 2 tbsp garlic (minced)
- ½ tsp black pepper

Instructions:
Mix elements in Vitamix on low to medium speed, then add to serving jar with pour spout, and refrigerate.

LIVE SAUCES

LIVE CATCHUP

No we didn't misspell one of the world's favorite condiments. We evolved it to represent our intention which is for the wolrd to 'catch up' to our innerstanding of putting an end to making condiments with toxic sweetenres like high fructose corn syrup, processed sugar, and even agave. Traditional ketchup acutally never had anything like this in it, but the GMO corn industry has infused their toxic product into every facet of our food infrastructure. So we had to create an evolution to catch up to the awakening of humanity, and we are honored to share it with you....

Creation time: 15 mins - preparation
- Lasts 1-2 weeks

Ingredients:

- 1 ½ cups SDT
- 2 cups fresh tomatoes (chopped)
- 3 tbsp shoya or umi plum vinegar
- ½ cup H20
- ¼ cup ACV
- 1/8 cup fresh orange juice
- 1/8 cup honey
- ¼ tsp black pepper
- 1 ½ tsp coriander

Instructions:
Mix elements with H20 in Vitamix on low to medium speed, then transfer to serving jar, and refrigerate.

CHAPTER 8 DRESSINGS, SAUCES, & SIDES

REAL MUSTARD

Real mustard is exactly that, and sadly in this day and age of fake manufactured high fructose corn syrup everything we had to specify. We had to bring back an old school formula like so many other magical things forgotten in this modern world and evolve it. Full of true mustard seed, spices and vinegar, this mustard is medicine.

Creation time: 15 mins - preparation
- Lasts 1-2 weeks

Ingredients:

- ½ cup black mustard seeds
- 1/3 cup yellow mustard seeds
- ½ cup white vinegar (raw)
- 2 tbsp Umi plum vinegar
- 1 clove garlic (minced)
- ¼ tsp coriander
- ¼ tsp cumin
- 1 shallot (2 oz minced)
- ½ tbsp sea salt

Instructions:
Mix elements in Vitamix on low to medium speed, then transfer to serving jar and soak in cool place for at least 48 hours and refrigerate.

MANDALA LIVING FOODS

MARAWNARA

Recreating this classic sauce was a passion for me both culturally and strategically as we have so many dises that a legitimate marawnara was foundational. From our pasta to our lasagna, I needed a marawnara that would make my Italian grandmother in heaven proud. Using sundried tomatoes in a sauce gives an experience of a roasted traditional tomato sauce, and when combined with all the classic Italian herbs of the providence, a beautiful creation took place that it's an honor to share with you.

Creation time: 15 mins - preparation
- Lasts 1–2 weeks

Ingredients:
- 2 cups SDT
- 4–5 cups fresh tomatoes
- ¼ cup nama shoyu or 4 tbsp Umi plum vinegar
- 2 tbsp garlic
- ½ cup H20
- 1/8 cup orange juice
- ¼ cup oregano
- ¼ cup basil
- ¼ cup thyme
- 1/8 cup rosemary
- 1 tsp black pepper
- ¼ tsp paprika
- ¼ tsp sea salt

Instructions:
Mix the sun-dried tomatoes first with the liquids in a food processor. Then add the fresh tomatoes, herbs, and the rest of the seasonings to blend them into a uniform sauce, Transfer to a serving jar, and refrigerate.

CHAPTER 8 DRESSINGS, SAUCES, & SIDES

CURRY MANDALA

Curry has become a more desired dish over the last few decades in the West, and with it may enthusiasts always looking to explore the next magical warming spice journey to satiate the tastebuds and the soul. Honoring the cultural sacred elements that create the "curry" experience and enhancing them was key, and that required much research and study of the sacred spices of the East. The end result is before you now on the page. Enjoy.

Creation time: 15 mins - preparation

- Lasts 1–2 weeks

Ingredients:

- 3 tbsp coriander (ground)
- 3 tbsp cumin
- 3 tsp turmeric (powder)
- 3 tbsp fresh turmeric (minced)
- 3/4 tsp cayenne
- 6 tsp sea salt
- 1½ tsp black pepper
- 3 tsp cardamom
- 3 tbsp organic SDT
- 1 tomato
- 3 tsp cinnamon
- 3 tbsp fresh ginger (minced)
- 6 cups Cloud milk (unsweetened)
- 3 cups Cloud cream
- 6 tbsp raw coconut oil
- 3 clove garlic
- 3/4 cup nutritional yeast
- 6 tbsp fresh lime juice
- 4 kefir lime leaves
- 6 tbsp fresh cilantro
- 9 tbsp nama shoyu

Instructions:
Mix elements in Vitamix on low to medium speed, then add to serving jar, and refrigerate.

SWEET & SOUR LIVE

Asian cuisine has always been one of my favorite cultural culinary art explorations. It's one of the most ancient dating back thousands of years. Flavors, spices, herbs all brought together in complex sauces and marinades bringing magic to every taste bud. So when creating one of the classics in a live version, we wanted to dive deep into the core foundations of flavors. We trust you'll enjoy it and use it on many things.

Creation time: 15 mins - preparation
- Lasts 1-2 weeks

Ingredients:

- ½ cup nama Shoyu
- 1 cup raw honey
- 1 clove garlic (minced)
- 2 tbsp ginger (minced)
- ¼ cup Umi plum vinegar
- ¼ cup apple cider vinegar
- 2 oz coconut oil
- 1 tbsp red pepper flakes

Instructions:
Mix elements in Vitamix on low to medium speed, then add to sauce bottle or serving jar with pour spout and refrigerate.

CHAPTER 8 DRESSINGS, SAUCES, & SIDES

PAD THAI SAUCE

Our live Pad Thai is one of our most beloved dishes and like most dishes, it's all about the sauce. I set my sights on creating the most amazingly fresh and fish sauce free version that would make our Pad Thai shine. This is what manifested, and we trust you'll enjoy it as much as our patrons do!

Creation time: 15 mins - preparation
- Lasts 1–2 weeks

Ingredients:

- 8 tbsp tamarind paste
- 4 cups hot H20 115
- 2 cups soy sauce
- 1/2 cup umi plum vinegar
- 4-10 fresh red chilies
- 1/2 cup sesame oil
- 2 cups raw honey
- 2 cups lime juice
- 1 cup toasted sesame oil
- 1 tsp seaweed of choice
- (optional)

Instructions:
Mix elements in Vitamix on low to medium speed, then add to serving jar with pour spout, and refrigerate.

MANDALA LIVING FOODS

LIVE PESTO

Pesto sauces was one of my first deep dives in the art of fresh sauce creation, and I have created so many versions over the years. It is a primarily raw or living sauce traditionally outside of the dairy that many add to it and was really fun to evolve it into the magical formula we are now sharing with you.

Creation time: 15 mins - preparation
- Lasts 1-2 weeks

Ingredients:

- 1 cup fresh cilantro
- 1 cup mac nuts
- ½ cup fresh basil
- ½ cup extra virgin olive oil
- ¼ cup lemon juice
- 3 tbsp garlic, minced
- 1 tsp sea salt
- 1 tsp black pepper
- ¼ avocado

Instructions:
Mix elements in Vitamix or food processor on low to medium speed, then add to sauce bottle or serving jar, and refrigerate.

CHAPTER 8 DRESSINGS, SAUCES, & SIDES

MACA NUT SAUCE

Maca is such a unique and powerful superfood. if you haven't explored all of its healing benefits in the superfood dictionary, be sure you check it out. On the side of flavor, it has been known to have a very similar resemblance to peanut butter. So how could we not make a hybrid medicinal peanutbutterless nut sauce with it? We couldn't, and so I give to you our Maca Nut Sauce. Amazing with summer rolls or Asian noodle dishes galore its rich, nutty, salty, and sweet with hints of garlic and coriander. This power packed sauce does not disappoint.

Creation time: 15 mins - preparation
- Lasts 1-2 weeks

Ingredients:

- 2 cups raw tahini
- 1 cup raw almond butter
- 12 tbsp raw maca powder
- 12 tbsp nama shoya
- 6 tbsp raw honey
- 1 cup fresh orange juice
- 8 oz coconut oil
- 4 tsp garlic minced
- 4 tsp coriander

Instructions:
Mix elements in Vitamix on low to medium speed, then add to serving jar with pour spout, and refrigerate.

MANDALA LIVING FOODS

THE ART & SCIENCE OF LIVING FOODS

ROSEBERRY SAUCE

What divine feminine doesn't love roses? I haven't found one, and that includes if it can be infused into gourmet food. It's one of my favorite essences and carries the highest vibration of all flowers. When combined with berries in a sauce for dessert, we have discovered a liquid form of heaven on earth that we are honored to share with you.

Creation time: 15 mins - preparation
- Lasts 1-2 weeks

Ingredients:

- 2 cups raspberries or strawberries
- (fresh or frozen)
- 1 ½ cups honey
- ½ cup lemon juice
- 2 tbsp raw coconut oil
- 4+ oz rose tincture

Instructions:
Mix elements in Vitamix on medium to high speed, then add to container, and refrigerate. For some sauces or larger batches use a food processor, and blend to puree consistency.

CHAPTER 8 DRESSINGS, SAUCES, & SIDES

LAVABERRY SAUCE

Our Lavaberry sauce is the key dessert sauce for so many of our magical desserts and is the perfect blend of sweet and acidic with a buttery undertone from the raw coconut oil. Very addicting in all the right ways and can be used on whatever you feel called to use it on as an alternative to honey with breakfast bowls as well as desserts.

Creation time: 15 mins - preparation
- Lasts 1–2 weeks

Ingredients:

- 2 cups raspberries or strawberries
- (fresh or frozen) if frozen, let thaw first
- 1 ½ cups honey
- ½ cup lemon juice
- 2 tbsp raw coconut oil

Instructions:
Mix elements in Vitamix on medium to high speed, then add to container, and refrigerate. For some sauces or larger batches use a food processor, and blend to puree consistency.

MANDALA LIVING FOODS

235

THE ART & SCIENCE OF LIVING FOODS

HOLY CACAO SAUCE

Cacao is another sacred and powerful superfood that has really exploded in the West. Dive into all of its medicinal magic int he superfood dictionary to get you excited to flip back to this recipe and create this holy cacao medicinal dessert sauce. It's our filling for the Chocolate Lava cakes and can be used for whatever your heart desires to add a splash of chocolate to the mix.

Creation time: 15 mins - preparation
- Lasts 1-2 weeks

Ingredients:

- 2 cup coconut H20
- 2 cup raw maple syrup
- 2 cup raw honey
- 2 ½ cups cacao powder
- 1 cup carob powder
- 2 tsp sea salt
- 4 tsp vanilla extract

Instructions:
Mix elements in Vitamix on low to medium speed, then add to sauce bottle or serving jar with pour spout and refrigerate.

CHAPTER 8 DRESSINGS, SAUCES, & SIDES

SACRED FIRE CACAO SAUCE

As if our Holy Cacao Sauce wasn't enough, we had to add some more fire to the mix and take it to another level for those with a taste for spice. With the essence of ginger and the pepper of your choice, this sauce is not for the faint of heart, and we trust you'll use it responsibly to light your sacred fire.

Creation time: 15 mins - preparation
- Lasts 1-2 weeks

Ingredients:

- 2 cups coconut H20
- 2 cups raw maple syrup
- 2 cups raw honey
- 2 ½ cups cacao powder
- 1 cup carob powder
- 2 tsp sea salt
- 4 tsp vanilla extract
- 1 tsp cayenne or Hawaiian chili pepper
- 1 tsp fresh ginger (minced)

Instructions:
Mix elements in Vitamix on low to medium speed, then add to sauce bottle or serving jar with pour spout and refrigerate.

MANDALA LIVING FOODS

ULU HUMMUS

If you're not familiar, Ulu is the Hawaiian word for bread fruit. Bread fruit is one of the native sacred staples of nutrition on the islands. It is like a very dense and moist potato when younger and becomes very soft and sweet as it ripens. It can be used for an assortment of dishes including breads, cookies, dips, and yes hummus. Here's our live version for you to enjoy if you can get your hands on some of this unique island produce.

Creation time: 15 mins - preparation
- Lasts 1-2 weeks

Ingredients:

- 1 ½ cups Ulu dehydrated or ripe
- ½ cup zucchini (chopped)
- 1 cup raw tahini
- ½ cup lemon juice
- 1/3 cup EVOO
- 2 tbsp garlic (minced)
- 3 tsp sea salt
- 1 tbsp cumin
- 1 ½ tbsp cinnamon
- ½ tsp coriander

Instructions:
- Mix elements in a food processor on low to medium speed, then transfer to serving container, and refrigerate.

CHAPTER 8 DRESSINGS, SAUCES, & SIDES

G-FREE HUMMUS

Hummus has always been a favorite in the traditional cultures of its creation but has exploded onto the scene in the West over the last ten years. So many styles and variations are out there, but this one is in a category of its own as it's garbanzo bean free! Garbanzo beans are challenging to digest for many, which is why even of you sprout them it's wise to cook them even on low heat. Well, this amazing hummus is free of the process while bringing all the magic you love from the classic spread.

Creation time: 15 mins - preparation
- Lasts 1-2 weeks

Ingredients:

- 2 cups zucchini
- 1 cup raw tahini
- ½ cup lemon juice
- 1/3 cup EVOO
- 2 tbsp garlic (minced)
- 3 tsp sea salt
- 1 tbsp cumin (ground)
- 1 ½ tbsp cinnamon
- ½ tsp coriander

Instructions:
- Mix elements in a food processor on low to medium speed, then transfer to serving container, and refrigerate.

RAWFRIED BEANS

Bean, beans magical fruit, the more you eat the more you…? So many people love refried beans, but even when soaked and cooked they are still not the most digestible. We have an amazing alternative that remarkably captures the texture and flavor that makes refried beans so loved by so many just without the beans. You will never look at pumpkin seeds the same again!

Creation time: 15 mins - preparation
- Lasts 1–2 weeks

Ingredients:

- 4 cups soaked pepitas
- 1/3 cup nutritional yeast
- ¼ cup raw coconut oil
- 3 tsp cumin
- 3 tsp chili powder
- 2 tsp coriander
- 3 tsp smoked paprika
- 1/8 tsp cayenne (optional)
- 3 tbsp shoyu

Instructions:
Mix elements with H20 in Vitamix on low to medium speed, then add to sauce bottle or serving jar with pour spout and refrigerate.

CHAPTER 8 DRESSINGS, SAUCES, & SIDES

GUACAMOLE

Who doesn't love guacamole? These days in the culinary world it's used for so much more than a plate of nachos. We didn't mess with tradition too much and kept all the sacred elements of what makes an amazing guacamole. Enjoy!

Creation time: 15 mins - preparation
- Lasts 1-2 weeks

Ingredients:

- 6 avocados, ripe
- ½ red onion, finely diced
- 4 tomatoes, diced
- 3 tbsp finely chopped fresh cilantro
- 1 jalapeno pepper, seeds removed
- and finely diced (optional)
- 3 garlic cloves, minced
- 2 limes, juiced
- 1 tsp sea salt

Instructions:
1. Mince cilantro & garlic and juice the limes.

2. Combine theme with diced onions, tomatoes, and sea salt in a mixing bowl.

3. Add avocados, and mash them with a spoon mixing it all together evenly.

4. Transfer to a container and refrigerate.

MANDALA LIVING FOODS

PICO DE GALLO

How could we not include our recipe for this classic element in Mexican cuisine that adds a boost of freshness to anything it touches. We've naturally evolved it with unique twists like ginger and Umi plum vinegar that honor the spectrum of spices and acidity, and only add to the magic.

Creation time: 15 mins - preparation
- Lasts 1-2 weeks

Ingredients:

- 5 cups fresh tomatoes (chopped)
- 1 cup red onion (minced)
- 1 cup cilantro (chopped)
- 6 tbsp fresh lime juice
- 4 tbsp extra virgin olive oil
- 2 tbsp garlic (minced)
- 1 tbsp Umi plum vinegar
- 4 tsp cumin
- 2 tsp ginger (minced)
- 2 tsp chili powder
- 2 tsp coriander
- 2 tsp sea salt
- ½ tsp - cayenne or chipotle

Instructions:

1. Mince cilantro & garlic and juice the limes.

2. Combine theme with diced onions, tomatoes, and sea salt in a mixing bowl, and mix them all together evenly.

3. Transfer to a container and refrigerate.

CHAPTER 8 DRESSINGS, SAUCES, & SIDES

CHEESY BRUSSEL SPROUTS

One of our favorite cheesy accents to literally any dish. Easy to make in large batches and lasts in the pantry for a month plus if you can keep from eating it all!

- Lasts 1 month +
- Makes one batch of cheesy brussel sprouts

Ingredients:

- 8 cups shredded brussel sprouts
- 2 cups alfredo sauce
- (alternative 2 cups of coconut cream or cloud + 1 ½ nutritional yeast cup)
- 2 tsp sea salt

Instructions:
STAGE 1:

1. In a food processor, pulse shred or hand shred brussel sprouts, and add to mixing bowl.

2. Add 2 cups of alfredo sauce or 2 cups of cream and nutritional yeast, and seat salt and mix evenly coating the brussel sprouts.

3. Spread brussel sprouts on dehydrator sheet / tray.

STAGE 2:

1. Dehydrate for 8–10 hours, and flip / stir until even dehydrated and fully crispy.

2. Let fully cool, transfer into container, and store in pantry.

MANDALA LIVING FOODS

THE ART & SCIENCE OF LIVING FOODS

CHICKPEA MISO SOUP

Our magic soy free miso is a wonderful evolution of traditional miso soup.

Creation time: 15 mins - preparation
- Lasts 1–3 weeks
- Makes 1 batch of miso soup

Ingredients:

- 8 cups H20
- 4 tsp dashi granules
- 6 tbsp chickpea miso paste
- 4 green onions (minced)
- 2 cups shiitake mushrooms (sliced)

Instructions:

STAGE 1:

1. Heat H20 to almost boiling with shiitakes, add to Vitamix straining mushrooms.

2. Add miso and dashi, and blend on low speed.

3. Transfer to hotpot or jar to cool and refrigerate and return mushrooms back into soup.

STAGE 2

1. Serve with green onions and dash of furikaki.

CHAPTER 8 DRESSINGS, SAUCES, & SIDES

RAINBOW SAUERKRAUT

Live sides are as underrated in mandala of living foods as the name "sides" itself, but they are some of our most favored culinary treasures that our pupus and entrees are just not the same without. They are in or served with pupus, entrees, and salads.

Creation time: 15 mins - preparation / 72 HRS - FERMENTATION

- Lasts 1-3 weeks
- makes 1 64 oz batch of sauerkraut - 72 hours +

Ingredients:
- 2 large cabbages (one Chinese/napa, one traditional)
- 2-3 medium carrots (grated)
- 2 tbsp fine sea salt
- 1 tbsp cane sugar or honey
- 1 oz Ume plum vinegar
- 2 tsp caraway seeds
- 1 tbsp coriander seeds
- 1 clove garlic, crushed
- ½ cup mustard seeds
- 4 oz sage tincture

Instructions:
STAGE 1:

1. Finely shred or slice cabbage and carrots in mixing bowl. Layer in salt and sweetener. Mix in seeds and spices. and mash with wooden spoon. Juice and brine begin to form, mix evenly.

2. Transfer to fermenting jar. Load cabbage into jar, mash into jar. Mash until cabbage is submerged under brine. Add essence if recipe calls. Once submerged, place an 8oz jar filled with H20 in the top of the 64oz jar. Cover with paper towel and mason lid ring. Sit out for 1-3 days

STAGE 2

1. Remove an 8oz jar each day, aerate sauerkraut with kebab poker. Rinse 8oz jar, refill with H20 and replace in jar. After fully fermented on day 3, seal and place in fridge

MANDALA LIVING FOODS

THE ART & SCIENCE OF LIVING FOODS

INDIGO SPICE KRAUT

Live sides are as underrated in mandala of living foods as the name "sides" itself, but they are some of our most favored culinary treasures that our pupus and entrees are just not the same without. They are in or served with pupus, entrees, and salads.

Creation time: 15 mins - preparation / 72 hours - fermentation
- Lasts 1-3 weeks
- makes one 64 oz batch of sauerkraut - 72 hours +

Ingredients:
- 2 medium/large purple cabbages (2.5 kg or about 5.5 lbs)
- 2-3 medium carrots, grated
- 2 tbsp fine sea salt
- 4 oz Monk Fruit syrup
- 1oz Ume Plum vinegar
- 6oz ginger tincture
- 2oz lavender tincture
- 1 clove garlic

Instructions:
STAGE 1:

1. Finely shred or slice cabbage and carrots in mixing bowl. Layer in salt and sweetener. Mix in seeds and spices. and mash with wooden spoon. Juice and brine begin to form, mix evenly.

2. Transfer to fermenting jar. Load cabbage into jar, mash into jar. Mash until cabbage is submerged under brine. Add essence if recipe calls. Once submerged, place an 8oz jar filled with H20 in the top of the 64oz jar. Cover with paper towel and mason lid ring. Sit out for 1-3 days.

STAGE 2

1. Remove an 8oz jar each day, aerate sauerkraut with kebab poker. Rinse 8oz jar, refill with H20 and replace in jar. After fully fermented on day 3, seal and place in fridge.

CHAPTER 8 DRESSINGS, SAUCES, & SIDES

SUSHI RICE LIVE

Can't have rice anymore or fast burning carbs in your diet? You can still have rice! At least this rice anyway, as it's not made from rice but is just as amazing! this is our live sushi rice recipe but can be used for any dish as a rice substitute.

Creation time: 25 mins - preparation
- Makes 1 batch of sushi rice
- Lasts 1 week

Ingredients:
- ¼ cup furi kake
- 3 cups cauliflower
- 3 cups older coconut (pulverized)
- ¼ cup hemp seeds
- 1 ½ tbsp fresh ginger (minced)
- ½ cup psyllium husk (binder)
- 3 tsp ACV or rice vinegar (sushi)
- ½ tbsp dulse flakes
- 2 tsp Umi plum vinegar
- ¼ tsp sea salt

Instructions:
STAGE 1:
In a food processor:

1. Process older coconut to a fine crumble until you have 1 cup total. Add to a bowl.

2. Process cauliflower, removing the majority of the stems. Pulse to a medium-fine crumble and add to the bowl. Add ½ cup more of the de-stemmed cauliflower and ¼ cup psyllium husk to the empty processor and process finely. Add to the bowl along with the remaining ingredients and press into container.

3. Seal, date, and refrigerate to set.

MANDALA LIVING FOODS

THE ART & SCIENCE OF LIVING FOODS

SPROUTED RICE

This is the only way you should ever eat rice! It activates it and turns it from a fast burning carb to a slow burning carbs and wholistic food.

Creation time: 15 mins - preparation / 72 hours - fermentation
- Lasts 1 week
- Makes 1 batch of sprouted rice

Ingredients:
- 6 cups brown or basmati rice
- 2 + cups H20

Instructions:
STAGE 1:

1. Soaking (3-day process). Add rice to a 64 oz jar. Fill with H20 to 2" above the rice

2. Cover with a screen (not sealed or airtight), label and dateEach day, dump the H20 only, rinse thoroughly with sink H20, and begin soaking again in hydrogen H20. After the 3rd day of soaking, strain, and refill with fresh H20. Ideally 3 days, 3 cycles

STAGE 2:

1. Strain rice, rinse thoroughly, and store in container for usage

STAGE 3:

1. Boil H20 with a proportion of 6 cups to 3 cups of rice. Turn to low temp once H20 boils. Cook rice at low temp until rice is fully cooked with lid on, stirring occasionally.

2. Once H20 is completely gone, keep lid on to steam. Alternative: use rice cooker; same measurements apply. Leave steaming until serving.

CHAPTER 8 DRESSINGS, SAUCES, & SIDES

SPROUTED MUNG BEANS

The most effective way to get the most bioavailable vegetarian protein is to sprout them and wake them up. This is your protein boost for the Green Goddess Soup, but can be used as a protein boost for any dish!

Creation time: 15 mins - preparation / 72 hours - fermentation
- Makes 1 batch of 64 oz sprouted rice
- Lasts 2 weeks

Ingredients:
- 6 cups mung beans
- 2+ cups H20

Instructions:
STAGE 1:

1. Soaking (2-day process). Rinse mung beans and add to a 64 oz jar.

2. Fill with hydrogen H20 to 2" above the mung beans. (They will rise in jar to the top)

3. Cover with a screen (not sealed or airtight), label and date.

4. Each day, dump the H20 only, rinse thoroughly with H20, and begin soaking again in hydrogen H20.

STAGE 2:

1. 2nd day, Strain mung beans, rinse thoroughly, and store in container for usage,

STAGE 3:

1. To prep beans to be more digestible, heat on low to medium heat 6–8 minutes to breakdown the starches & proteins.

2. Strain, store, or add to batch of Green Goddess soup.

MANDALA LIVING FOODS

THE ART & SCIENCE OF LIVING FOODS

FAB FIVE GRAIN YOGI CEREAL

Makes 1 batch of sprouted 5 grain cereal

- lasts 1-2 weeks
- must be fresh and stocked daily

Ingredients:
DRY GRAIN MIX RATIO

- ½ cups red wheat berries
- ½ cups rye berries
- ½ cups barley
- ½ cups Kamut
- ½ cups whole oat berries

SPROUTING RATIO

- 6 cups yogi grain cereal
- 2 cups H20

Instructions:
STAGE 1:

1. Add grain mix to a 64 oz jar, fill with hydrogen H20, and cover with a screen (not airtight

2. Soak for 8-10 hours.

STAGE 2:

1. Strain grain, rinse thoroughly, and store in container for usage.

STAGE 3:

1. Prep grains to be more digestible by heating on low to medium heat 6-8 minutes to breakdown the fiber & proteins.

2. Strain, store, and serve.

THE ARTS & SCIENCE OF LIVING FOODS

CHAPTER 9
BREAD & SNACKS

LIVE PIZZA CRUST / BURGER BUNS

We have a created a miraculous alternative to baked pastries that is nothing short of living foods perfection using creative ingredients like our nut pulps, coconut, zucchini, flax seeds, and psyllium husk. The result is an amazing line of unbaked goods and pastries that make up many of our entrees and desserts.

Creation time: 25 mins - preparation / 12 hours - dehydration
- Lasts 1–2 weeks

Ingredients:
- 4 cups medium-older coconut meat (pulp)
- 4 cups zucchini (pulp)
- ½ cup psyllium husk, mixed evenly
- 2 tsp sea salt
- 1 tbsp garlic (minced)
- 1 tsp black pepper
- 1 tsp coriander

Instructions:
STAGE 1:

1. In a food processor, breakdown older coconut to a crumble until you have 4 cups total, then clear the processor.

2. Process chopped zucchini/squash, pulsing in a food processor to a course hand-squeezing most of the juice out of it until you have 4 cups total.

STAGE 2:

1. Mix pulp in a mixing bowl together with other ingredients evenly, adding the psyllium husk gradually kneading it into the pulp until a dough consistency is achieved. Spread on dehydrator sheets into pizza crust or into 5–6 inch diameter buns. You should be able to fit 16 buns per tray. Dehydrate at 117 degrees for 8 hours.

2. Flip buns or pizza crust and dehydrate another 4–6 hours depending on thickness of the buns. Remove and let cool, then store in sealed container in pantry.

CHAPTER 9 BREAD & SNACKS

MANDALA LIVING FOODS

TOSTADAS / TACO SHELLS / NACHO CHIPS

Creation time: *8 hours - sprouting / 25 mins - preparation / 12 hours - dehydration*

- Makes 15 Tostadas or taco shells, or 4-5 sheets of nachos
- Lasts 1-2 weeks

Ingredients:
- 6 cups soaked golden flax seeds
- 2 cups sunflower seeds
- 6 tbsp nama Shoyu
- 2 tsp sea salt
- 2 tbsp cumin
- 2 tbsp coriander
- 2 tbsp chili powder
- 2 tbsp paprika
- ½ cup orange juice
- 4 cups corn kernels
- ½ cup red onion
- 3 cloves garlic

Instructions:

STAGE 1:

1. Soak flax & sunflower seeds 6-8 hours and mix thoroughly. In a blender: orange juice, 4 cups corn kernels, red onion, garlic, and seasonings. Blend to a liquid consistency and add to the batter. Mix thoroughly into an even dough.

STAGE 2:

1. Tostadas: On a dehydrator tray with a sheet, spread the mix into thin tostada shapes. 9 tostadas per tray, edges should be touching each other. Dehydrate 8-10 hours then flip and dehydrate another 4-6 hours or until crispy.

2. Taco Shells: when you flip them after initial dehydrate, place them on taco forms to dehydrate the remaining 4-6 hours until crispy/hard.

3. Nacho Chips: On a dehydrator tray with a sheet, spread the batter in a thin layer to cover the entire sheet. With a fine-edged utensil, gently press lines into the batter that divide it into fourths, eighths, and onward until you have a matrix sheet of diamond shaped chips. Within the four new squares, make more perforations. Dehydrate 8-10

CHAPTER 9 BREAD & SNACKS

hours then flip and dehydrate another 4-6 hours until crispy. Nacho chips break apart and store in container.

STAGE 3:

4. Let cool and transfer to storage containers and stock in pantry.

LIVE PASTA

Our live alternative to traditional gluten pasta is light, delicious, and easy to make. Made from zucchini and kelp noodles, this pasta is every bit as amazing as traditional pasta, and better for the digestion!

Creation time: 25 mins - preparation
- Lasts 1 week
- Makes 9-10 servings

Ingredients:
- 6 cups zucchini (sliced w spirally)
- 6 cups kelp noodles
- 4 tbsp cold pressed olive oil
- 4 tbsp lemon juice
- 2 tbsp Umi plum vinegar
- ½ tsp sea salt
- 2 cloves garlic

Instructions:

STAGE 1:

1. With a spirally or shredding device make zucchini noodles of the whole zucchini. Combine these noodles with the kelp noodles in a large container to marinate.

STAGE 2:

1. Blend EVO oil, lemon, sea salt, and garlic in a blender, add to noodles, and mix evenly allowing to marinate for at least 3-4 hours or overnight in the refrigerator.

2. Serve in 10 oz portions for pasta live bowl with sauce and Rawcotta.

CHAPTER 9 BREAD & SNACKS

MANDALA PAD THAI

One of our fan favorites at Mandala is this recreation of the classic favorite Pad Thai. All the amazing elements of a Pad Thai, with our live noodles and vegan Pad Thai sauce taking you deep into the cultural magic of this dish.

Creation time: 25 mins - preparation
- Lasts 1 week
- Makes 9–10 servings

Ingredients:
- 6 cups spiralized zucchini/squash
- 6 cups kelp noodles
- 6 cups bean sprouts
- 4 cups carrot, shredded
- 3 cups green beans, chopped
- 3 cups red bell pepper, minced
- 1 ½ cups red onion (minced)
- 1 cup cilantro (chopped)
- 3 green onions (chopped)
- 3 ¼+ cups pad Thai sauce

Instructions:
STAGE 1:

1. With a spirally or shredding device make zucchini noodles of the whole zucchini. Combine these noodles with the kelp noodles in a large container to marinate.

STAGE 2:

1. Add Live Pad Thai sauce to noodles and mix evenly allowing to marinate for at least 3–4 hours or overnight in the refrigerator.

2. Serve in 10 oz portions for Mandala Pad Thai bowl on top of rice.

MANDALA LIVING FOODS

LIVE LASAGNA NOODLES

Another amazing reinvention of the pasta wheel, or noodle more accurately. These noodles are used for our Live Lasagna and are easy to make with a mandolin and marinade.

Creation time: 25 mins - preparation
- Lasts 1 week
- Makes 9-10 servings

Ingredients:
- 6-10 of zucchini (sliced w/ spirally)
- 4 tbsp cold pressed olive oil
- 4 tbsp lemon juice
- 2 tbsp Umi plum vinegar
- ½ tsp sea salt
- 2 cloves garlic

Instructions:
STAGE 1:

1. With a mandolin or shaving mechanism make thin shaved whole slices of the zucchini creating noodles of the whole zucchini. Layer these in a container to marinate.

STAGE 2:

1. Blend EVO oil, lemon, Umi, sea salt, and garlic in a blender, add to noodles, and mix evenly allowing to marinate for at least 3-4 hours or overnight in the refrigerator.

2. Use in Live Lasagna recipe in Entrees.

GRAWNOLA

Creation time: 6 hours sprouting / 25 mins - preparation / 12 hours dehydration

- Makes 15 + cups of Grawnola or Cloud Grawnola
- Double recipe for larger batches
- Lasts 1–2 months

Ingredients:
- 6 cups soaked/sprouted groats
- 6 cups soaked oats
- 2 cups dry shredded coconut
- 2 cups nuts of choice, chopped2 cups seeds (optional)
- 2 cups dried fruit of choice (optional)
- 1.5 cups honey or 4 droppers of stevia
- 2 droppers vanilla stevia
- 1 cup (8oz) Cloud yogurt (optional Cloud Grawnola)
- 1/8 cup coconut oil
- 2 tbsp vanilla extract
- 1 ½ tsp sea salt
- 6 oz Flower essence (optional)

Instructions:
STAGE 1:

1. In a bowl, mix the soaked oats, groats, and all ingredients into and even consistency. Add cup of Cloud in if making Cloud Grawnola.

STAGE 2:

1. On dehydrator trays with sheets: Spread Grawnola mix to a medium thickness. Use your fingers to make craters and mini clumps, ensure that thickness stays relatively uniform.

2. Place trays back in the dehydrator on a setting that stays below 117 degrees. Set for max time limit.

STAGE 3:

1. Remove the trays/sheets with granola from the dehydrator. Carefully flip the entire sheet with the granola over onto an empty tray, keeping the granola intact.

2. Once face down on an empty tray, carefully peel off the dehydrator sheet from the granola, moving from one side to the other.

3. Place trays back in dehydrator, on a setting that stays below 117 degrees. Set for max time limit.

STAGE 4:

1. Remove the trays with granola from the dehydrator. Test the granola for moisture, ensuring that it's fully dehydrated, especially in thicker spots.

2. Let granola cool down completely. Add granola to containers, preserving the largest pieces/chunks possible without breaking them down. Label, date, and store in the proper cabinet.

CHAPTER 9 BREAD & SNACKS

LIVE PIE CRUST - 1

Creation time: 25 mins preparation
- Makes 1 Live pie crust
- Lasts 1-2 weeks

Ingredients:
- 2 cups raw almonds (finely ground)
- 2 cups dates
- 1 cup shredded coconut
- ¼ cup honey raw
- ¼ cup raw coconut oil
- 1 tsp sea salt

Instructions:
STAGE 1:

1. Pulse almonds and shredded coconut into fine flour in food processor, and blend sea salt into mix evenly.

2. Add dates, honey, and coconut oil, and process until evenly mixed into live dough.

STAGE 2:

1. Roll dough out into a flat 14 inch diameter circle.

2. Oil a pie pan or cheesecake pan.

3. Carefully peel dough off board, lay dough over top of pan, and press into pie dish or pan.

STAGE 3:

1. Refrigerate to set into form before filling.

MANDALA LIVING FOODS

LIVE PIE CRUST - 2

Creation time: 25 mins - preparation
- Makes 1 Live pie crust
- Lasts 1-2 weeks

Ingredients
- 1 ½ cups almonds (finely ground)
- 1 ½ cups of granola of choice
- ½ cup shredded coconut
- 3 cups dates
- ¼ cup honey
- ¼ cup coconut oil
- 1 tsp sea salt

Instructions:

STAGE 1:

1. Pulse almonds, shredded coconut, and Grawnola into fine flour in food processor, and blend sea salt into mix evenly.

2. Add dates, honey, and coconut oil, and process until evenly mixed into live dough.

STAGE 2:

1. Roll dough out into a flat 14 inch diameter circle.

2. Oil a pie pan or cheesecake pan.

3. Carefully peel dough off board, lay dough over top of pan, and press into pie dish or pan.

STAGE 3:

1. Refrigerate to set into form before filling.

CHAPTER 9 BREAD & SNACKS

LIVE TOAST

Creation time: 25 mins - preparation
- Makes 24 pieces of Live Toast
- Lasts 1-2 weeks
- Must be fresh and stocked daily

Ingredients:
- 6 cups flax (soaked)
- 3 cups sunflower seeds (raw)
- 3/4 cup orange juice (fresh)
- 1 cup name shoyu
- ¾ cup minced red onion
- 3 tbsp garlic (minced)
- 6 tbsp poppy seeds
- ¾ cup herbs of your choice
- 3 tbsp coconut oil
- 1 cup nutritional yeast (cheese toast) (optional)

Instructions:
STAGE 1:
1. Soak flax & sunflower seeds 6-8 hours and mix thoroughly.
2. In a blender: orange juice, red onion, herbs, and garlic. Blend to a liquid consistency and add to the batter.
3. Mix thoroughly into an even dough.

STAGE 2:
1. Spread all dough into just under half inch thick layer on dehydrator sheets, lightly salt, and dehydrate 6-8 hours, flip and dehydrate another 4-6 hours until crispy.

STAGE 3:
1. Let cool, gently break into individual pieces, and transfer to storage containers, Stock in pantry.

MANDALA LIVING FOODS

LIVE SCONE

Creation time: 25 mins - preparation
- Makes 1 batch of scones or pastries
- Lasts 1-2 weeks
- Must be fresh and stocked daily

Ingredients:
- 6 cups almond pulp
- 2 cups mac nut pulp
- ½ cup psyllium husk
- 2 tsp sea salt
- 4 cup shredded coconut (pulverized)
- 3 tbsp olive oil

Savory cheese scone
- ¼ or ½ cup alfredo sauce (depends on recipe)
- herbs (optional)

Sweet fruit scone
- 1 cup honey
- 2 tbsp vanilla extract
- 2 cups dried berries or fruit
- 2 droppers vanilla stevia
- 4 oz flower extract (optional)

Instructions:

STAGE 1:

1. In a food processor, add shredded coconut and process to a fine pulp until you have 4 cups.

2. In a bowl mix 6 cups almond pulp, 3 cups mac nut pulp, pulverized coconut, ½ cup psyllium husk, and the remaining ingredients depending on if you're going sweet or savory. Knead thoroughly mixing the live batter.

STAGE 2:

1. Scoop 8 oz (1 cup) balls and press out 16 scones per dehydrator tray. Perforate holes in them after they're all formed and laid out. Dehydrate for 6-8 hours.

STAGE 3:

1. Flip them and dehydrate another 4-6 hours or until done. This depends on the individual scone and its ingredients.

CHAPTER 9 BREAD & SNACKS

LIVE SWEET TOAST

Creation time: 30 mins - preparation / 6 hours - refrigeration
- Makes 1 batch of Live Sweet Toast
- Lasts 1-2 weeks

Ingredients:
- 4 cups coconut meat pulp
- 3 cups almond pulp
- ½ cup psyllium husk
- ¼ cup raw honey
- ¼ cup maple syrup
- 2 tbsp vanilla extract
- 2 tbsp cinnamon
- 1 tsp sea salt
- ½ tsp Ume plum vinegar
- 2 droppers vanilla stevia

Instructions:
STAGE 1:

1. In a food processor, add older coconut meat and process to a fine pulp until you have 3 cups. In a bowl mix 3 cups coconut meat pulp, 3 cups nut pulp, ½ cup psyllium husk. Then add the raw honey, maple syrup, vanilla extract, sea salt, cinnamon, Ume plum vinegar, and vanilla stevia. Knead thoroughly mixing the live batter.

STAGE 2:

1. Press into bread pan with a dehydrator sheet lined across the bottom with the sides coming out from the edges of the pan to the thicknesloaf andead loaf and refrigerate for at least 6 hours. The dehydrator sheet will support where you can peel off the mold and the loaf stay firm and intact.

STAGE 3:

1. Remove from the refrigerator and the bread pan using the leverage for the dehydrator sheet. Slice into individual slices of sweet toast and place in container. Label/date/store in an airtight container or plastic wrapped pan. Refrigerate or serve.

MANDALA LIVING FOODS

UNBAKED CAKE RECIPE

Creation time: 30 mins - preparation / 1 hour - refrigeration
- Makes 1 cake or batch of cupcakes or pastries
- Lasts 1-2 weeks

Ingredients:
- 3 cups coconut meat pulp
- 3 cups nut pulp
- ½ cup psyllium husk
- 2 tbsp raw honey
- 2 tbsp maple syrup
- 2 tbsp vanilla extract
- 1 tsp sea salt
- ½ tsp Ume plum vinegar
- 2 droppers vanilla stevia

Instructions:
STAGE 1:

1. In a food processor, add older coconut meat and process to a fine pulp until you have 3 cups. In a bowl mix 3 cups coconut meat pulp, 3 cups nut pulp, ½ cup psyllium husk. Then add the raw honey, maple syrup, vanilla extract, sea salt, Ume plum vinegar, and vanilla stevia. Knead thoroughly mixing the live batter.

STAGE 2:

1. Press into cupcake molds in a cupcake pan to a thickness where you can peel off the mold and the cake stays firm. Remove molds and label/date/store in an airtight container or plastic wrapped pan. Refrigerate for at least 1 hour to set cake.

STAGE 3:

1. Assembly: Carefully halve the cake to make a top and bottom layer.
2. Add coconut whipped cream or frosting and 2-3 sliced strawberries to the middle layer
3. Add the top layer of cake. Frost cake or serve as angel food cake with a scoop of whipped cream and a sliced strawberry fan garnish to the top
4. Optional: Add a super light fruit drizzle across or around the cake.

CHAPTER 9 BREAD & SNACKS

LIVE COFFEE CAKE

Creation time: 30 mins - preparation / 4–6 hours - refrigeration
- Makes 1 cake or batch of individual cakes or pastries
- Lasts 1–2 weeks

Ingredients:
- 6 cups coconut meat older
- 1 cup younger coconut meat
- 1 cup mac nut pulp
- ½ cup psyllium husk
- 2 tbsp vanilla extract
- 1 ½ tsp sea salt
- 1 cup raw maple syrup
- ¼ cup coconut oil
- 2 droppers vanilla stevia
- 2 tbsp cinnamon
- 1 tbsp cardamon

Cinnamon sugarless crumble topping
- 2 cups raw honey
- 2 cups shredded coconut (pulverized)
- 1 tsp sea salt
- 2 tbsp cinnamon

Instructions:
STAGE 1:

1. In a food processor, add younger and older coconut meat and process to a fine pulp. In a bowl mix 7 cups coconut meat pulp, 1 cup nut pulp, ½ cup psyllium husk. Then add the maple syrup, vanilla extract, sea salt, spices, and vanilla stevia. Knead thoroughly mixing the live dough.

STAGE 2:

1. Press into a cake pan to 2 inch thickness and press the cake stays firm. Flip the pan over a tray so the cake cleanly comes out of the cake pan. Label/date/store in an airtight container or plastic wrapped pan. Refrigerate 4-6 hours to set cake.

STAGE 3: Topping:

1. In a food processor, blend the honey, pulverized coconut, mac nuts, sea salt, and cinnamon into a sweet crumble. Pull the coffee cake back out of the refrigerator, top it with the crumble, wrap it. Return to the refrigerator to set for at least 3 hours.

MANDALA LIVING FOODS

LIVE CINNABONS

Makes 1 batch of Cinnamons
- Lasts 1-2 weeks

Ingredients:
DOUGH:
- 4 cups coconut ground to fine pulp
- 4 cups almond pulp
- ¾ cup psyllium husk
- 2 tablespoons vanilla extract
- 1 tsp sea salt
- 3/ droppers vanilla stevia
- 1 tbsp cinnamon
- 1 tsp cardamom
- ¼ cup maple syrup

FILLING:
- 1 cup dates mixed with
- 1 cup of H20 8oz
- 1 ½ tbsp cinnamon
- 1 tsp cardamom
- 1 tsp sea salt
- 1/8th cup coconut oil
- Blend and add to mixture

Instructions:
STAGE 1:
1. Mix Cinnabon dough in a large mixing bowl evenly.
2. In a blender or food processor purées cinnamon filling.

STAGE 2:
1. Roll dough out on baking sheet evenly to ½ inch thickness.
2. Spread filling layer on top.
3. Roll up dough into even cylinder and slice individual rolls.

STAGE 3:
1. Make honey cinnamon frosting - (see recipe)
2. Frost Cinnamons, transfer to container, label, and refrigerate 2-6 hours to set.

CHAPTER 10
BULK PROTEINS

GARDEN ISLAND BURGER

Our Live proteins are the heart of our nutrition for our pupus and entrees and are a foundational building block of sustenance in a vegan living food diet. They are in or served with pupus, entrees, and can be ordered ala carte to boost protein in any dish.

Creation time: 8 hours - sprouting / 45 mins - preparation / 14 hours - dehydration
- Makes 14–15 GI burgers
- last 1–2 weeks

Ingredients:
- 3 cups - soaked walnuts
- 2 cups - coconuts (crumble pulp)
- 2 cups - marinated mushrooms (juiced out)
- 1 cup - shredded carrots
- 1 cup - shredded beets
- ¼ cup - green onion
- 1/8 cup - sun dried tomatoes
- 1-2 cloves garlic
- ½ cup - parsley, minced
- ½ cup - cilantro, minced
- 2 tsp - smoked paprika
- 2 tsp - chili powder
- 2 tsp - cumin
- ¼ cup (4 tbsp) - nama shoyu
- ¼ cup - coconut oil
- ¼ cup - psyllium husk, added slowly while mixing

Instructions:
STAGE 1:

1. In a food processor, add older coconut meat and process to a fine pulp until you have 3 cups. In a bowl mix 3 cups coconut meat pulp and other ingredients. Mix pulp together with other ingredients evenly, adding the psyllium husk gradually kneading it into our ground burger.

STAGE 2:

1. Scoop healthy 8 + oz balls on dehydrator sheets and form into 6 inch diameter burgers. You should be able to fit 12 per tray. Take a fork and poke holes in the patties to support even dehydration. Dehydrate at 117 degrees for 8 hours.

2. Flip burgers and dehydrate another 6-8 hours depending on thickness of the burgers. Remove and let cool, then store in sealed container in pantry.

THE ART & SCIENCE OF LIVING FOODS

MICAH SKYE

LIVE MEATLOAF

How could we not make a meatloaf vegetarian and Live? It's such a smart unit of protein in a diet meal plan. This one is an impressive hybrid.

Creation time: 8 hours - sprouting / 30 mins - preparation / 16 hours - dehydration
- Makes 1 Meatloaf - 12–14 slices
- lasts 1 week

Ingredients:

- 1 ½ cups coconut meat
- 2 ½ cups walnuts (soaked)
- 1 ½ cups marinated portobellos (chopped)
- ½ cup SDT
- ½ cup red onion
- ½ cup parsley (chopped)
- 2 cloves- garlic (minced)
- ¼ cup olive oil
- 2 tbsp cumin seeds
- ½ tsp cayenne
- 2 tbsp thyme
- 1 ½ cup celery
- ¼ cup - psyllium husk
- 6 oz - Live catch up (topping)

Instructions:

STAGE 1:

1. In a food processor, add older coconut meat and process to a fine pulp until you have 3 cups. In a bowl mix 3 cups coconut meat pulp and other ingredients. Mix pulp together with other ingredients evenly, adding the psyllium husk gradually kneading it into our ground burger.

STAGE 2:

1. Roll into loaf and form on dehydrator sheet / tray. Take a fork and poke holes in the patties to support even dehydration. Dehydrate at 117 degrees for 8 hours.

2. Flip loaf carefully, and dehydrate another 6–8 hours depending on thickness of the loaf. Remove and let cool, serve or store in refrigerator.

CHAPTER 10 BULK PROTEINS

SLOPPY JOY MIX

Our Live protein Sloppy Joe mix is a hearty classic reinvented with a walnut meat base combined with our Live catchup and does not disappoint. You can always modify it with more mesquite to give it a more smokey twist.

Creation time: 8 hours - sprouting / 30 mins - preparation
- Makes 12–14 Sloppy Joys
- Lasts 1–2 weeks

Ingredients:

- 6 cups - raw walnut (soaked)
- 6 cups - live catchup
- 6 tsp - cumin
- 2 tsp - mesquite or 4-5 drops Cade
- 2 tsp - smoked paprika
- 4 tsp - chili powder
- 2 tsp - coriander
- ¼ cup - honey
- 6 tbsp - nama shoya

Instructions:
STAGE 1:

1. In a food processor, add walnuts and pulse to a medium crumble without any large nut chunks. Add Live catchup and other ingredients and mix pulp together evenly.

STAGE 2:

1. Transfer to a container and serve or refrigerate.

CHAPTER 10 BULK PROTEINS

WALNUT CARNE

Creation time: 8 hours - sprouting / 30 mins - preparation
- Makes 12 - 14 Sloppy Joys
- Lasts 1-2 weeks

Ingredients:

- 6 cups - soaked walnuts
- 1 cup - live catchup
- ½ cup - raw coconut oil
- 3 tbsp - cumin
- 3 tbsp - chili powder
- 2 tbsp smoked paprika
- 4 tsp coriander
- 1 tsp - cayenne or chipotle
- 6 tbsp - nama shoyu

Instructions:

STAGE 1:

1. In a food processor, add walnuts and seasonings, and pulse to a medium crumble without any large nut chunks. Transfer to mixing bowl, add the live catchup and mix evenly place in container and refrigerate or serve.

STAGE 2

1. You can also dehydrate the walnut crumble as a dry crumble by transferring to a dehydrator sheet, spread crumble out evenly, and dehydrate for 8 hours. Stir the crumble and continue dehydrating for another 4–5 hours or until complete. Transfer to a container and st.

MANDALA LIVING FOODS

ITALIAN RAWSAGE

Creation time: 8 hours - sprouting / 30 mins - preparation / 10-12 hours dehydration

- Makes 12 - 14 Sloppy Joys
- Lasts 1-2 weeks

Ingredients:

- 6 cups - soaked walnuts
- ½ cup - coconut oil
- 4 tbsp - fresh oregano, minced
- 4 tbsp - fresh thyme, minced
- 4 tbsp - fresh basil, minced
- 1 tbsp - anise seed
- 1 tsp - caraway seed
- 3 cloves garlic, minced
- 5 tbsp nama shoyu

Instructions:

STAGE 1:

1. In a food processor, add walnuts and seasonings, and pulse to a medium crumble without any large nut chunks. Transfer to container and refrigerate or serve.

STAGE 2

1. You can also dehydrate the walnut crumble as a dry crumble by transferring to a dehydrator sheet, spread crumble out evenly, and dehydrate for 8 hours. Stir the crumble and continue dehydrating for another 4-5 hours or until complete. Transfer to a container and store.

THE ART & SCIENCE OF LIVING FOODS

SWEET & SOUR CRUMBLE

Creation time: 8 hours - sprouting / 30 mins - preparation / 10-12 hours dehydration

- Makes 48 oz of S & S crumble
- Lasts 1-2 weeks

Ingredients:

- 6 cups - soaked walnuts
- 1 cup - S & S Live dressing

Instructions:

STAGE 1:

1. In a food processor, add walnuts and dressing, and pulse to a medium crumble without any large nut chunks. Transfer to container and refrigerate or serve.

STAGE 2

1. You can also dehydrate the walnut crumble as a dry crumble by transferring to a dehydrator sheet, spread crumble out evenly, and dehydrate for 8 hours. Stir the crumble and continue dehydrating for another 4-5 hours or until complete. Transfer to a container and store.

CHAPTER 10 BULK PROTEINS

MAGI SHROOM BURGER

Creation time: 30 mins - preparation / 8-12 hours - marination
- Makes 8–12 shroom burgers
- Lasts 1-2 weeks

Ingredients:

- 8 - 12 whole portobello mushrooms
- ½ cup - Extra Virgin Olive Oil
- 6 tbsp - Nama Shoyu
- 3 tbsp - Apple Cider Vinegar
- 4 oz - Ume plum vinegar
- ½ tsp - sea salt
- ½ cup - balsamic vinegar
- ½ cup - fresh herbs (e.g., basil, fennel/dill, cilantro, rosemary)
- 2 tbsp - fresh garlic, minced
- 2 tbsp - raw honey
- 2 tsp - black pepper
- 2 tsp - paprika
- 1 cup - H20

Instructions:
STAGE 1:

1. Mix thoroughly, and add mix to silicone bag, airtight container, or Ziploc bag.

2. Label, date, and store in the fridge at an angle where all mushrooms are soaking evenly.

3. (If storing in a Ziploc bag, place bag in bowl for protection.)

STAGE 2:

1. Transfer to a container and refrigerate

MANDALA LIVING FOODS

COCONUT BACON

Creation time: 30 mins - preparation / 2-12 hours marination / 4-5 hours - dehydration

- Makes 8 - 12 shroom burgers
- Lasts 1-2 weeks

Ingredients:

- 8 cups - adolescent coconut meat
- ½ cup - nama shoyu - soy sauce
- ½ tsp - sea salt
- 2 tsp - paprika
- 2 tbsp - smoked paprika
- 1 tsp - mesquite powder

Instructions:

STAGE 1:

1. Slice the coconut in thin strips

2. Mix marinade evenly and add to Ziploc with coconut strips. make sure marinade is evenly distributed in coconut meat. Refrigerate overnight

STAGE 2:

1. Remove coconut from the refrigerator and marinade in the bag (which can be used for multiple batches), and transfer meat to a dehydrator sheet. Spread out evenly and dehydrate for 8 hours. flip and continue dehydrating for another 4-5 hours or until complete. Transfer to a container and store in pantry.

COCONUT SCRAMBLE

Creation time: 30 mins - preparation
- Makes 64 oz Coconut Scramble
- Lasts 1-2 weeks

Ingredients:

- 8 cups - adolescent coconut meat
- 2 cup - H20
- 2 tsp - sea salt
- ½ cup - nutritional yeast
- 1 tsp - paprika
- 1 cup - red bell peppers
- ½ cup - red onion
- 1 cup - green bell peppers

Instructions:
STAGE 1:

1. Pulse coconut with sea salt, H20, and nutritional yeast in food processor into chunky pulpy scrambled egg consistency. Transfer to a mixing bowl.

STAGE 2

1. Dice veggies and mix into the coconut scramble with the paprika. Salt to taste. Transfer to storage container and place in refrigerator. Label, date, and serve.

CHAPTER 10 BULK PROTEINS

GREEN GODDESS SOUP

Creation time: 8–12 hours sprouting / 30 mins - preparation
- Makes 64 oz - 4 - 16 oz bowls of soup
- Lasts 1 week

Ingredients:

- ¼ cup - lemon juice (without seeds)
- 3 Swiss chard leaves
- 1 cup - carrots, cut into chunks
- 2 cups - sprouted Mung Beans
- 2 tbsp - ginger tincture or fresh ginger
- 2 tbsp - turmeric
- 1 small clove Garlic
- ½ cup - parsley, basil, cilantro
- 3 tbsp - chickpea Miso
- 1 tsp - Umi plum vinegar
- One piece of kombu (soaked 5 mins)
- 5 - 6 cups - H20
- 8 oz - sprouted rice or sushi rice
- (optional - added charge)

Instructions:
STAGE 1:

1. Prepare sprouted mung beans, by heating them on low to medium heat for 6-8 minutes to breakdown cellular integrity for easy digestion.

2. Strain, and add to blender with the other ingredients, and H20.

STAGE 2

1. In Vitamix, blend briefly on high to chop vegetables, then leave blending on medium-high until evenly pureed. Label, date, and store or serve.

MANDALA LIVING FOODS

CHAPTER 11
HEALFAST

CLOUD BOWL

One of the most important windows of nourishment is breaking the fast after recharging with sleep from your last meal the previous day. Or preferably healing the fast, which is what our rising menu of living foods, smoothies, and tonics is intended to do.

Creation time: 15 mins - preparation
- lasts 3-5 days after preparation
- Recipe for one serving

Ingredients:

- 6 oz - Live milk of choice
- 4 oz - Cloud Yogurt
- 3/4 cup - Grawnola
- 1 banana (1/3 cup)
- ¼ cup - blueberries
- ¼ - papaya
- 1/8 cup - bee pollen
- 1/8 cup - macadamia nuts (chopped)
- 4 oz - fruit chia compote (optional)

Instructions:

Start with the scoop of Grawnola, add fresh fruit, nuts, and live milk of choice. Add the scoop of Cloud on top, and dress with hemp seeds or bee pollen, and fruit dressing.

CHAPTER 11 HEALFAST

YOGI RISING BOWL

Yogi grain mix: sprouted kamut, barley, rye, and quinoa (heated at 110 degrees to break down the proteins), two fruits du jour, raw maple syrup, and a topping of one other Cloud raw yogurts.

Creation time: 15 mins - preparation
- lasts 3-5 days after preparation
- Recipe for one serving

Ingredients:

- 1 cup - Fab 5 Grain Yogi cereal
- ¼ cup - walnuts (chopped)
- 1 banana (1/3 cup+)
- ¼ cup - blueberries
- ¼ cup - papaya
- 1Tbl - of raw honey
- ¼ cup - coconut meat chunks
- ¼ cup - bee pollen
- 1 tbsp - hemp hearts
- 1 tbsp - chia seeds
- ½ cup of live milk of choice
- Pinch of sea salt

Instructions:
Start with the scoop of FAB5 grain mix, add fresh fruit, nuts, coconut, and live milk of choice. Dress with hemp, bee pollen, honey design.

*Top with Cloud for additional probiotic boost.

MANDALA LIVING FOODS

THE ART & SCIENCE OF LIVING FOODS

LIVE SWEET TOAST

Mandala Raw Toast, two fruits de jour, raw maple syrup, and a topping of whipped cream or one of our Cloud yogurts.

Extra toppings: chia seeds, raw mac nuts, coconut, raw almond butter, cacao nibs, seasonal toppings.
Creation time: 15 mins - preparation
- lasts 3-5 days after preparation
- Recipe for one serving

Ingredients:

- 3 pieces of Sweet Toast
- 4 oz - whipped cream
- 4 oz - fresh papaya (chopped)
- 4 oz - banana
- 2 oz - strawberry (Chopped)
- 1 oz - bee pollen

Instructions:
Place three pieces of Sweet Toast on a plate in a trinity, dress with fresh fruit, and top with whipped cream. Place strawberry on top of the whipped cream and sprinkle with bee pollen.

CHAPTER 11 HEALFAST

HEALFAST PARFAIT

Raw coconut cream layered with Mandala Grawnola, fruit du jour, and fruit chia compote. Extra toppings: chia seeds, raw mac nuts, coconut, raw almond butter, cacao nibs, seasonal toppings.

Creation time: 15 mins - preparation
- lasts 3-5 days after preparation
- Recipe for one serving

Ingredients:

- 8 oz - coconut cream
- 6 oz - Grawnola
- 6 oz - fruit chia compote
- 4 oz - Cloud yogurt
- ½ cup - blueberries
- ¼ cup - raspberries
- 1 tsp - cacao nibs
- 1/8 cup - blackberries

Instructions:
Start with a layer of coconut cream, followed by fruit compote, then Grawnola, then fresh fruit, and repeat till the glass is full. Top with Cloud and fresh fruit, and sprinkle with cacao nibs.

MANDALA LIVING FOODS

GREEN GODDESS SOUP

This powerfully healing soup is the foundation for our detox/ healing program with a hydrogen H20 base, chickpea miso, sprouted mung beans (heated at 110 degrees to break down the proteins), Swiss chard, kale, cilantro, parsley, basil, mint, lemon, sliver of garlic (optional), turmeric, ginger, Umi plum vinegar, and sea salt.

Creation time: 15 mins - preparation
- lasts 3-5 days after preparation
- Recipe for one serving

Ingredients:

- 16 oz - Green Goddess soup
- 1 oz - walnut carne
- 1 oz Parmrawsen crumble
- 6 oz - sprouted rice or sushi rice (optional- additional charge)

Instructions:
Pour soup, garnish and serve. If rice requested, place rice in the bottom of the bowl first and the pour the soup over it. Garnish with walnut carne and Parmrawsen and serve.

CHAPTER 11 HEALFAST

LIVE CINNABON

One of the most important windows of nourishment is breaking the fast after recharging with sleep from your last meal the previous day. Or preferably healing the fast, which is what our rising menu of living foods, smoothies, and tonics is intended to do.

Creation time: 15 mins - preparation
- Lasts 3-5 days after preparation
- Recipe for one serving

Ingredients

- 1 live Cinnabon
- 4 oz - fresh fruit
- 2 oz - candied walnuts

Instructions:
Place Cinnabon on a plate, garnish candied walnuts and with side of fresh fruit. Serve.

* Dishes can be EVOLVED with extra toppings per individual's preference.

THE ART & SCIENCE OF LIVING FOODS

MANDALA HEALFAST BURRITO

Coconut scramble, coconut bakin' or healfast rawsage, avocado, tomato, taro hash or breadfruit (when available).

Creation time: 15 mins - preparation
- Lasts 3-5 days after preparation
- Recipe for one serving

Ingredients:

- 1 - collared green or hibiscus leaf
- 3 oz - rawfried beans
- 4 oz - coconut scramble
- 2 oz - Pico de gallo
- 3 oz - coconut bacon or walnut carne
- 2 oz - nacho cheese
- 3 oz - avocado
- 1 tbsp - cilantro

Instructions:
Place green leaf, lay out ingredients in, fold in the sides and wrap over applying pressure while you roll. Serve with a small salad.

* Wraps can be EVOLVED with extra toppings per individual's preference.

CHAPTER 12
PUPUS

THE ART & SCIENCE OF LIVING FOODS

MANDALA SIDE

Local mixed greens, shredded carrots, cucumbers, red cabbage, sauerkraut, seeds, & sprouts. Served the Garden Goddess Dressing.

Add nut meats, Parmrawsan crumble for protein boost...
Creation time: 20 mins - preparation
- Lasts 3–5 days after preparation
- Recipe for one serving

Ingredients:
- 2 cups - mixed greens
- 3 oz - shredded carrots
- 3 oz - shredded cabbage
- 3 oz - sliced cucumbers
- 3 oz - Rainbow kraut
- 2 oz - sunflower seeds
- (cheesy if stocked)
- 3 oz - sprouts

Instructions:
Fill bowl with mixed greens, garnish like a mandala with various veggies, seed and sprouts

* Bowls can be EVOLVED with extra toppings per individual's preference.

CHAPTER 12 PUPUS

SUMMER ROLLS

Sprouted wild rice, coconut meat, carrots, kelp noodles, Thai basil, mind, sunflower sprouts, marinated shiitake mushrooms, avocado, and Mandala siracha sauce, wrapped in raw noodle paper. Served with Thai tahini dipping sauce.

Creation time: 15 mins - preparation
- Lasts 3 days after preparation
- Recipe for two roles - make in large batches

Ingredients:
- 2 rice noodle paper sheets
- (rinse or dip in H20)
- 4 oz - sushi rice
- 2 medium thin avocado strips
- 4 oz - sunflower sprouts
- 2 oz - marinated shiitake mushrooms
- 2 oz - shredded carrots
- 3 oz - marinated kelp noodles
- 3 oz - sweet and sour crumble
- 4 Thai basil leaves

Instructions:
1. Get large plate and put 2 oz of H20 on the plate, and dip rice noodle paper in H20. Place on clean rolling surface. Lay rice down then veggies layered on to the sides and on top finishing with two basil leaves alongside each other.

2. Fold the sides of the noodle paper in and roll up, sealing cleanly. Cut in half and serve with sauce.

MANDALA LIVING FOODS

LIVE PASTA

Our Live pasta and kelp noodles marinated and served with your choice of pesto, coco-mac nut alfredo, or our Marawnara sauce. Or mix them up.

Creation time: 15 mins - preparation
- Lasts 1 week
- Makes 9-10 servings

Ingredients:
- 6 cups of zucchini (sliced w spiralli)
- 6 cups of kelp noodles
- 4 tbsp – cold pressed olive oil
- 4 tbsp - lemon juice
- 2 tbsp - Umi plum vinegar
- ½ tsp - sea salt
- 2 clove garlic

Instructions:
STAGE 1:

1. With a spiralli or shredding device make zucchini noodles of the whole zucchini. Combine these noodles with the kelp noodles in a large container to marinate.

STAGE 2:

1. Blend EVO oil, lemon, sea salt, and garlic in a blender, add to noodles, and mix evenly allowing to marinate for at least 3 - 4 hours or overnight in the refrigerator.

2. Serve in 10 oz portions for Pasta LiVE bowl with 4 oz of pasta sauce - Alfredo or Marawna. Top with Rawcotta, and Rawmesan.

3. Dinner portion - 14 oz topped with 8 oz pasta sauce - Alfredo or Marawnara sauce, topped rawcotta, and Rawmesan.

CHAPTER 12 PUPUS

ISLAND QUICK SLICE

We have a created a miraculous alternative to baked pastries that is nothing short of living foods perfection using creative ingredients like our nut pulps, coconut, zucchini, flax seeds, and psyllium husk. Living thin crust or deep dish pizza, lined with collard leaf, covered in Marawnara, marinated veggies, fresh herbs, Rawsage Italiano, & Rawmesan crumble.

Creation time: 15 mins - preparation
- Lasts 1 week
- Makes 1 pizza slice

Ingredients:
- 1 slice pizza crust
- 1 collard green
- ¼ cup - marawnara sauce
- ½ cup - marinated mushrooms
- ¼ rounded cup - Rawcotta cheese
- ¼ cup - red bell pepper slices
- ¼ cup - green bell peppers (minced)
- 1 oz - red onion (minced)
- ½ tsp - basil (fresh)
- ½ tsp - oregano (fresh)
- 1 tbsp - kalamata/black olives

Instructions:
STAGE 1:

1. Lay the crust on top upside down and cut extra leaf off of the front two sides, leaving leaf around the crust. Flip slice back over and spread sauce evenly on slice.

2. Add mushrooms, bell peppers, onions, black onions, and Rawcotta.

STAGE 2:

1. Top with herbs and Rawmesan.

MANDALA LIVING FOODS

ISLAND SUSHI ROLL

Live cauliflower coconut sushi rice wrapped around avocado, marinated Shiitake mushroom, raw coconut, cucumber, pickled carrot, sweet & sour crumble, marinated kelp noodles, and cilantro.

Creation time: 15 mins - preparation
- Lasts 3 days
- Makes 1 sushi roll

Ingredients:
- 1 sheet nori
- ½ cup: Sushi rice
- 3 slices - avocado, cut lengthwise
- 2 slices - cucumber, cut lengthwise
- ¼ cup - shredded carrots
- ½ cup - marinated mushrooms
- ½ cup - sweet and sour crumble
- Optional: 1 tsp pickled ginger as a side

Instructions:
STAGE 1:

1. On a bamboo rolling mat. Spread all ingredients evenly to get uniform pieces of sushi. Start with sushi rice and spread as wide, even sheet that takes up about 2/3 of the nori sheet. Press in evenly.
2. Lay vegetables, mushrooms, avocado, and S & S crumble on top of presses sushi rice.

STAGE 2:

1. Lift the end of the bamboo mat upward and roll firmly to tuck the nori into itself.
2. Gently separate the bamboo from the nori once tucked in.
3. Gently spread 1 tsp H20 along the remaining nori that hasn't been rolled up yet.
4. Finish the roll and hold in place for a few seconds.
5. Remove the bamboo entirely and slice with no downward pressure, only a gentle sawing motion.
6. Plate in a creative and clean way. Include 2oz of Sauce in a small dish.

CHAPTER 12 PUPUS

GARDEN ISLAND TOAST

Living cracker, lined with collard leaf, covered in living hummus or cloud chevre, sunflower sprouts, marinated vegetables & sauerkraut, fresh herbs. Topped with nut meats, Rawmesan crumble.

Creation time: 15 mins - preparation
- Lasts 3 days
- Makes 1 sushi roll

Ingredients:
- 1 Garden Island Toast Cracker
- 4 oz - G-free hummus or chevre
- 3–4 slices - avocado
- 2 slices - red onion
- 2 oz - sunflower sprouts
- 2 slices - tomato
- 3 oz - marinated mushrooms
- 2 oz - rawtalian sausage
- 1 oz - rawmesan crumble

Instructions:
STAGE 1:

1. Spreads G-free hummus or chevre on Live toast cracker.

2. Lay vegetables, mushrooms, avocado, and Italian rawsage crumble on top.

STAGE 2:

1. Top with sprouts and Rawmesan crumble and serve.

MANDALA LIVING FOODS

THE ART & SCIENCE OF LIVING FOOD

MICAH SKYE

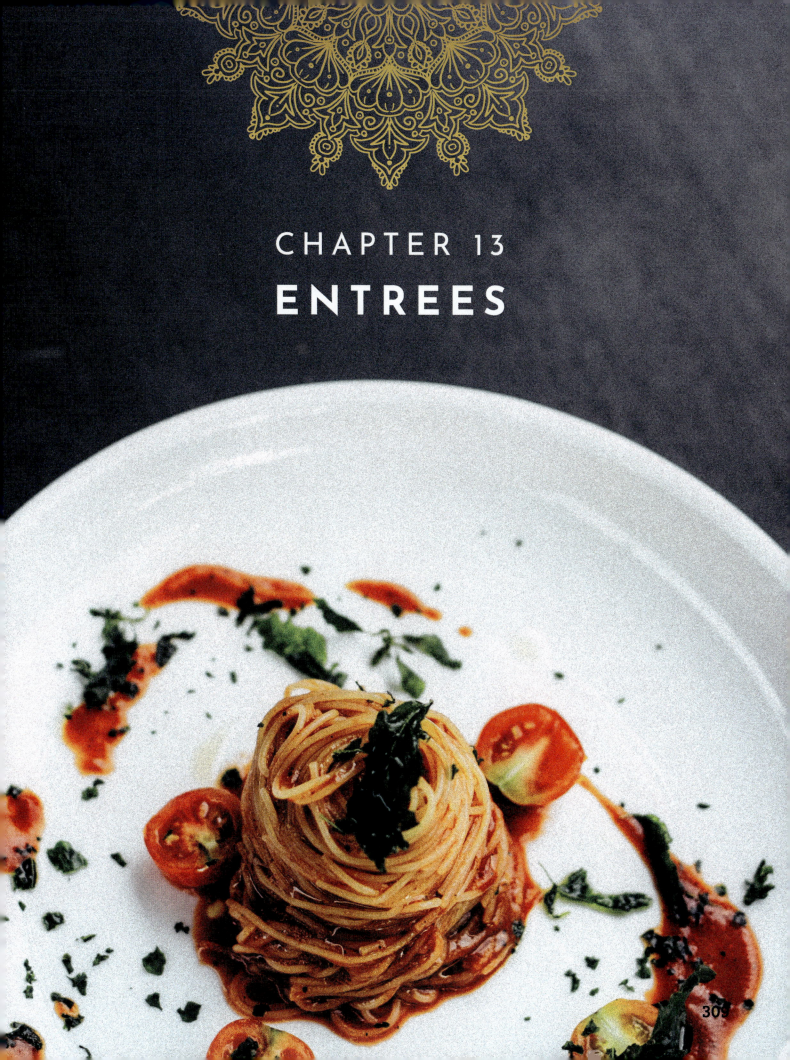

CHAPTER 13
ENTREES

THE ART & SCIENCE OF LIVING FOODS

RAWKIN' HARD SHELL TACOS

2 corn flaxseed hardshell taco shells, lined with collard greens, rawfried beans, taco crumble, shredded lettuce and cabbage, Pico de gallo, raw nacho cheese. A small side salad.

Creation time: 15 mins - preparation
- Lasts 3 days
- Makes 2 hard shell tacos

Ingredients:
- 2 hard shell tacos®
- 8 oz - Walnut Carne®
- 4oz - nacho cheese
- 6oz - lettuce (shredded)
- 3 oz - purple cabbage (shredded)
- 4 oz - Pico de gallo
- 4oz - Cloud Sour Cream (optional EVOLVE)
- 6 oz - mixed greens
- 1oz - MLF dressing of choice

Instructions:
STAGE 1:

1. Fill two hard shell tacos with walnut carne.

2. Add shredded lettuce, cabbage, and Pico de gallo.

3. Top with Nacho cheese drizzle.

STAGE 2:

1. Place mixed greens on plate, dress salad with MLF dressing of choice.

2. Place tacos leaning on either side of the salad. Serve.

* For take out, place tacos separate from salad undressed.

MICAH SKYE

CHAPTER 13 ENTREES

LIVE LASAGNA

Layers of zucchini noodles and collard greens with our marawnara, Italian walnut rawsage, rawcotta cheese, fresh basil, balsamic mushrooms, bell peppers, and topped with our Parmrawsan cheese and fresh herbs. One of our house favorites!

Creation time: 15 mins - preparation
- Lasts 1 week +
- One slice of Live Lasagna

Ingredients:
- 1 slice of Live lasagna
- 8 oz - mixed greens
- 1 oz - MLF dressing of choice
- 2 oz - Rawmesan crumble

Instructions:
STAGE 1:

1. Place one slice of Live Lasagna on center of plate.

2. Add mixed greens around or under the lasagna.

3. Drizzle dressing around on mixed greens.

4. Top lasagna with Rawmesan crumble and or cheesy brussel sprouts if available.

* For take out, place lasagna separate from salad undressed.

MANDALA LIVING FOODS

NACHOS MANDALA

Corn flaxseed chips covered in rawfried beans, taco crumble, raw coco nacho cheese, Pico de gallo, chopped cilantro.

Creation time: 15 mins - preparation
- Lasts 2 days +
- One plate of Nachos Mandala

Ingredients:
- 12 oz - Live Nacho chips (1 ½ cups)
- 5 oz - nacho cheese ®
- 5 oz - Rawfried Beans ®
- 5 oz - Walnut Carne ®
- 5 oz - Pico de gallo ®
- 4 oz - Cloud Sour Cream ®
- 1 oz - cilantro (minced)
- 2 oz - black olives
- 1 oz - jalapenos
- 2 slices - avocado (cut into chunks)

* EVOLVE with 4 oz guacamole

Instructions:
1. Place nacho chips on center of the plate.
2. Add Rawfried beans, walnut carne, Pico de gallo, olives, and avocado.
3. Drizzle nacho cheese all over nachos, and sprinkle cilantro on top.
4. Top with sour cream, and jalapeno slices as well as hot sauce if requested spicy.

TOSTADA MANDALA

Corn flaxseed tostada lined with a collard green leaf, topped with raw fried beans, taco crumble, shredded lettuce and cabbage, raw nacho cheese, Pico de gallo.

Creation time: 15 mins - preparation
- Lasts 2 days +
- One Tostada Mandala

Ingredients:
- 1 Live Tostada
- 5 oz - nacho cheese ®
- 5 oz - Rawfried Beans ®
- 5 oz - Walnut Carne ®
- 5 oz - Pico de gallo ®
- 5 oz - handful of shredded greens
- 4 oz - Cloud Sour Cream ®
- 1 oz - cilantro (minced)
- 1 oz - jalapenos
- 2 slices - avocado (cut into chunks)

Instructions:
1. Place Live Tostada on center of the plate, and place collard green leaf cute to circle on top.

2. Cover in Rawfried beans spread, add walnut carne crumble, and gentle press into beans.

3. Add handful of greens on tostada and add Pico de gallo and avocado.

4. Drizzle nacho cheese all over tostada, and sprinkle cilantro on top.

5. Top with sour cream, and jalapeno slices as well as hot sauce if requested spicy.

LIVE BURRITO

A fresh collard green or one of our coconut wraps filled with raw fried beans, taco crumble, shredded lettuce, purple cabbage, raw nacho cheese, and topped with guacamole, Pico de gallo, and Cloud sour cream.

Creation time: 15 mins - preparation
- Lasts 2 days +
- One Live Burrito

Ingredients:
- 1 Live Tostada
- 5 oz - nacho cheese ®
- 5 oz - Rawfried Beans ®
- 5 oz - Walnut Carne ®
- 5 oz - Pico de gallo ®
- 5 oz - handful of shredded mixed greens
- 4 oz - Cloud Sour Cream ®
- 1 oz - cilantro (minced)
- 4 oz - guacamole
- 2 slices - avocado (cut into chunks)

Instructions:
STAGE 1:

1. Place collard green leaf on cutting board, lay out Rawfried beans spread, add walnut carne crumble, and gentle press into beans.

2. Add handful of greens on tostada and add Pico de gallo and avocado.

3. Drizzle nacho cheese all over burrito, and sprinkle cilantro on top.

STAGE 2:

1. Fold ends of the collard leaf in symmetrically and roll burrito firmly into form.

2. slice in half and angle on the plate.

3. Top with sour cream, and jalapeno slices as well as hot sauce if requested spicy.

CHAPTER 13 ENTREES

GARDEN ISLAND BURGER

Mandala living patty, on a living bun, garnished with live catchup, live coco-mayo, mustard, lettuce, tomato, and pickles. Side salad.

Creation time: 15 mins - preparation
- Lasts 4 days +
- One Live GIL Burger

Ingredients:
- 2 live buns
- 1 GIL Burger
- 2 slices tomato
- Sunflower or clover sprouts
- Thin-sliced red onion
- ½ oz - Live Catchup
- ½ oz - Live Mustard
- ½ oz - Coco Mayo
- 6 oz - mixed greens
- 1 oz - MLF dressing of choice

Instructions:
STAGE 1:

1. Place bottom bun with layer of mayo and mustard. Add lettuce, onion, and tomato.

2. Add burger patty on top - add cheese EVOLVE if requested.

3. Top with sprouts, and top bun after spreading Live Catchup, mustard and coco mayo on it.

STAGE 2:

1. Place burger on the plate with mixed greens to the side.

2. Dress salad and serve.

* For take out, place burger separate from bun, dressings, and salad undressed.

MANDALA LIVING FOODS

315

MANDALA PAD THAI

Sesame zucchini noodles, mung bean sprouts, carrots, red cabbage, cilantro, lime, Umi plum vinegar, coconut oil, Kauai honey, garlic essence, raw mac nuts, Hawaiian chili.

Creation time: 15 mins - preparation
- Lasts 4 days +
- One bowl of Pad Thai

Ingredients:
- 10 oz - Mandala Pad Thai
- 6 oz - sprouted or sushi rice
- 1 nori sheet
- 1 rice noodle
- 1 bunch of bean sprouts
- 2 oz - mac nut crumble
- 1 oz - furikaki seasoning

Instructions:
STAGE 1:

1. Place nori sheet in the bottom of the bowl, and place rice on top pressing a flat plateau for a base of the Pad Thai to be placed on.

2. Place 10 oz of Pad Thai on top of the rice forming it into a dome. Dress with zig zag of siracha.

STAGE 2:

1. Wet the rice noodle lightly and place it over covering the dome of Pad Thai. Take a paring knife and poke a small hole in the top.

2. Sprinkle with mac nut crumble & furikaki sesame, and finish with putting the bean sprouts up right through the hole at the top into the dish as displayed above.

3. Serve immediately.

CHAPTER 13 ENTREES

MANDALA SUSHI PLATE

Live sushi roll, live miso, and Asian salad.

Creation time: 15 mins - preparation
- Lasts 4 days +
- One Live Sushi Plate

Ingredients:
- 1 Live Sushi roll - cut
- 8 oz - Miso soup
- 1 Mandala Side

Instructions:
STAGE 1:

1. Place sushi on plate around nama shoyu dressing, and garnish with pickled ginger.

2. Add Mandala Side to the plate, and cup of Miso soup. Garnish with green onion and furikaki.

MANDALA LIVING FOODS

THE ART & SCIENCE OF LIVING FOODS

CHAPTER 14
DESSERTS

THE ART & SCIENCE OF LIVING FOODS

CHAPTER 14 DESSERTS

LIVE APPLE PIE

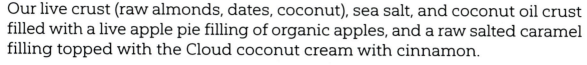

Our live crust (raw almonds, dates, coconut), sea salt, and coconut oil crust filled with a live apple pie filling of organic apples, and a raw salted caramel filling topped with the Cloud coconut cream with cinnamon.

Creation time: 45 mins - preparation
- Lasts 1 week +
- One Live Apple Pie

Ingredients:
- 2 Live Pie Crusts - recipe 1
- 5-6 Apples (Peeled, cored, and sliced)
- 4 cups (48oz) hot H20
- 2 cups - room temp H2O
- ½ cup - lemon juice
- 3 tbsp - cinnamon
- ½ cup - coconut oil
- ¼ cup - raw honey
- 1 tbsp - ACV - apple cider vinegar
- 2 tbsp - fresh ginger
- 1 tsp - sea salt
- ½ tsp - cloves
- 2 cups - pitted dates

Instructions:
STAGE 1:
1. Bring H20 to boil, then turn off and add apples, lemon juice, and 1 tbsp of cinnamon. Cover and let sit 20-30 mins while making the Live pie crusts - recipe 1.
2. Leave one of them rolled out and the other in the pie dish refrigerating.
3. In food process blend the dates, 2 tbsp cinnamon, coconut oil, raw honey, ACV, ginger, sea salt, cloves to a caramel consistency adding ½ a cup of the hot lemon H20 to support puree.
4. Strain apples and return to mixing bowl. Add caramel filling to apples and mix thoroughly.

STAGE 2:
1. Remove pie crust from the refrigerator and add the filling into the pie crust.
2. OPT 1 - Place rolled out pie crust on top, fusing the edges cleanly to the top of Pie crust
3. OPT 2 - Cut the rolled out pie crust into strips and interweave them into the top of the Pie crust. Fuse edges. Refrigerate to set.

MANDALA LIVING FOODS

CHAPTER 14 DESSERTS

GRASSHOPPER PIE

Live coconut cream fused with chlorella, spirulina, chlorophyll mint, & vanilla, cacao, carob, & sea salt with our live crust.

Creation time: 30 mins - preparation
- Lasts 1 week +
- Makes one Grasshopper Pie

Ingredients:
- 1 Live Pie Crusts - recipe 1
- 1.5 cups (12oz) - coconut H20
- 1 and 1/3 cup - raw coconut oil
- 4 cups - fresh poi or coconut cream
- ½ cup - coconut butter
- 1 cup - raw honey
- 5 tbsp - green spirulina
- 5 tbsp - moringa powder
- 5 tbsp - carob Powder
- 4 tbsp (¼ cup) - cacao powder
- ¼ cup - fresh lemon juice
- 1 tsp - blue algae/spirulina powder
- 1 tsp - sea salt

Instructions:
STAGE 1:

1. Make Live Pie Crust 1 or 2.

STAGE 2:

1. Blend filling in food processor to a creamy puree.
2. Remove pie crust from the refrigerator and add the filling into the pie crust.
3. Refrigerate overnight to set.

STAGE 3:

1. Serve with sprinkle of cacao nibs
2. EVOLVE with a scoop of whip cream if requested.

MANDALA LIVING FOODS

CHAPTER 14 DESSERTS

BLUE DREAM PIE

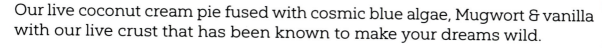

Our live coconut cream pie fused with cosmic blue algae, Mugwort & vanilla with our live crust that has been known to make your dreams wild.

Creation time: 45 mins - preparation
- Lasts 1 week +
- Makes one Blue Dream Pie

Ingredients:
- 1 and ¼ cup (10oz) - coconut H20
- 1 and 1/3 cup - raw coconut oil
- 4 cups - fresh poi or coconut cream
- ½ cup - raw honey
- ½ cup - coconut butter
- ¼ cup - fresh lemon juice
- 3 tsp - blue algae
- ½ tsp - sea salt
- 6oz - mugwort essence
- 1 tbsp - vanilla extract
- 2 droppers - vanilla Stevia
- 1.5 tsp - pearl Powder

Instructions:
STAGE 1:

1. Make Live Pie Crust 1 or 2.

STAGE 2:

1. Blend filling in food processor to a creamy puree.

2. Remove pie crust from the refrigerator and add the filling into the pie crust.

3. Refrigerate overnight to set.

STAGE 3:

1. Serve with sprinkle of cacao nibs

2. EVOLVE with a scoop of whip cream if desired.

CHAPTER 14 DESSERTS

MANDALA BROWNIE LIVE

Raw walnuts, coconut, cacao, carob, cacao butter, coconut oil, Kauai honey, dates, sea salt. Topped with a cacao syrup drizzle, and the fresh fruit (seasonal).

Creation time: 30 mins - preparation
- Lasts 2 weeks +
- Makes one tray of brownies

Ingredients:
- 5 cups - raw walnuts, process to fine chunks (not powder)
- 1/8 cup - coconut oil
- 3 cups - dates, pitted
- 2 cups raw cacao powder
- ¼ cup carob powder
- 2 tsp vanilla extract
- 1 tsp sea salt
- 6 tbsp honey
- Optional: Superfood powder

Instructions:
STAGE 1:

1. In a food processor, blend walnuts to a fine to crumbled pulp, add cacao, carob, and sea salt. Blend evenly.

2. Next add honey, coconut oil, vanilla, and begin adding dates gradually blending them all into chocolate brownie dough.

STAGE 2:

1. Remove dough from food processor, and press into coconut oiled baking pan or dish. Press in evenly to thickness of a ½ inch. Top with chopped walnuts. Refrigerate overnight to set.

STAGE 3:

1. Remove from refrigerator and cut into even squares.

2. Serve with fresh raspberries or strawberries and Lavaberry sauce.

3. * EVOLVE with a scoop of whip cream if desired.

CHAPTER 14 DESSERTS

NY STYLE CHEESECAKE

The Cloud fermented coconut cream, stevia, vanilla, sea salt, coconut oil, coconut butter with live almond, date, & coconut crust.

Creation time: 45 mins - preparation
- Lasts 2 weeks +
- Makes one whole NY Style Cheesecake

Ingredients:
- 5 cups - coconut meat
- 1 ½ cup - of coconut oil
- 1 tsp - sea salt
- ½ cup - honey
- 2 droppers - vanilla stevia
- 1 tbsp - vanilla extract
- 2 cups - H20
- ¼ cup - lemon juice
- ½ cup - coconut butter
- 1 tsp - cloud culture
- 1 live pie crust (see recipe)
- 12 oz - Fruit de jour

Instructions:
STAGE 1:

1. Make Live Pie Crust 1 or 2.

STAGE 2:

1. Blend filling in food processor to a creamy puree.

2. Remove pie crust in a spring pan from the refrigerator and add the filling into the pie crust.

3. Refrigerate overnight to set.

STAGE 3:

1. Slide a butter knife around the edge of the spring ban to make sure the crust stays in integrity when releasing the pan off the sides.

2. Serve with fresh strawberries, sprinkle of cacao nibs, and Lavaberry sauce.

3. EVOLVE with a scoop of whip cream if desired.

MANDALA LIVING FOODS

CHAPTER 14 DESSERTS

FLOUR-LESS LAVA CAKE

Coconut, almond, cacao powder, coconut oil, cacao butter, honey, vanilla, sea salt, and the Cloud. Topped with a sea salted chocolate drizzle and fruit.

Creation time: 45 mins - preparation
- Lasts 2 weeks +
- Makes one batch of Lava Cakes

Ingredients:
- 4 cups - nut pulp (almond, mac nut, or hazelnut)
- 1 cup - older coconut
- ½ cup - carob
- 1.5 cups - cacao
- ½ cup - psyllium husk
- 1 tsp - sea salt
- 1 tsp - vanilla extract
- 2 droppers - vanilla stevia
- ½ tsp - Umi plum vinegar
- ¼ cup - raw maple syrup
- ¼ cup - raw honey
- 2 ½ cups - Holy Cacao Sauce

Instructions:
STAGE 1:

1. In food processor, break down the coconut to a fine pulp. Gradually add in psyllium husk.

2. Add nut pulp to coconut pulp, along with cacao powder, carob powder, sea salt, and remaining ingredients. Mix into an even dough, and transfer to a mixing bowl. Evenly continue to knead and mix. Pull out cup cake pan lined with silicon liners. Pack the cake batter in the cups leaving a hollow inside. pack the edges just above the liners.

3. Press out batter on a sheet and cut circular bottoms to the cakes to be pressed on sealing them along the edges.

STAGE 2:

1. Make Holy Cacao Sauce and fill the cups. Make sure they're below the edge of the cake sides.

2. Press bottoms consciously on to the cakes along the edges sealing the filling in the cakes. Refrigerate overnight.

3. Serve with fresh strawberries, sprinkle of cacao nibs, and Lavaberry sauce.

4. EVOLVE with a scoop of whip cream if desired.

MANDALA LIVING FOODS

CHAPTER 14 DESSERTS

STRAWBERRY SHORTCAKE

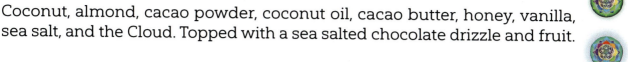

Coconut, almond, cacao powder, coconut oil, cacao butter, honey, vanilla, sea salt, and the Cloud. Topped with a sea salted chocolate drizzle and fruit.

Creation time: 45 mins - preparation
- Lasts 2 weeks +
- Makes one batch of Strawberry Shortcakes

Ingredients:
- 3 cups coconut meat pulp
- 3 cups nut pulp
- ½ cup psyllium husk
- 2 tbsp - raw honey
- 2 tbsp - maple syrup
- 2 tbsp vanilla extract
- 1 tsp sea salt
- ½ tsp Ume plum vinegar
- 2 droppers vanilla stevia
- 2 + cups - whipped cream
- 2 + cups - sliced strawberries
- 4 oz - cacao nibs
- 8 oz - lavaberry sauce

Instructions:
STAGE 1:

1. In food processor, break down the coconut to a fine pulp. Gradually add in psyllium husk.

2. Add nut pulp to coconut pulp, along with ingredients. Mix into an even dough, and transfer to a mixing bowl. Evenly continue to knead and mix. Pull out cup cake pan lined with silicon liners. Press into cupcake molds in a cupcake pan to a thickness where you can peel off the mold and the cake stays firm.

3. Remove molds and label/date/store in an airtight container or plastic wrapped pan.

STAGE 2:

1. Carefully halve the cake to make a top and bottom layer. Add coconut whipped cream and 2-3 sliced strawberries to the middle layer and add the top layer of cake.

2. Add a dollop of whipped cream and a sliced strawberry fan garnish to the top, and a super light fruit drizzle across or around the cake.

3. Serve with fresh strawberries, sprinkle of cacao nibs, and Lavaberry sauce. Serve.

MANDALA LIVING FOODS

THE ART & SCIENCE OF LIVING FOODS

MICAH SKYE

CHAPTER 14 DESSERTS

VANILLA LAVENDER POI CHEESECAKE

The Cloud fermented poi cream, stevia, vanilla, sea salt, coconut oil, coconut butter with live almond, date, & coconut crust.

Creation time: 30 mins - preparation
- Lasts 2 weeks +
- Makes one whole poi pie /cheesecake

Ingredients:
- 1 ¼ cup - coconut H20
- 1 1/3 cup - raw coconut oil
- 4 cups - fresh poi
- ½ cup - raw honey
- ½ cup - coconut butter
- ¼ cup - fresh lemon juice
- ½ tsp - sea salt
- 6oz - lavender essence
- 1 tbsp - vanilla extract
- 2 droppers - vanilla stevia
- 1.5 tsp - pearl powder

Instructions:
STAGE 1:

1. Make Live Pie Crust 1 or 2.

STAGE 2:

1. Blend filling in food processor to a creamy puree.

2. Remove pie crust in a spring pan from the refrigerator and add the filling into the pie crust.

3. Refrigerate overnight to set.

STAGE 3:

1. Slide a butter knife around the edge of the spring ban to make sure the crust stays in integrity when releasing the pan off the sides.

2. Serve with sprinkle of cacao nibs, and Holy Cacao sauce.

3. EVOLVE with a scoop of whip cream if requested.

MANDALA LIVING FOODS

CHAPTER 14 DESSERTS

LIVE PUMPKIN PIE

Our Live Pumpkin pie is a magical living revival of a classic holiday favorite and is nothing short of a gift to humanity with a live almond, date, & coconut crust.

Creation time: 45 mins - preparation
- Lasts 2 week +
- Makes one whole Live Pumpkin Pie

Ingredients:
- 3 cups - raw pumpkin (chopped)
- ½ cup - coconut meat younger
- 1 ½ cups - dates (soaked)
- 1 cup raw coconut oil
- 1 cup - coco H20
- 1 tsp - sea salt
- 1 tsp - nutmeg
- 1 tsp - ground cloves
- 1 tsp - all spice
- 1 tsp - fresh ginger (minced)
- 2 tsp - cinnamon
- ½ tsp - coriander
- 1 live pie crust
- 2 droppers - vanilla stevia
- ¼ cup - raw honey

Instructions:
STAGE 1:

1. Soak the raw chopped pumpkin in hot water for at least 20 minutes to break down the pumpkin, while you make Live Pie Crust 1 or 2.

STAGE 2:

1. Blend filling in food processor to a creamy puree.

2. Remove pie crust in a spring pan from the refrigerator and add the filling into the pie crust.

3. Refrigerate overnight to set.

STAGE 3:

1. Slide a butter knife around the edge of the spring ban to make sure the crust stays in integrity when releasing the pan off the sides.

2. Serve with a scoop of whip cream.

THE ART & SCIENCE OF LIVING FOODS

MICAH SKYE

CHOCOLATE FUDGE PIE

One of the richer and more decadent of Mandala's pies. This chocolate fudge pie doesn't disappoint. With layers of chocolate, vanilla, sea salt, and coconut butter, it's as dense as it is rich in chocolate magic accented with a live almond, date, & coconut crust.

Creation time: 45 mins - preparation
- Lasts 2 week +
- Makes one whole Chocolate Fudge Pie

Ingredients:
- 3 cups coconut meat
- 2 cups coco oil raw
- 1 cup coco butter raw
- 2 cups cacao powder
- 3 tbsp vanilla extract
- 2 tbsp sea salt
- 2 cups honey
- 1 cup coco H20
- 1 live pie crust

Instructions:
STAGE 1:

1. Make Live Pie Crust 1 or 2.

STAGE 2:

1. Blend filling in food processor to a creamy puree.
2. Remove pie crust from the refrigerator and add the filling into the pie crust.
3. Refrigerate overnight to set.

STAGE 3:

1. Serve with sprinkle of cacao nibs and either Holy Cacao Sauce or Lavaberry Sauce
2. EVOLVE with a scoop of whip cream if desired.

THE ART & SCIENCE OF LIVING FOODS

CHAPTER 14 DESSERTS

COCONUT CREAM PIE

The ultimate coconut cream pie living in all the hearts of all those who love classic coconut cream pie. Rich, fluffy, and creamy with a live almond, date, & coconut crust.

Creation time: 45 mins - preparation
- Lasts 2 weeks +
- Makes one whole coconut cream pie

Ingredients:
- 2 cups young coco meat
- 2 cups older coco meat
- 1 ½ cups coco oil
- 1 cup shredded coconut
- ½ cup coconut butter
- 1 tsp sea salt
- 1 cup raw honey
- 1 tbsp lemon juice
- ½ tsp cloud culture
- 1 cup coco H20
- ½ cup cacao nibs
- (optional topping)
- 1 live pie crust

Instructions:
STAGE 1:

1. Make Live Pie Crust 1 or 2.

STAGE 2:

1. Blend filling in food processor to a creamy puree.

2. Remove pie crust from the refrigerator and add the filling into the pie crust.

3. Refrigerate overnight to set.

STAGE 3:

1. Serve with sprinkle of cacao nibs and either Holy Cacao Sauce or Lavaberry Sauce

2. EVOLVE with a scoop of whip cream if desired.

MANDALA LIVING FOODS

REFLECTIONS OF A LIVING FOODS CHEF...

Our relationship to what we eat is a reflection of ourselves and our relationship to loving our self. It's so much more than, "you are what you eat", and yet it's quite literally the case. For this reason, our food supply has been under attack for decades with GMOs, chemical, and pharmaceutical manipulation, as well as preservative and bio-chemical additive-based bombardment of our food supply. It's been going on for generations and is all but designed as part of a dysgenics program to control the populations of the world. From the "Fat Free Era" in the 90s that resulted in a whole generational increase in ADD and ADHD in the generations to follow to the processed soy milk alternative era that has led to generations of more feminized boys and men to the latest push for everyone to eat bugs as an alternative along with lab grown meats made from fecal matter. There is an agenda deeply organized beneath all of this, and it's not to save the planet or your health and wellness. We have unfortunately all fallen into some diet psychosis or toxic food consumption, and for many a solid detox is a great precursor to evolving to a new conscious journey of awakened food exploration. Just remember when fasting...

When the human body is hungry, it eats itself, it does a cleansing process, removing all sick cells, cancer, aging cells and Alzheimer's; keeping young and fighting diabetes. Making special proteins that only form under certain circumstances. And when they are made, the body selectively gathers around dead cancer cells, dissolves them and restores the state from which the organism benefits. This is what recycling looks like. Scientists have found through long and specialized research that the process of autophagy requires atypical conditions that force the body to do this process. These circumstances consist of abstaining from eating and drinking for 16 hours (Cycle 8/16). A human should function normally during this period. This process should be repeated for some time to reach the body for maximum use and not let sick cells reactivate. It is recommended to repeat the hunger and thirst process two or three days a week.

Yoshinori Ohsumi - Nobel Prize Winner in Physiology and Medicine.

Your relationship with food is sacred and personal to you and biochemistry. Only you can discover what synthesizes best for you, and that takes something way more involved than just following what someone else tells you to consume. It takes you being willing to experiment and see what works for you and doesn't work for you, and that's a life long journey! It can also be an adventure that's so much fun and full of amazing surprises. You are worth it, and so is your health and wellness. May this book be a guide and inspiration for you to discover your food medicine formula that awakens your highest mental, physical, and vibrational experience. Only you will know, by exploring and expanding your art and science of living foods!

REFLECTIONS OF A LIVING FOODS CHEF...

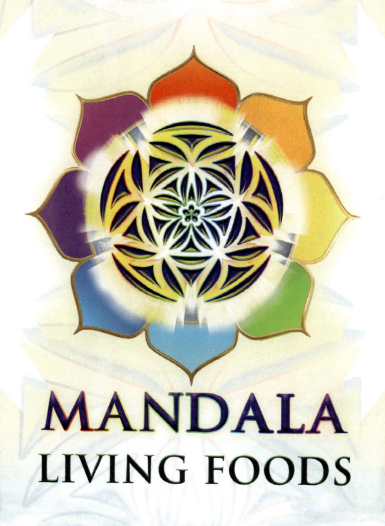

MANDALA
LIVING FOODS

Made in the USA
Las Vegas, NV
21 November 2023